AF352723

The Way of Reason
in Religion and Politics

The Way of Reason in Religion and Politics

The Philosophy of Franklin I. Gamwell

DANIEL A. DOMBROWSKI

SUNY
PRESS

Published by State University of New York Press, Albany

EU GPSR Authorised Representative:
Logos Europe, 9 rue Nicolas Poussin, 17000, La Rochelle, France
contact@logoseurope.eu

For information, contact State University of New York Press, Albany, NY
www.sunypress.edu

Library of Congress Cataloging-in-Publication Data

Name: Dombrowski, Daniel A., author.
Title: The way of reason in religion and politics : the philosophy of
    Franklin I. Gamwell / Daniel A. Dombrowski.
Description: Albany : State University of New York Press, [2026]. | Includes
    bibliographical references and index.
Identifiers: LCCN 2025041313 | ISBN 9798855806366 (hardcover : alk. paper) |
    ISBN 9798855806380 (epub) | ISBN 9798855806397 (PDF)
Subjects: LCSH: Metaphysics. | Religion and politics. | Political science—Philosophy. |
    Gamwell, Franklin I.
Classification: LCC BD111 .D66 2026
LC record available at https://lccn.loc.gov/2025041313

Contents

List of Abbreviations   vii

Introduction   1

Chapter 1   Liberalisms   17

Chapter 2   Process Metaphysics   29

Chapter 3   Two Metaphysical Claims   43

Chapter 4   Contingency and Necessity   59

Chapter 5   Aristotle, Kant, and Modern Moral Theory   73

Chapter 6   MacIntyre, Rorty, Apel, and Habermas   89

Chapter 7   Politics as a Vocation   103

Chapter 8   Justice as Compound   115

Chapter 9   Religious Freedom   129

Chapter 10   A Rawlsian Response   145

Chapter 11   American Intellectual History   167

Chapter 12   Community   181

Chapter 13   Applied Ethics   203

Chapter 14   The Method of Reflective Equilibrium   217

Coda   239

Works Cited   241

Name Index   249

List of Abbreviations of
Works by Franklin Gamwell

BP   *Beyond Preference*

BTP   *By the People*

DG   *The Divine Good*

DP   *Democracy on Purpose*

EG   *Existence and the Good*

MN   *On Metaphysical Necessity*

MRF   *The Meaning of Religious Freedom*

PCV   *Politics as a Christian Vocation*

WTP   *Religion among We the People*

Introduction

This is a work in *metaphysics*, but there are two different senses of what it means to engage in metaphysical thinking. On the one hand, metaphysics involves the explication of the necessary character of all existence (i.e., metaphysics in the *strict* sense). On the other hand, metaphysics explicates the necessary character of subjective existence or of life with conscious purpose. We will see that metaphysics in the latter sense implies, but is not implied by, metaphysics in the strict sense. Whereas metaphysics in the strict sense involves an explication of the characteristics of all possible reality or existence as such, the other sort of metaphysics involves an explication of all possible subjectivity or subjectivity as such. Both types of metaphysics are *transcendental* in the sense that they are involved in explicating the *necessary conditions* of reality as such or subjectivity as such (*EG*, ix; *WTP*, 217; *MN*, 1–2).

While human beings are well aware of the fact that they live within limits, they also are aware of alternative ends. Our lives are moral enterprises because these alternatives require decisions from us by way of evaluation. Further, we also have the capacity to raise questions regarding the entirety of things. One expression of this capacity is found in religion, but there is another expression of this capacity found in discourse typically called metaphysics. Indeed, metaphysics explores religious truths at the highest level of abstraction. In the modern period, however, there has been widespread doubt cast on metaphysics as the discipline that studies the most general characteristics of existence. Sometimes this doubt surfaces (especially in the Kantian tradition) as a trimmed-down version of metaphysics that includes only the necessary conditions of subjectivity (i.e., metaphysics in the *restricted* sense), independent of any necessary conditions of existence as such. A more extreme sort of doubt is found when both sorts of metaphysics are rejected. In the present book I will be attempting to explicate and defend Franklin "Chris" Gamwell's redemption of metaphysics in a twofold sense (*EG*, 17–22; *MRF*, 235).

But it is also a work in *political philosophy*, specifically in the connection between metaphysics and political thought. It is the purpose of the first two chapters of the book to introduce these two major themes: political liberalism and process metaphysics. Subsequent chapters will return to these two themes, and to the connections between them in Gamwell's thought, in deeper and sometimes unexpected ways. Although I was initially tempted to gather together all of the chapters dealing with metaphysics into a first part of the book, with all of the chapters dealing with political philosophy gathered into a second part, I decided against such an arrangement. The close connection between metaphysics and political thought in Gamwell is better served, I think, by going back-and-forth between these two topics from chapter to chapter and, in some cases, within an individual chapter.

In the remainder of this introduction I would like both to summarize each chapter of the book so as to prepare the reader for what follows and also to indicate why transcendental argumentation is necessary in religion and politics by pointing out the dire consequences if it is either ignored or rejected.

In chapter 1 I will deal with several different meanings of "liberalism," distinguishing between nineteenth-century or libertarian or neoliberal liberalism (as exemplified by Milton Friedman) and twentieth-century or welfare or redistributive liberalism (as exemplified by Alan Gewirth). We will see that Gamwell refers to *both* of these as versions of *established* liberalism, in contrast to his own *reformed* or *substantive standard* liberalism. This latter view is one that is given metaphysical backing in terms of a comprehensive telos wherein all human activity ought to pursue maximal creativity of all future activities or of the future as such. One makes the most of the opportunity one's past delivers when one seeks to make the most of the opportunity one delivers to one's successors (including to future phases of one's own life). In different terms, one is an individual-in-community rather than primarily (as in established liberalism) a maximal preference satisfier.

An introduction to process metaphysics is offered in chapter 2, where Gamwell's debt to Alfred North Whitehead and Charles Hartshorne, especially the latter, is made explicit. Here it is clear that there is a significant difference between local and cosmic (i.e., between nonmetaphysical and metaphysical) variables. Local variables may or may not be exemplified, but cosmic, metaphysical variables cannot not be exemplified. The connection with political thought is made explicit here. Consider the greatest happiness principle, which operates in several moral/political theories. Although human beings can talk *about* this principle, no human being could actually experience the greatest happiness. Only an omnipresent, omniscient (properly defined), and omnibenevolent being could do this. Only a comprehensive individual in whom every realization of value is united could do this. This is a cosmic variable that is operative in both metaphysics and politics. I will argue that this theory requires Hartshorne's distinction, adopted by Gamwell, between divine *existence* (*that* God exists) and divine *actuality* (*how* God exists from moment to moment). As a perfect being, God's existence is necessary, but not God's actuality, the latter of which constantly changes because time is the process by which possibilities are actualized. With Whitehead as his guide, Gamwell insists that the notions of right and wrong depend on this (neoclassical) theistic background, otherwise our activities are passing whiffs of insignificance. In response to the objection that the capacity to give reasons and to assess them is *always* indexed to some argumentation community, it should be noted that this claim itself implies a universal character of argument (i.e., its indexicality). The ways in which neoclassical or process metaphysics is and is not indebted to ancient Greek philosophers (especially Plato) will also be treated in this chapter, as well as the process critique of the bifurcation of nature found in dualism. Metaphysical dualism is incoherent in that metaphysics deals with universal characteristics of the real but, on the dualist hypothesis, there are no universal or ultimate characteristics of the real but two sets of characteristics that are in conflict with each other. One of the very abstract features that operates transcendentally on all of reality is the temporal structure of existence, which is constituted by determinate realities from the past, future determinables, and the present process by which determinables are made determinate. We will see that these metaphysical considerations prevent democracy from losing its security of intellectual justification.

It can be said that chapters 3 and 4 are the core of the book in that in these chapters arguments for two key metaphysical claims are offered. Both "something exists" and "God exists" are necessarily true, as argued in chapter 3. These conclusions are reached on the basis of metaphysics seen as the study of nonrestrictive existential statements. Distinctions among partially restrictive existential statements, completely restrictive existential statements, and completely nonrestrictive existential statements are explicated in this chapter, as is the character of neoclassical (or process) metaphysics as both "neo" and "classical." The hope is that a defensible third alternative between classical metaphysics and skepticism regarding metaphysics can be found in the neoclassical or process view. The propositional content of a metaphysical statement (e.g., "something exists") is such that its denial is self-contradictory or meaningless. Further, the contradiction involved can be either semantic or pragmatic or both, as I will argue. Metaphysical necessity refers to those conditions or characteristics of existence that cannot fail to obtain or that cannot fail to be exemplified. The aforementioned claim that "God exists" will be defended via a modal (Hartshornian) version of the ontological argument where the familiar misconception that this argument moves illegitimately from the abstract to the concrete will be challenged. This challenge is once again the result of Hartshorne's distinction, adopted by Gamwell, between (necessary) existence and (contingent) actuality.

The fourth chapter continues the work of the third by exploring the concept of contingency and the ways in which it limits or complements transcendental argumentation. Neoclassical metaphysics centers on the dipolar contrast and complementarity between the necessary and the contingent. Although eminent reality exists necessarily, it also necessarily has some contingent features or other. Neoclassical metaphysics exists so as to restore a reticulative perspective whereby we can understand reality as both somewhat predictable *and* creative. However, to see *all* truth as metaphysical in a sort of intellectual imperialism is not to take the unique contribution of metaphysics seriously. Metaphysics cannot long survive if it swallows up science and the empirical method will soon falter if it tries to adjudicate metaphysical disputes. The necessity that there be *some* contingent things or other is entirely consistent with the genuine contingency of these things. It will nonetheless be emphasized that our very efforts to persuade each other of what we take to be necessary truths have a contingent character.

In chapter 5 I will examine the two greatest options in the history of Western philosophical ethics: Aristotle and Kant. Whereas Gamwell largely sides with Aristotle regarding desire (or better, regarding excellence of desire), he sides with Kant regarding the a priori or transcendental characteristics that must be accounted for in ethics. Thus, his view is indebted to both premodern and modern sources. Gamwell seems to subscribe to the imperative to act in a way that is consistent with the proper exercise of practical reason and that exemplifies moral and intellectual virtues. It also seems fair to say that Gamwell is an ardent supporter of Enlightenment rationality. What leads him to be critical of the Enlightenment is not its emphasis on reason, but rather the belief that religious truths cannot be supported by theoretical reason. Strange as it sounds, in this regard Gamwell is more of an Enlightenment thinker than Kant! In addition, Gamwell does not think that autonomy is necessarily compromised by theism. Because Kant defines noumena in strictly negative terms (as nonphenomena), this stance reminds us of the problems detailed in chapter 3 regarding runaway negativity. Likewise, although Kant is instructive regarding the need to be worthy of happiness, he is not as informative about the positive highest good or ultimate purpose. It should be emphasized that Gamwell does not so much reject Kant's attenuated version of metaphysics as he incorporates it within a larger whole of metaphysics in the strict sense. Although Kant's view has radical implications for the *existence* of God, it is also crucial to notice that his *concept* of God is the frustrating one of classical theism. That is, due to Kant's influence, it is common to see thinkers criticizing classical theism and reaching the erroneous conclusion that they have criticized theism itself.

Chapter 6 examines four contemporary thinkers who philosophize in the wake of Aristotle and Kant and who have in turn influenced Gamwell. Alasdair MacIntyre in many ways continues the Aristotelian tradition, but he sees all theories and states of character as historically specific. One wonders how one could even know that one's thought is tradition-dependent if one did not have *some* sense of what it would mean to speak of necessary or universal truth. Richard Rorty's empirical moral theory is even more extreme than MacIntyre's in that he wants to altogether drop the vocabulary of necessary and contingent. The difficulty Rorty faces is that if he tries to advance a philosophic *argument* regarding the alleged negative consequences of transcendental pursuits, he will enter into the very transcendental discussion he despises. Further, falsification with assurance requires intellectual foundations of at least a modest sort. One wonders what sort of claim Rorty is making when he says that moral truth *does not have* an essence. Karl-Otto Apel is much closer to Gamwell than MacIntyre or Rorty because he embraces transcendental arguments. Both Apel and Gamwell think that to *deny* the conditions of rational discourse is to contradict oneself. Arguable claims are fallible claims and transcendental philosophy is an attempt to understand the nature of argumentative discourse as such wherein one gives reasons that command the assent of rational subjects. That is, practical reason presupposes commitment to the transcendental or ideal communication community, which, in turn, points us in political philosophy toward democracy when seen as an inclusive ideal for the associative order of society. The *moral* meaning of democracy is integrally connected to the telos of a maximal (or optimal) public world. Gamwell's major disagreement with Apel is that the latter continues the Kantian tradition of refusing altogether metaphysics in the strict sense. The fourth contemporary philosopher treated in this chapter is Jurgen Habermas, who, like MacIntyre, assumes that conceptions of the good *cannot* transcend a particular lifeworld (thereby engaging in transcendental reasoning in spite of themselves). Gamwell, by contrast, sees the real threat to democracy, in addition to authoritarianism, in withdrawing from discourse regarding contested ends, in withdrawing from even the possibility of defending adequately a conception of common purpose. Metaphysical conceptions of the good are neither "baggage" in the pejorative sense nor, in partial agreement with Habermas, blank checks to run roughshod over opponents.

Politics as a vocation is the topic of chapter 7. Theists are called to politics because their lives should be oriented toward the common good; they are called to democratic politics in particular because they are called to pursue a community of love. The vocation of which Gamwell speaks is given two roughly equivalent labels: the way of reason and the humanistic commitment. He is impressed, as we should be, by the incisive cadences of Martin Luther King Jr. that are testimony to the theses that metaphysical theism prescribes democracy and that the question of God is a rational one. (Gamwell participated in the historic march from Selma to Montgomery, Alabama, in 1965 with MLK.) In fact, raising the question *critically* regarding whether religious or metaphysical claims can be assessed through rational discourse commits one to a positive response to the question. Skepticism regarding the role of reason in religion is often, as Gamwell correctly notes, really skepticism regarding the cogency of classical theism, hence the need for a more defensible version of metaphysical theism. The view of politics as a vocation is seen in this chapter against the Augustinian background to the thought of Reinhold Niebuhr (who was, incidentally, one of Barack Obama's favorite thinkers). Gamwell's view of politics as a vocation is very much a Niebuhrian one purged of classical theism. He even ventures the opinion that Niebuhr would have endorsed the neoclassical alternative if he had been presented with it.

Chapter 8 indicates that, despite the fact that transcendental arguments are at the core of Gamwell's philosophy, there are also limits to transcendental argumentation. But these limits are less restrictive in Gamwell than in almost all other contemporary thinkers. As a general rule, it can be stated with equanimity that transcendental arguments deal well with the most abstract issues in metaphysics, but their applicability is attenuated as the issues become more and more concrete. For example, the transcendental argument in favor of the maximal good by and for the widest number of subjects does not tell us everything we need to know about the details of the moral/political life. Justice has a compound character in Gamwell. It involves the distinction between abstract *formative* principles of a democratic constitution and more concrete *substantive* principles. Of course, democratic discourse cannot be solely about the formative character of the discourse, given the concrete problems faced in any society, but such a formative principle is nonetheless a necessary condition for a just society. Formative philosophical conditions are those that characterize full and free political discourse and are strongly analogous to constitutional essentials in the legal realm, in contrast, say, to substantive principles and norms at a more concrete level that do not rise to the level of constitutional essentials. There is something amphibious about justice when it is considered that it both swims in the waters of the formative comprehensive order of reflection and walks on the substantive ground of practical reason. Deontic norms can be part of this further specification, norms that can be eased under the pressure of *in extremis* conditions, as many committed deontologists themselves admit.

Chapter 9 deals with Gamwell's approach to religious freedom (with my critique of this approach postponed to the next chapter). Gamwell characteristically wants to call attention to more general or philosophical (indeed metaphysical) aspects of the classic debate between separationists and religionists regarding the first amendment to the United States Constitution. His approach militates against the widely held view (among religious skeptics and religious believers alike) that religious beliefs cannot be the subject of public debate or rational assessment. He argues that religious freedom is ultimately constituted by free and full discourse in a democracy. It is high time, Gamwell seems to say, for democratic societies *and religions* to grow up and face the comprehensive question in terms of rational assessment, rather than in terms of either dogmatic assertion or trivializing neglect. In preparation for the critique of Gamwell's nuanced view in the following chapter, this chapter details some of the contrasting views of John Rawls (the "privatist" view), John Courtney Murray (the "partisan" view), and Kent Greenawalt (the "pluralist" view).

In chapter 10 I will order Gamwell's criticisms of Rawls's view of the relationship between religion and politics and offer a spirited Rawlsian response to Gamwell's criticisms. I lay out eight criticisms that I detect in Gamwell's profound reading of Rawls, five of which are directed specifically at Rawls and three of which point the way toward Gamwell's own view. Gamwell thinks that the very idea of *separation* of justice from the good militates against Rawlsian comprehensiveness. Several of my criticisms of Gamwell's view are actually friendly amendments to his stance. One of these is to say that it makes sense to take the truth or falsity of comprehensive doctrines off the table *in politics*, making it possible to rationally assess them in other areas: academe, churches, responsible journalism, the arts, et cetera. That is, it would be a mistake to see Rawls's view as a sort of secularism in that the just society he defends could just as easily be described as post-secular as post-religious. What we want are all defenders of *reasonable* (as this technical term is used in Rawls) comprehensive doctrines to be treated fairly, whether the comprehensive doctrine is theistic or not. It would also be a mistake to say that the Rawlsian view is antiteleological. In fact, one could see it as hyper-teleological in that it permits as many ends as are compatible with justice. Further, the problem with labeling Rawls's view as "privatist" is explored in terms of Rawls's translation proviso, where the terms of one's comprehensive doctrine are permitted into the public square so long as they are presented in such a way that adherents to contrasting comprehensive doctrines could understand and possibly accept. There is no incoherence in eschewing any particular metaphysical or religious view *in politics* while permitting one, encouraging one, and perhaps even requiring one elsewhere! In political liberalism a theory of justice is "freestanding" in the sense that it does not depend on *any particular* metaethical view, but not in the sense that it could dispense with *all* metaethical views or comprehensive doctrines. The crucial *pro tanto* character of political philosophy is also explored in this chapter.

In chapter 11 I examine Gamwell's appropriation of several thinkers in the American intellectual tradition, including Thomas Jefferson and Abraham Lincoln (as interpreted by John Burt), along with historian David Strauss, who introduces dynamism into scholarship regarding the US Constitution and who provides a bridge between Jefferson and Lincoln. A precursor to Rawlsian overlapping consensus is found in the moral precepts thought by Jefferson and others to be common to all religions, precepts that are different from the dogmas of religion that divide various sects. The key for Gamwell is to stay locked together in argument. Errors cease to be dangerous when they can be corrected over time by rational criticism engaged against the background of an omniscient knower. Reasonable parties agree that there are grains of truth in both the separationist *and* religionist perspectives on religious freedom. Of course, Jeffersonian values were violated by Jefferson himself regarding the institution of slavery, an institution that over time has ironically not withstood the test of Jeffersonian rationality. It will be emphasized that Lincoln never had a political feeling that did not spring from the sentiments in the Declaration of Independence: human equality, inalienable rights, and consent of the governed. Throughout the chapter a distinction from the philosopher of law H. L. A. Hart is crucial: a *concept* is a deep value that more particular *conceptions* are meant to serve. Various conceptions of equality are efforts to understand better the underlying and elusive concept of equality that is our goal. Although we do not always act from pristine motives, some of our reasons do in fact rely on the better angels of our nature, to use Lincoln's famous phrase. The chapter concludes with a consideration of the thought of Jeffrey Stout in relation to Gamwell's views.

Because Gamwell wishes to defend a version of political liberalism, it will be worthwhile to respond to the influential criticisms that liberalism is a ruse for possessive individualism and that liberalism involves a retreat from community. My defense of Gamwell will emphasize the importance of community (and cognate conceptions) in his thought as well as the degree to which his view is more similar to Rawls's view than Gamwell is often willing to admit; hence careful attention will be paid to Rawls in chapter 12. That is, Rawls and Gamwell can serve to mutually illuminate and support each other, as was also emphasized in chapter 10. Gamwell's and Rawls's view of community is a moderate one between two extremes: Hobbesian stances wherein there is only a *modus vivendi* among parties who do not share a sense of justice and Aristotelian stances that prescribe a unity constituted by widespread acceptance of a particular conception of the good life. These views can be called weak and strong communitarianism, respectively. Several other topics related to the concept of community will be treated in this chapter: the process of individuation of citizens through community, the complementarity of citizens in community, the virtues requisite in a politically liberal society, and the relationship between communal love/benevolence and Gamwellian/Rawlsian justice.

In chapter 13 a Gamwellian approach to issues in applied ethics will be explored. This approach relies on the crucial distinction in Gamwell between abstract *formative* principles and more concrete *substantive* principles, on the one hand, and Hart's aforementioned distinction (endorsed by Gamwell) between relatively abstract *concepts* and more particular *conceptions*, on the other. To these very helpful distinctions we can add the equally helpful Rawlsian four-stage sequence. In each case, the indeterminacy of theory is not itself a defect, but is rather an understandable feature of abstraction: its need for particular, contingent exemplification. Gamwell's theory clearly goes deeper than Rawls in the effort to articulate the metaphysical basis of both politics and comprehensive doctrines; hence his theoretical ambitions are more extensive than those found in Rawls. But Gamwell is also more ambitious than Rawls at the most concrete end, given Rawls's general reluctance to join the fray at the level of applied ethics. I will deal with four topics in Gamwell's applied ethics: abortion, animal rights (and environmental ethics), affirmative action, and distributive justice.

In the final chapter I defend the views that: (1) reflective equilibrium should be seen as the overall method at work in philosophy, a method that is explicit in Rawls and, I will argue, implicit in Gamwell; and (2) reflective equilibrium should be seen as an ongoing process. The latter thesis is a novel one that both helps to clarify what reflective equilibrium is and establishes the cogency of the former thesis. It is precisely the processual character of reflective equilibrium that forges a crucial link between liberal political philosophers like Rawls and liberal metaphysicians like Whitehead, Hartshorne, Gamwell, and me. In order to establish this link, however, it will be fruitful to first understand Nicholas Wolterstorff's interpretation of Rawls's theory, an understanding that will in turn help us to better understand Gamwell, in particular. Like chapters 10 and 12, the last chapter of the book attempts to better grasp Gamwell's thought through close association with Rawls. Gamwell's metaphysically ambitious project involves a layered concern for issues with varying degrees of abstractness and concreteness, making his version of reflective equilibrium somewhat distinctive. Rapprochement between processual reflective equilibrium and Gamwellian transcendental argumentation in metaphysics can be reached precisely because the former can be seen to *include* the latter in that it is a commonplace in Gamwell's philosophy to invite *dialogue*, even in metaphysics. A brief coda follows.

Prior to his death in 2023 at the age of eighty-five, Gamwell was the Shailer Mathews Service Professor Emeritus of Religious Ethics, Philosophy of Religions, and Theology at University of Chicago, where he was a faculty member for several decades. He also served for a decade as dean of the Divinity School at University of Chicago. As hinted at above, throughout his life he was involved in economic and racial justice work. He was a beloved teacher at University of Chicago precisely because of his meticulous care at understanding others' arguments and his remarkable clarity at expressing his own views. That is, Gamwell's own life was a consistent embodiment of his intellectual commitment to rational dialogue on the most abstract and the most concrete problems with which human beings are confronted.

David Tracy expresses well what is perhaps the most remarkable thing about Gamwell's intellectual achievements, specifically his view regarding the connection between metaphysics and politics, an achievement that the present book is meant to explicate in the hope that Gamwell's thought will become better known among both metaphysicians and political theorists: "His is the strongest argued intellectual challenge to the common misbelief that, in the modern world, religion is merely private, and the equally unfortunate belief of the Christian political right that Christianity (or any other religion) should dominate public discourse. . . . He has provided a third and persuasive way of thinking about religion in the public realm beyond these blind alleys" (quoted in Lee 2023). I think it is fair to say that I am an admirer of Gamwell's work, but it will become clear that I also have criticisms of his thought, which will become especially apparent regarding his at times adverse relationship with Rawls, the greatest political philosopher of the twentieth century. I will argue that, despite appearances, Gamwell was closer to Rawls than he realized and that he actually adds something significant to the Rawlsian project in political liberalism. I will also criticize Gamwell's manner of appropriating ancient philosophy. Although I was never a student or colleague of Gamwell's, I have read his magisterial books very carefully and, I hope, judiciously. The present work is an attempt to demonstrate this.

A key feature of this book is a defense of transcendental arguments, a defense that is often indicated in the text by the use of italics for words like *all, necessity, never, cannot, obligation*, et cetera. I will try to convince readers that they should care about the issues raised in transcendental arguments for the sake of both religion/metaphysics and politics. It is not merely desirable or wise that we pay attention to these issues, but *rationally necessary* to do so. As Gamwell sees things, rightly I think, one is morally *obliged* to maximize the good and to show communicative respect to one's interlocutors in a democracy. These are not mere options for a rational being. In the course of the book I will at several points detail the negative consequences of failing to consider transcendental arguments.

One way to see the importance of transcendental arguments in politics is to compare and contrast Gamwell and Rawls. Although they agree about the general contours of a just society, with Gamwell largely agreeing with Rawls's famous principles of justice, there are differences between the two regarding the place of these principles in the wider scheme of things. The principles of justice constitute the highest level of abstraction with which Rawls is willing to engage *as a political philosopher*. But he does point us toward what he calls a "four-stage sequence" where, in descending order, political questions are dealt with in more and more concrete terms: original position, constitutional convention, the legislative process populated by legislators and voters, and court decisions. It should be noted that Rawls sees two moral powers in human beings: the ability to develop a concept of justice and the ability to develop a concept of the good life. It is the former with which he is concerned as a political philosopher and where he is in agreement with Gamwell. The latter—a concept of the good as found in any one of a number of comprehensive doctrines—is left for citizens to decide on their own in some nonpolitical way. Rawls permits, encourages, even requires a concept of the good when dealing with questions that are not strictly speaking part of public discourse, but, he thinks, it is not his job as a political philosopher to direct citizens regarding how to respond to questions about the good life. It is for this reason that Gamwell (not entirely accurately) labels Rawls's stance "the privatist view." Rawls's main concern regarding comprehensive doctrines and the concept of good contained in them is that they not impede the principles of justice.

Gamwell has a quite different view in that, in addition to being a political thinker, he is also a theistic metaphysician concerned with several levels of discourse more abstract than the principles of justice. These levels are unfortunately largely left untouched by Rawls and most other political thinkers. Here it is relevant to consider one of the key distinctions in Gamwell, that between very abstract *formative* principles and more concrete *substantive* principles. Gamwell's most distinctive contributions to political thought consist in what he has to say very abstractly about formative metaphysical principles that guide more concrete substantive ones. A related distinction points to the contrast between *necessary* truths and *contingent* ones. By "religion" Gamwell means that area of human interest that is primarily concerned with the comprehensive question or a human being's ultimate concern, and metaphysics is the discipline that deals with religious questions at the most abstract, formative level. We have seen that justice, by way of partial contrast, is an amphibious concept. For example, exactly what should the income tax rate be? It should be high enough to ensure that everyone in society is provided basic goods, but low enough to still provide incentives for talented people to work hard so as to benefit both themselves *and others* in society. Gamwell thinks that contemporary American society is in no danger in the immediate future of having levels of taxation that are too high.

This amphibious quality to justice Gamwell calls "the compound character" of this concept. A variation of this compound character can be found in the distinction between constitutional essentials and particular laws. Gamwell's overall method, like Rawls's, is that of reflective equilibrium or a processual version of Aristotelian dialectic where, over time, human beings may asymptotically approach truth and justice via the exchange of rational arguments about both abstract and more concrete issues. However, there are levels of abstraction in political thought largely ignored by Rawls and almost all other contemporary political thinkers.

Consider a possible gap between Rawlsian political liberalism and Gamwellian reformed liberalism wherein the latter is explicitly teleological, whereas the former is alleged to be nonteleological due to the pervasive influence of Kant. This gap can be easily exaggerated when it is considered that both types of liberalism can legitimately be characterized as hyper-teleological, given the many different ends that can be pursued by citizens in a democratic society. But there really is something distinctive about Gamwell's stance that, among these various reasonable ends, which must be tolerated in a just society, there can also be *at a higher level of abstraction* a truly inclusive end, a common good (of common goods). Likewise, some might drive a wedge between political liberalism and reformed liberalism due to the defense of freestandingness in the former. But Gamwell would be quick to point out that to say that the government should be freestanding *in the sense that* it is not to be hemmed in by any particular comprehensive doctrine does not mean that there is no need for *any* metaphysical backing for principles of justice.

Rawls himself seems to admit this when he says that his view is *pro tanto*. Literally these Latin words mean to pay in part, as when in a legal context someone in debt escapes penalty by paying part of the debt on the pledge to pay the remainder at a later time. *Pro tanto* pledges are quite different from bankruptcies, where one is under no obligation to repay the remaining debt. Given this distinction, one can interpret Rawls to be saying that one pays one's "debt" in moral philosophy in two stages (or better, in two different ways, in that I am speaking of logical stages here and not temporal ones). "First" one needs to get clear on the abstract principles of justice that would guide a democratic society in a condition of reasonable pluralism; "then" one needs to deal with all of the other questions in moral philosophy and religion that are not primarily questions regarding justice. It must be admitted, however, that Gamwell is much more forthright than Rawls regarding this second stage of reasoning about the comprehensive question. For example, one of Rawls's most important statements of his response to the comprehensive question as it relates to the inviolable dignity of human beings occurs in a footnote (Rawls 1971, 505–6) in contrast to Gamwell's frequent and explicit treatment of this question in several of his books by way of transcendental argumentation concerning the necessary features of rational subjectivity.

Gamwell thinks it crucial to defend the concept of necessary truth (in contrast to most political thinkers) even if most of the truths that one could defend are contingent. The most abstract principles in religion are found in metaphysics, which, we have seen, is a discipline that admits of two sorts, both of which involve transcendental argumentation regarding necessary conditions. It should be emphasized that by "metaphysics" Gamwell does not refer to a region beyond the physical; nor does he mean by "transcendental" a type of reasoning that pole vaults us, as it were, into another world beyond this one, the one in which we live. Rather, metaphysics in a *strict* sense studies the necessary features of reality as such, whereas metaphysics in a *restricted* or *nonstrict* sense (Gamwell misleadingly calls it metaphysics in a *broad* sense) studies arguments that characterize the necessary features not of reality as such but of subjectivity as such, or more precisely, of human subjectivity as such, including the human ability to exhibit rationality. Because Kant famously (or infamously) rejected metaphysics in the strict sense (even if he accepted it in the nonstrict sense) and because prevailing philosophical *and* theological opinion rejects metaphysics in both senses, there is something heroic about Gamwell's defense of metaphysics in both senses. He is almost alone in arguing that every moral claim eventually must include a consideration of its metaethical character. This consideration is one instance of the comprehensive order of reflection that is integral to what Gamwell calls the humanitarian ideal, the way of reason mentioned in the title of the present book.

It is a hallmark of rational human beings that they make claims. A claim is something very much like a promise in that the claimant in effect is promising to give reasons in favor of the claim if it is challenged. When one makes a claim it is understandable for one's interlocutor to ask "why?" A proper response to this question involves the giving of reasons (in contrast, say, to making threats) until any dispute between the two interlocutors can be adjudicated. The giving of reasons for one's claims, especially for a contested claim, is what it *means* to be rational. Gamwell thinks that it follows from this that one of the necessary (i.e., metaphysical) features of rational subjectivity is that one adhere to a principle of *communicative respect*, a principle that is integrally connected to an ethos of toleration and the sense that, even when dealing with contested claims, indeed *especially* when dealing with contested claims, we are *locked together in argument*. The telos of such argument is nothing other than a just society, a maximal (or better, optimal) public world.

In response to the criticism that Gamwell is too far out on a limb by engaging in transcendental argumentation regarding the necessary features of human subjectivity in its connection to rationality, Gamwell is rhetorically astute to turn the tables on the critic. When, for example, it is claimed, as it is almost axiomatically in contemporary academe, that *all* truth is historically contingent or that there is *no* intelligible discourse outside of some contingent linguistic community, there is the formidable difficulty involved in explaining the legitimacy of terms like "all" or "none." That is, opposition to transcendental analysis itself is subject to transcendental analysis because, for example, relativism itself makes a claim to necessary truth: the claim that *all* truth is relative. Likewise, if one tries to advance an *argument* against transcendental pursuits, one will enter into the very transcendental discussion that one opposes. Gamwell's challenge to opponents of transcendental reasoning has not yet received a detailed, convincing reply.

The way of reason, including the use of transcendental argumentation, is a crucial antidote to what I see as a dangerous misology that is prevalent on both the political left and right, although I would like to avoid the charge of false equivalence by admitting that the current danger from the authoritarian right is the far greater problem. This misology is characterized by three claims, all of which should be contested, as I see things:

1. There is no objective truth and there are no universal moral/political values.

2. All claims to truth or goodness are relative and are strictly subject to perspectival limitation.

3. When conflicts regarding truth claims or moral/political values occur, the resolution of such conflicts occur more through power relations than through epistemic considerations or justificatory warrant.

It will be the purpose of the present book to offer a quite different and superior view. I should note, however, that the present work is only an initial attempt to analyze Gamwell's major works. My hope is that this book will be supplemented and corrected by others who are also interested in this remarkable thinker.

CHAPTER 1

Liberalisms

It will be the purpose of the first two chapters to *introduce* two of the major themes in Gamwell's thought: political liberalism and process metaphysics. The first of these will be treated in the present chapter. Subsequent chapters will return to these two themes, and to the connections between them, in deeper and sometimes unexpected ways.

It is unfortunate today that there are many people who, when they hear the word "liberalism," immediately think of "neoliberalism," the latter of which is close to the libertarian view of Milton Friedman, as found in two of his well-known books: *Capitalism and Freedom* and *Free to Choose*. Gamwell also calls this view "nineteenth-century liberalism," a stance that involves minimal government and maximum independence for individuals and for voluntary associations. Further, Friedman's stance is based on a preferential view of self-interest, which Gamwell is intent to criticize. On Gamwell's view, freedom involves more than absence of coercion on the part of government. In fairness to Friedman, it should be noted that, despite the fact that he is suspicious of the state because it is inherently coercive, he is not an anarchist, because maximal freedom for individuals and voluntary associations is not possible without the social order made possible by the minimal state. But government coercion is warranted only if it prevents greater coercion in its absence. The legitimate tasks for government, according to Friedman, are, first, national defense against extrasocietal coercion and acting as an umpire regarding domestic disputes; and second, acting as an intervener when voluntary exchange is either impossible or very costly, as in the regulation of public utilities (*BP*, 13–16).

One might wonder why freedom should be the ultimate goal if it is defined in a strictly negative way as the absence of coercion. Is there anything positive involved? From Friedman's point of view, there is no moral criterion with which wants can be evaluated in that they are solely matters of individual preference. That is, on Friedman's view there is no normative distinction between genuine and merely putative wants, hence the title to Gamwell's first book by way of reaction: *beyond* preference. Friedman would permit (but not require) charity, but only if it is voluntary. Forced charity is, on Friedman's view, (in)famously described as "theft." And Friedman is clear that one should be discouraged in a persuasive way from being charitable to people who are capable of voluntary exchange but who, for some reason or other, decide (prefer) not to work or to be underemployed. There can be improper charitable activity, he thinks, in addition to there being improper government activity. The private activity of individuals is the game of pursuing wants; government provides the context within which this game is played with minimum coercion. As Friedman sees things, politics is an instrumental good that is requisite for, but is not itself a part of, human flourishing (*BP*, 17–28).

The main distinguishing feature of the reformed liberalism defended by Gamwell is its opposition to the preferential view of happiness. Unfortunately, Friedman gives no indication that his own preferential view needs justification. But it *does* require justification, as Gamwell rightly argues. In effect, Friedman has assumed that ethics, in general, and political philosophy, in particular, are simple extensions of classical economic theory where consumer preferences are taken as given. The fact that this view is not as self-evident as Friedman thinks it is comes into focus when we notice that the dominant alternatives in Western philosophy, informed as they are by ancient and medieval ethical traditions, hold that certain things *ought* to be wanted and others *ought not*. This distinction sometimes involves the contrast between the truly human and the bestial and at other times involves the contrast between conformity to, or violation of, a religious ideal, but some such distinction has been seen historically as essential to a good life. By contrast, Friedman's now popular view sees no objective moral criterion. Gamwell, contra Friedman, thinks that a just social order is one that facilitates the realization of higher human possibilities (*BP*, 29–33).

Friedman commits what Gamwell calls the "partialist fallacy," where a part of the story is taken for the whole. No doubt even on, say, an Aristotelian view of happiness human wants are *part* of the story that must be told about a good life, but Gamwell is not convinced by Friedman's view that they are the whole story. If human activities as wholes cannot be moral, neither can the parts (wants or preferences). Friedman's assertion to the contrary is fallacious, Gamwell thinks. He is also understandably skeptical of Friedman's implication that all (or almost all) human wants are *equally* good. That is, even if self-interest in some way involves preference, it does not follow that it is *solely* a matter of preference. There is no escaping the need, once again contra Friedman, to distinguish between genuine and putative self-interest. Friedman does not even permit a moral criterion by which to make such a distinction. As I write, however, there are literally thousands of people on the streets in the city in which I live (Seattle) with addiction problems who provide very strong evidence for the need for the aforementioned distinction. Many people act on wants or preferences that are obviously *not* in their long-term self-interest (*BP*, 34–35).

In different terms, Friedman commits the partialist fallacy by claiming that, even if one (abstract) part of an act can be moral, the act as a whole is amoral pure preference. Gamwell rightly thinks that these two are incompatible: the former presupposes a comprehensive standard, whereas the latter is divorced from a comprehensive standard. We will see that both types of traditional liberalism commit this fallacy. Further, Kantian and other nonteleological theories also commit this fallacy in a different manner when they concentrate on only the abstract, formal aspect of ethics to the exclusion of the whole. In this regard, the partialist fallacy is an instance of what Whitehead famously calls the fallacy of misplaced concreteness; or better, the partialist fallacy *is* the fallacy of misplaced concreteness as it is found in ethics (*DP*, 42; *EG*, 103).

It would be a mistake to think that Gamwell's critique of liberalism ends with his case against Friedman. He also criticizes "twentieth-century liberalism," as exemplified in the thought of Alan Gewirth in his work *Reason and Morality*. Gewirth is different from Friedman in thinking that essential to human action is both voluntariness *and* purposiveness, both of which are assumed to be directed toward the good by any human agent who acts, on Gewirth's view. In addition to basic goods, which are necessary preconditions to action, there are also different sorts of nonbasic goods that are connected to an agent's purpose. Some of these are additive goods, in Gewirth's terminology, which an agent adds to other goods so as to increase *purpose-fulfillment*. Freedom *and* well-being are important to both Gewirth and Gamwell. Further, Gewirth is well-known for his principle of generic consistency whereby whatever is right for one person must be right for any similar person in similar circumstances. This deontological principle has both egalitarian and universalist elements which, along with his emphasis on purposiveness and the importance of well-being, distinguish his view from Friedman's (*BP*, 36–42).

If voluntariness refers to means, purposiveness refers to the end of well-being. It is not surprising that, in contrast to Friedman's *minimal* state, Gewirth calls for a *supportive* state that not only supplies and enforces uniform rules, but also ensures the material conditions required for purposive action conducive to well-being for all citizens. Income is, to a certain extent, constitutive of basic well-being, but it is also at a certain level part of additive well-being and becomes a morally permissible (rather than required) good (*BP*, 43–54).

However, Gamwell views *both* nineteenth- and twentieth-century liberalisms as types of *established* liberalism in need of critique. His primary reason is that even Gewirth's type of liberalism relies too heavily on the preferential view of happiness. The common preferential view of happiness in both Friedman and Gewirth excludes a moral criterion, as Gamwell sees things. It refuses to define the good for an individual, even at a very abstract level. Gamwell is aware that such a definition would indeed have to be very generic, as in Aristotle's saying that the good life includes nutritive, sentient, and rational flourishing. Quite understandably, Gamwell wants to be able to distinguish between putative self-interest, as in someone thinking that taking a mind-stultifying drug promotes self-interest, and genuine self-interest. He quite legitimately wants to point out that "self-interest" is ambiguous (*BP*, 54–55).

Clearly Gamwell is here at odds with Friedman, but it might be asked: How are his concerns at odds with those of Gewirth? The principle of generic consistency does not, despite appearances, provide a criterion for genuine self-interest in that flourishing is still viewed in terms of personal preference. The principle assumes that individuals *have* purposes, but it does not *prescribe* any, hence it fails as a normative theory. Further, Gewirth, along with Friedman, commits the partialist fallacy, as we will see. Or again, Gewirth and other twentieth-century liberals notice that citizens have *particular* purposes, but they do not say anything about *general purposiveness* or what Gamwell calls a "constitutive choice" regarding matters of ultimate concern. Constitutive choice regarding a supreme moral principle is hardly a mere preference, as Gamwell sees things (*BP*, 56–66).

We have seen that Gamwell thinks it is fallacious to assert that human activities can exist in part, but never as parts *of wholes*. If wholes cannot be moral, then neither can the parts, he thinks. It should be noted that the partialist fallacy is integrally connected to the view that self-interest is solely a matter of very particular preferences. But the supreme moral principle, to be discussed in due course, is not particular. It is, he thinks, *categorically required* (*BP*, 34, 68–69, 85, 90).

It is true that Gewirth asserts a universal principle of the good—the aforementioned principle of generic consistency—but this is not so much a comprehensive good as a piece of procedural advice regarding the good seen as preference satisfaction. We pay too stiff a conceptual price, Gamwell thinks, if we remain indifferent to the question as to whether human beings have an overall purpose. If the difference among human preferences makes no difference, then this assertion itself *is* a moral evaluation. To be specific, it is a moral evaluation in favor of relativism. In different terms, Gewirth's nonteleological theory appears to be agnostic regarding the human good, but he *does* implicitly take a stand on this issue: human preferences are on a par. On this basis, it is hard to see how Gewirth can justify his own universal principle of generic consistency.

We now have on the table a key idea explored by Gamwell throughout his career that I will later assess in light of his criticisms of another twentieth-century liberal: John Rawls. This key idea is that any universalist nonteleology in which all permissible conceptions of the comprehensive good are *merely* morally permissible is self-refuting and is bound implicitly by a prior (relativistic) conception of the good (*DP*, 256–62).

It cannot be the case that "all truth is relative" because this very assertion is stipulated to be nonrelative. That is, relativism is self-refuting because it is a type of nonrelative theory. Of course, conditions of choice vary widely among individuals and across cultures. Gamwell's point is that there is a *categorical* problem with relativism in that it collapses into its supposed opposite. Relative variables, real as they are, need a more general moral context because a relative variable cannot even be identified as such without a more general moral context (*BP*, 76, 81).

There are obviously many different meanings to the term "liberalism." In popular discourse (at least in the United States), the term contrasts with "conservatism," but Gamwell is looking at things with a wider historical lens where nineteenth-century laissez faire liberalism contrasts with twentieth-century egalitarian or welfare liberalism. In effect, contemporary conservatism is often the liberalism of an earlier period. Gamwell lumps both of these together under the label *established* liberalism, in contrast to the *reformed* liberalism that he would like to defend, otherwise called *substantive standard* liberalism. This view does not entail that pursuit of self-interest is necessarily selfish or morally wrong, but such pursuit can only be understood in terms of a larger whole. To think otherwise is to commit the partialist fallacy and to collapse the crucial distinction between putative and genuine self-interest. Indeed, it is to deny any substantive moral principles and to suggest the meaninglessness of "*x* is a categorically required choice," as we will see. Admittedly, *some* human choices are matters of preference and *some* alternatives are comparatively equal. But this does not mean that the alternatives are neither good nor bad in themselves or that they are solely matters of preference (*BP*, 7–12, 87, 89).

There are also distinctions within reformed liberalism. Gamwell views John Dewey's political theory as a type of reform or substantive standard liberalism, but one that is nonetheless defective in certain ways. That is, his liberalism is a step in the right direction, as Gamwell sees things, but only a step. Dewey is a thoroughgoing process philosopher, especially in his *Reconstruction in Philosophy*, which is to Gamwell's liking, but it is only in an attenuated sense that we can see him as a metaphysician. This is a problem given Gamwell's quest for the metaphysical basis for democratic society. At the very least, Dewey denies to metaphysics the pride of place as first philosophy. But Dewey *does* orient us toward a substantive standard, with philosophy and science partnering so as to lead us—individually and collectively—to a practical telos. Dewey's reconstruction of philosophy makes all thought instrumental in the interest of democracy, with "democracy" referring to both a form of government and a social ideal at the associational level. In this regard democratic political theory is the inclusive philosophical enterprise (*BP*, 92–99).

Dewey's reformed or reconstructed liberalism is obviously quite different from nineteenth-century laissez faire liberalism, where the inegalitarian consequences of the economic order work against the democratic ideal. America had unfortunately become a pecuniary culture, according to Dewey. The marketplace is not as natural as laissez faire defenders imagine. The scientific community points us toward a more humane age in which human individuals inherit from *and creatively contribute to* each other in intelligent association. There really is no such thing as a separate individual, on Dewey's view. The telos of social life is nothing other than maximal individuality-in-association, in contrast to nineteenth-century liberalism's individualistic consumption-regarding ethos. Dewey and Friedman are not only different from each other; they are dramatically opposed. For one, the commercial sector is subservient to a communal telos; for the other, associational and governmental activity are subservient to the profit-seeking sector (*BP*, 100–113).

One standard criticism of Friedman's view that is *not* emphasized by Gamwell is that nineteenth-century liberalism is plagued by "individualism." The issue is complicated because, although there is a significant amount of attention paid to individuals in Friedman, there is also a significant amount of attention paid to voluntary associations (or nonprofit organizations or "the third sector" that is nongovernmental and noncommercial), of the sort that Alexis de Tocqueville noticed as crucial in American culture and in the nascent American intellectual tradition (*BP*, 1–5, 154). As far back as one of the classics in early liberalism (John Locke's "A Letter concerning Toleration") it was not only individual freedom that mattered in liberal theory, but also associational freedom, especially for religious associations. It is not primarily "the individual" in Friedman that Gamwell finds problematic so much as the overconcentration on individual *preferences* at the expense of other principles.

The distinction between reform liberals like Dewey and Gamwell, on the one hand, and established liberals, like Friedman and Gewirth, on the other, is that the former develop a moral criterion, a comprehensive moral principle, by which happiness can be defined, which implies a distinction between putative and genuine self-interest. Admittedly, Dewey worked on the problem of bridging science and value throughout his career, as the great scholar of American philosophy, John Smith, attests. But he was never tempted by relativism. He is clear that maximal individuality is *constituted by* association with others, whereas in established liberalism, even of the twentieth-century sort, associational life is largely instrumental to successful fulfillment of preferences. Dewey is famous for seeing means and ends on a continuum because every means is also an end and vice versa (*BP*, 114–18).

Due to the processual nature of the real, as Dewey sees things, one can speak of ends-in-view, but not static ends-in-themselves. He was not clear, however, as Gamwell and Smith interpret him, on the question of *ultimate* ends, whether processual or static. Growth in terms of individuals-in-society constitutes the human telos in Dewey's version of reform liberalism, in contrast to both forms of established liberalism. But his metaphysics, if we can call it that, consists in the claim that all things are contingencies-in-association. That is, metaphysical traits are strictly contingent. Dewey is a philosopher who restricts generalizations to the empirical features of the items that he just so happens to have considered. This is in contrast to the truly metaphysical characteristics of all actual and possible items of experience, as we will see. Empirical generalization is not the same as the effort to find necessarily true statements about traits of existence. Further, the "common faith" to which

Dewey adhered is a nontheistic religion. This is because belief in God would signal for him a surrender of universal contingency-in-association. Although Dewey confusedly thought that even metaphysical traits were contingent, we will see that Gamwell provides a great service to scholars by clarifying the idea that the metaphysical trait of contingency-in-association *is itself necessary* in that all possible realities must exhibit it. But this gets us ahead of the story I would like to tell (*BP*, 119–22; *EG*, 36).

The version of reform liberalism defended by Gamwell is one backed by a comprehensive moral principle, according to which alternatives for choice are compared, contrasted, and evaluated. In simple terms, every self-understanding or self-conscious choice implies a standard and this standard must be morally evaluative. If human activity were completely determined, there might not be a need for such a comprehensive moral principle. However, human beings have an insistent sense that *choices* have to be made, hence the need for a moral standard. Gamwell likes to illustrate this point by appeal to the famous lines from the Robert Frost poem "The Road Not Taken," where two roads diverged in a wood. Frost cannot understand himself accurately unless he knows that he *could have chosen* the well-worn path rather than the one that was less traveled yet chosen by him. Further, the claim that the two paths are morally indifferent both contradicts our experience of moral choice and itself implies a morally evaluative judgment (*BP*, 74, 80; *EG*, 86; *MRF*, 216; *DP*, 38).

Comparing choice alternatives and realizing (often after the fact) that some choices are *better* than others requires an objective standard, which Gamwell usually calls a comprehensive variable. In addition, this variable itself cannot be a matter of choice because, if it were a matter of choice, there could be no correct understanding and no poor choices. But there *are* poor choices. Nor should we forget the aforementioned argument that *all* truth cannot be relative because the claim that it is so is itself nonrelative. Relativism is nonrelative and hence self-refuting (*BP*, 73–77).

Gamwell does not shy away from calling the comprehensive moral principle a *supreme* evaluative variable. He uses this word because he thinks that what is needed is a principle that can operate when comparing similarities and differences in choices that are *categorical*, rather than those that deal with concrete particulars. Principles that are operative at a specific level require another principle at a higher level of generality, of which those operations at a more concrete level are specifications. It is also insightful of Gamwell to notice that if we identify exceptions to principles operative at a specific level, as we often do, then this requires a more general principle so as to account for our "reasons to the contrary." We see here yet another example of Gamwell's persistence and thoroughgoing consistency in his transcendental reasoning: if it is claimed, as it often is, that *all* moral principles are exception*able*, then it is crucial to notice that this claim itself is exception*less* (*BP*, 80, 83, 91).

Gamwellian freedom includes the idea that the evaluation of specific alternatives for choice can occur only against the background of a comprehensive telos. We are moral beings precisely because we can make bad choices and are not programmed to do only the good. We will see that there are similarities between Gamwell's view of freedom and Immanuel Kant's partially contrasting view. The main difference between the two lies in the fact that Kantian freedom subsists in the sheer absence of comprehensive purpose. Gamwell refers to the human capacity to make choices as *original freedom*, a designation that no doubt is meant to counterbalance the more famous (or infamous) theological doctrine of original sin. He frequently reminds us of human fragmentariness and fallibility (which are hallmarks of original sin), but in Gamwellian fashion he emphasizes that these characteristics of human understanding and choice can be seen as such only against a background that is comprehensive, thus reinforcing his stance regarding the transcendental conditions of subjectivity. We do not adequately understand ourselves as human persons if we are not cognizant, whether explicitly or implicitly, of ourselves as possessive of original freedom, which is something much deeper than preference satisfaction, considering the latter's compatibility with determinism (*DP*, 47–57).

Freedom in Gamwell is positively correlated to the public world to which one is related, once again contra the preference satisfaction view. The concept of comprehensive purpose, as we will see, is compatible with a wide range of moral standards of lesser generality, but these less abstract standards nonetheless require a comprehensive telos as background and as a standard for evaluation. The (process) metaphysical character of reality is tightly connected to Gamwell's concept of freedom. This is due to the fact that any actual occasion of experience both prehends (grasps) past influences on it and functions as a cause facing its future. This requires that each occasion is to a certain degree self-determining. In fact, Gamwell agrees with Hartshorne's characterization of prehension as a sort of creative synthesis. The present *must* be different from the past. If it were not different, it would be solely a repetition and could not be distinguished from the past. But we *do* quite easily distinguish the present from the past. As Whitehead famously put the point, "The many become one, and are increased by one"

(Whitehead 1978, 21). Neither complete other-determination nor complete self-determination make sense; indeed, they are self-contradictory notions. Complete other-determination would imply that the present is not different from the past (but it obviously *is* different), and complete self-determination would imply that there is no past (but there obviously *is* a past). The unification of past influences is, Gamwell thinks, an exercise in freedom. In effect, the word "complete" is at odds with both concepts: other-determination and self-determination. *Complete* self-determination denies the insistent causal efficacy of the past (*BP*, 152–53; *DG*, 180).

Greater creativity or freedom is made possible by a prehension or synthesis of greater diversity of influences. It is astute of Gamwell to argue that, because greater creativity or freedom is the unification of more diverse influences, each activity partially creates the degree of freedom that will obtain in the future. This is why rational freedom is greater than that typically found in the subhuman world. Because *every* activity of an actual occasion of experience affects succeeding activities, this transcendental condition of reality counts against (Gamwell says "convicts") Kantian nonteleology. That is, an exercise of freedom is the affirmation of *some* telos or purpose. Indeed, an individual with practical reason is one who chooses among possible purposes (*DG*, 180–81).

At this early point in the book, I would like to be explicit about the comprehensive telos that Gamwell defends. It goes as follows:

> The telos that all human activity ought to pursue is the maximal creativity of all future activities or of the future as such. Moreover, it is precisely the pursuit of maximal future creativity in or through which present activity maximizes its own creativity. One makes the most of the opportunity one's past delivers when one seeks to make the most of the opportunity one delivers to one's successors. This must be the case because creativity is the comprehensive variable in terms of which present activity, as all activity, is evaluated. (*DG*, 182)

Regarding this comprehensive telos, the idea of "better" refers to that which contributes more to the supreme diversity that is supremely unified in the concept of God. The transcendental telos is the divine good. The divine relativity (the phrase Gamwell borrows from Hartshorne) must mean a profound range of alternatives, but this does not open Gamwell (or Hartshorne) to the charge of arbitrariness in that one constant is that God, as the greatest conceivable, ever exemplifies the good. Human goodness is constituted by its relation to the above comprehensive (divine) telos (*DG*, 182–84).

Although Gamwell's terminology alters a bit throughout his career, the contrast between the two liberalisms remains. In a later work, *Politics as a Christian Vocation*, he refers (perhaps as a concession to popular culture) to the libertarian view as the conservative ideal of community and the welfare view as *the* liberal view. As he notes, there is a certain fluidity in the ways both scholars and citizens generally use these terms. What he calls the conservative view in *PCV* is one that asks for minimal government and maximal individual liberty. By contrast, the liberal view calls for more extensive government activity. Despite the label changes, Gamwell continues to view these stances as related beneath the surface, as when "separate" aquatic plants are connected beneath the surface of the water by a common root system. The common root here is a common purpose in terms of the satisfaction of private (or associational) interests and ends. Goods and services are instrumental to consumer preferences when these two positions are tightly allied to the economic order. As before, the common root is problematic because principles of justice cannot be separated from the common good. The "conservative" and "liberal" views share a conception of the good in terms of maximal economic prosperity so as to satisfy consumer preferences. Gamwell admits that the conservative ideal has its own virtues, but these are private virtues tied to efficient preference satisfaction. For example, strength of character is needed to discipline wanton appetite that gets in the way of long-term preference satisfaction. Ironically, some conservatives urge the government to enforce such discipline and to encourage family responsibilities for the same reason. These private virtues, conservatives tend to think, are best cultivated in local communities. Admittedly, there is an understandable difference between private interests and private virtue, but this distinction is nonetheless compatible with the view that the good life is individualistic or, at most, associational in families and local communities (*PCV*, 117–22).

Unfortunately, Gamwell may be correct that individualism may very well be the most pervasive communal ideal in American history, an individualism that (in different ways) characterizes the conservative and (unreformed) liberal views. His own stance, which he identifies as compatible with the authentic Christian one, sees an individual as more accurately described as an individual-in-community. That is, Gamwell's reformed liberalism and authentic Christianity converge in the critique of maximal want satisfaction. Private virtues, as important as these are, are not sufficient for the good life in that public virtue is also required. Conservatives *and* (unreformed) liberals sell us short in that even the latter see community as instrumental to want satisfaction. But complicity between Christian churches and the conservative ideal is especially bothersome to Gamwell. The reason for this is that the conservative ideal does not conform to the thesis that the good life is one that is conducive to maximizing access to *general* conditions of creativity equally available to *all*, as we will see. To put the point in the starkest terms, the conservative ideal is a misrepresentation of both (neo-classical) metaphysics and Christianity. Indeed, it is insightful of Gamwell to argue that the (unreformed) liberal and especially the conservative ideals of community show complicity with social and political conditions that betray the presence of individuals who are more economically and socially advantaged (*PCV*, 123–129).

Much more work is needed to understand Gamwell's moral and political philosophy and to appreciate his contributions to this discipline. Much of this work involves a consideration of his commitment to process metaphysics, a topic to which I now turn. This work will, along with Brian Barry, assume that reasoning about justice will have no alternative to democracy of some sort. But, unlike Barry, Gamwell will not conclude that any discourse about the good will be uncertain and speculative in the pejorative sense. Gamwell does not, like Barry, assume that the overwhelming evidence is in favor of skepticism. That is, Gamwell does not think that pervasive pluralism in society *necessitates* skepticism. If it did, there would be a contradiction between the words "skepticism" and "necessity" (*DP*, 244–46, 263–65).

CHAPTER TWO

Process Metaphysics

In addition to the previous chapter's introduction to Gamwell's political philosophy, the present chapter will introduce his views on metaphysics. Both of these chapters together will set the stage for more detailed consideration of his views in subsequent chapters.

Dewey's contingency-in-association is given a quite different backing by Gamwell than the backing given to it by Dewey himself. In a word, Gamwell's approach is *metaphysical*. As before, it will be my aim in the present chapter to introduce Gamwell's process metaphysics, which is heavily indebted to the thought of Alfred North Whitehead and Charles Hartshorne, neither of whom developed a comprehensive political theory, although it can be stated with assurance that both Whitehead and Hartshorne were political liberals of some sort, as Randall Morris and I have argued in detail in different ways. Metaphysical characteristics are those that are necessary rather than contingent. This does not mean that there is no appeal to experience in metaphysics, because a metaphysical characteristic is one that must be present in *all* experienced realities. That is, there is no possible experience that fails to exhibit a metaphysical characteristic.

A reality in which contingency-in-association is absent is inconceivable. Hartshorne's way of putting the relevant distinction, agreed to by Gamwell, is between local and cosmic (i.e., between nonmetaphysical and metaphysical) variables. Local variables may or may not be exemplified, but cosmic, metaphysical variables cannot not be exemplified. Further, like Whitehead and Hartshorne, Gamwell thinks of metaphysical characteristics as value-laden, at the very least because the justification of moral claims (once again, universal comparison is involved at least implicitly in every self-understanding and every self-conscious choice) depends upon a metaphysical principle. Gamwell's pithy way of putting the point is to say that the metaphysical variable *is* an evaluative principle (*BP*, 123–29).

Metaphysical principles, to be discussed in more detail later, are those needed in order for reality to be comprehensively understood *and evaluated*. A powerfully persuasive "ought" grows out of a comprehensive factual "is." At the most basic level, fact and value are coimplicative. Assuming that human beings are influenced by their pasts and environments (i.e., assuming that they are partially determined), we can conclude that they are at least partially constituted by relations with others, both others that have influenced them and others whom they will influence. Due to the fact that this determination is only partial, human beings necessarily face contingency. Gamwell thinks we cannot even imagine a reality in which contingency-in-association is absent. Such a reality would have to be, *per impossibile*, either completely other-determined or completely self-determined. In some forms of theism (not defended by Gamwell), God determines everything, a view that will be criticized later; and some might implausibly defend solipsism as a type of complete self-determination. But a reality that is *completely* self-chosen would have nothing to choose among, it would have no past or future to control. At the other extreme, a *complete* determination by another would have nothing that was determined, an alternative that is indistinguishable from the posit of absolute nothingness (*BP*, 130–32).

A reality that is *completely* necessary does not even allow for the possibility of some other reality. This is because any implication of this reality would also be necessary. Gamwell defends the Hartshornian view that causal explanation is incurably pluralistic and incurably contingent, as least in part. On the basis of many past events, one must account for a single present event, but there is no airtight logic for such a derivation. What is needed, in addition to partial determination, is some sort of creation. All concrete singular realities are to some degree self-determinative. What is distinctive about human beings is the way in which they can become self-conscious of this process of choice. *All* concrete singulars, however, are partially self-determined (and hence partially other-determined). In a way, freedom within limits has no alternative if *complete* self-determination and *complete* other-determination are impossibilities (*BP*, 133–34).

Whitehead, Hartshorne, and Gamwell define reality in terms of "actual occasions" or "concrete events" or "units of process" that are partially determined by prior causes and partially self-determined in their unifications of relations with these prior causes. Each unit of process begins as a partial effect of its past and ends as a partial cause of some future units of process. All of these self-determinations are unifications. The comprehensive principle of evaluation, given the processual character of the real, is *maximal* unity-in-diversity or *maximal* contingency-in-association (to use Dewey's label). There is a correlation between other-determination and self-determination in the sense that greater complexity in the former allows greater scope and intensity in the latter. Here we should note a crucial point of connection to the previous chapter: if the good of human individuals (when seen as streams of units of process with a line of inheritance among the actual occasions of its existence) is maximal unity-in-diversity, then the good for such an individual is *not* a matter of mere preference (*BP*, 134–38).

Happiness is maximal growth, given the particular other-determination an individual experiences. One can think of the life of a human individual as an aesthetic whole that is other-determined by its relations with the wider world and capable of self-determined contributions beyond itself. Human individuals are temporally ordered societies of actual occasions. The moral task for human beings is to harmonize the maximal growth of individuals with the telos of the universe, which consists in maximal unity-in-diversity at a cosmic level. Such harmonization produces a profound sense of peace. This peace involves a satisfaction deeper than any particular joy or sorrow because it deals with comprehensive or cosmic rather than merely local concerns. Happiness at its deepest level for human beings involves the realization of maximal unity-in-diversity in harmony with the same at the most general level (*BP*, 138–39).

As the book proceeds I will be concentrating on the connection between process metaphysics and political theory and the ways in which such a metaphysics contributes teleologically to maximal happiness. Thus far, however, we are in a position to say that the distinction between putative and genuine self-interest consists in the former's failing to maximize one's own unity-in-variety or beauty or happiness and in the latter's success in these regards. This success involves not freedom in the sense of absence of coercion (or at least not primarily this sort of freedom), but the freedom that comes from realizing that one is contributing to the achievement of effective unity-in-variety both for oneself and for others in the future. The democratic ideal implies that the telos of the social order is to maximize community-regarding goods, including the flourishing of individuals-in-community. Of course, such a telos requires that one be free to choose the associations to which one belongs, both due to the flourishing such choice facilitates in individuals and for the sake of the public world. What we want in the public world is both greater width (more individuals and associations contributing to the maximization of happiness) and greater depth (with such contributions emanating from individuals committed to character development rather than to mere want satisfaction). There is no avoiding the fact that comparatively private worlds are preconditions for the maximal public world (*BP*, 142–50).

We should be well aware of the objection that, because both human understanding is fragmentary and a comprehensive moral principle is very general, the joining of these two might not yield fruitful practical deliberation. The proper response is to readily admit the need for more particular moral standards, a need that will be addressed later. Moral discourse needs to occur at several different levels of generality/specificity. Another likely criticism is that there is an implied religious character to the comprehensive metaphysical variable discussed by Gamwell. This religious character, indeed the theistic character of the process view, will also be discussed throughout the book. The process or neoclassical concept of God is not lurking implicitly behind the scenes but will be made explicit. The maximal public ideal finds its justification in the neoclassical God, if not in the inadequacies of the God of classical theism (*BP*, 151).

If unity-in-diversity is a metaphysical characteristic of actualities, in general, God as a perfect actuality would exhibit this characteristic preeminently. Consider the utilitarian greatest happiness principle (although other moral principles would work as well). Although human beings can talk *about* this principle, no human being could actually experience the greatest happiness. Only an omnipresent, omniscient (properly defined), and omnibenevolent being could do this. Only a comprehensive individual in whom every realization of value is united could do this. Human activities are necessarily fragmentary, in contrast to a comprehensive individual in whom various human and other achievements could be measured. Gamwell views Hartshorne as the philosopher who has offered the most thorough and systematic explication of this comprehensive individual, which Hartshorne calls "the divine relativity." We are related to some actualities and these only inadequately. God is related to all actualities and ideally so. The distinction between an individual who is related to some and an individual who is related to all is a metaphysical one such that God is the one metaphysical *individual* (as opposed to a metaphysical *principle*). On this account, there can be no God without a world with which to be related. That is, the class of nondivine individuals cannot be empty (*DP*, 139–42).

Hartshorne is also famous for his distinction between divine existence (*that* God exists) and divine actuality (*how* God exists from moment to moment). As a perfect being, God's *existence* is necessary, but not God's *actuality*, the latter of which constantly changes because time is the process by which possibilities are actualized. Widespread rejection of theistic teleology is largely due to classical theistic assumptions, in contrast to the process or neoclassical concept of God found in Hartshorne and Gamwell. Classical theistic omnipotence, and the resultant nastiest version of the theodicy problem, is one of the key problems here, along with classical theistic insistence that God is a strictly permanent being who is not at all changed by creaturely suffering. The distinguishing characteristic of the neoclassical God, in Gamwell's view, is God's necessarily comprehensive and omnibenevolent purpose. In a sense one can say legitimately that something is good because God wills it, but Gamwell avoids the Euthyphro problem by also claiming that a perfectly good being would will something because it is itself moral. In this way Gamwell also mediates between voluntarists and intellectualists regarding the concept of God.

With Whitehead as his guide, Gamwell holds that the insistent notions of right and wrong depend on this (neoclassical) divine background; otherwise our activities are passing whiffs of insignificance. We complete what the past begins in us, but we are left in the present with a decision between authenticity and duplicity, with the latter involving either a lie or self-contradiction. Gamwell has a special talent, detailed throughout the present book, at pointing out our self-contradictions. Religious thought, broadly construed, is an attempt to direct our attention to the final real things (actual occasions, including divine actual occasions). Each of our experiences unifies relations to the past by means of a creative de-cision (literally, a cutting off of some possibilities so that others remain). These decisions, however trivial, condition the future. The moral law, as Gamwell sees it, is to pursue the maximal divine good, with "maximal" qualified by the process commonplace that with each new moment new possibilities for human and divine greatness come to the fore, such that the terms "maximal" or "comprehensive" are not to be equated with "total" or "totality" (*DP*, 143–49).

To those who *deny* the existence of the sort of universal norm defended by Gamwell, he makes the following telling reply: such a denial is self-refuting because the denial itself indicates a belief about all true understandings. Gamwell is well aware of the fact that many thinkers claim not to believe in God or in any universal norms. In fact, such denials are themselves ironically now the norm. He is claiming, however, that there are theistic *implications* of every belief. Any claim to truth involves an implied premise that, if the claim is contested, it can be redeemed by the communal practice of rational argument. Granted, it is common to hear that the capacity to give reasons and to assess them is always indexed to some specific argumentation community. But those who emphasize this point usually fail to notice that this claim *itself* implies that the understanding of argument it purports to denigrate points to a universal character of argument (i.e., its indexicality). Those who continue to undermine argument in this way, it seems, can do so only by retreating into nonrational ideology or dogmatism. This criticism applies as well to defenders of "reformed epistemology" (like Nicholas Wolterstorff), the innocent until guilty view that people should be free to believe anything they want until their beliefs are shown to be contradictory or inadequate to the facts. But in asserting that one need not have reasons for one's beliefs one contradicts oneself by purporting to designate a universal feature of beliefs (i.e., their innocent until proven guilty quality) (*DP*, 151–67).

Gamwell seeks rapprochement with both those who defend the correspondence theory of truth and those who defend a coherence theory. The latter may come as a surprise, given what has been said above regarding the need for a (divine) universal standard. But Gamwell notes that the very truth of a true opinion has an effect on an argumentation community when such a community is construed as an ideal community of communication spread out over time and including all rational inquirers. A true understanding *is* true (in a correspondence sense), but this understanding of truth surely ought to have an impact on what *would be* agreed to by rational inquirers over the long haul, when petty passions and impediments to clear-headedness are evened out. The activities of this long-term collection of ideal knowers can be seen as an analogy for the activity of the metaphysical individual, who knows what would be agreed to by this community of human knowers over time when adjustments are made for their cognitive impediments. To believe something is to implicitly make a claim to truth and to authenticity in pursuit (without duplicity) of the divine good (*DP*, 168–75).

These first two chapters have *introduced* both Gamwell's political liberalism and his process theism. In subsequent chapters I will explore how his humanitarian ideal (otherwise known as the way of reason), when backed by neoclassical theism, fares when compared with various other stances: for example, the view of moral and political principles as nonuniversal (as in different post-Enlightenment thinkers), the view of such principles as universal but nontranscendental (as in utilitarian thinkers), the view of such principles as transcendental but nonteleological (in the Kantian tradition), the stance that sees moral and political principles as metaphysical but nontheistic (as in Iris Murdoch), and the view of such principles as classically theistic (as in Reinhold Niebuhr) (*WTP*, 223).

Gamwell's stance is that neither nonteleology nor teleology without metaphysics can provide the ground for democratic political theory. With David Hume and Immanuel Kant, however, Hartshorne and Gamwell think that not much help comes from classical theism, which the latter thinkers allege is an incoherent position. If the preeminent being is in *all* respects eternal (in the sense of being outside of time altogether) and changeless, then the distinctions between absolute and relative, necessary and contingent, are equivalent to the distinction between eminent and lesser reality, respectively. But there *are* eminent cases of being related to others. There are also cases of being admirably re-sponsive to the contingent features of the world. Classical theism offers only unintelligible divine atemporal "indesponses" to what happens in the world of temporal change (*DG*, 17–18).

A helpful way of organizing Gamwell's ideas can occur when they are seen in terms of a series of logically exhaustive choices, a series that shows the influence of Hartshorne's position matrices: either there is no metaphysical ground for moral-political claims or there is such a ground. If there is no such ground, then the eventual result is amoralism in that the moral-political claims cannot last for long if suspended in midair without metaphysical support, as we will see. If there is such a ground, then the ground is either teleological or nonteleological. If it is nonteleological, then something like Kant's position results. If it is teleological, then this teleological ground is either a transcendental telos or a nontranscendental telos. If it is nontranscendental, then one ends up with an empirical teleology, perhaps of the sort defended by Alasdair MacIntyre. If there is a transcendental telos, then the telos is either metaphysical or nonmetaphysical. If it is nonmetaphysical, then one is likely to end up with a hermeneutical telos of the sort defended by Karl-Otto Apel. But because of the defects of all of these views (more later on Kant, MacIntyre, and Apel), Gamwell thinks it is wise to defend a *transcendental teleology* as the ground for moral and political philosophy (*DG*, 155–57); indeed, such a view is a metaphysical necessity.

One is morally obliged to maximize the good. This involves the attempt to identify what things or what kinds of things are metaphysically basic. The final real things, on the process view, are actualities, or better, actual occasions.

This conflicts with the view that the final real things are rocks, plants, and chairs. This widely held, but mistaken, view commits what Whitehead calls the fallacy of misplaced concreteness, where mere aggregates of the true concrete singulars are taken to be the fundamental realities, as opposed to the abstract collections that they are. The above examples are all composites rather than concrete actualities or concrete singulars. A metaphysical ethics is one that tries to identify both actualities and composite states of affairs that maximally exemplify the good. It should be remembered that as an everyday occurrence we evaluate items as better or worse: gems, apples, pets, furniture, and fellow people. The conviction that practical reason can reach rationally defensible answers to these evaluative questions unwittingly supplies a premise for a theistic argument for the neoclassical God, who is a comprehensive actuality of which all things actual and possible are parts, an all-inclusive exemplification in which real things can be compared and hence evaluated (*DG*, 164–69).

Hartshorne and Gamwell refer to the divine relativity, which is related to all actuality *and possibility* in that reality without possibility is nonsensical. This is because to eliminate all possibility would be to signal the end of temporal process altogether. But time goes on. A reality devoid of possibility would mean that nothing could conceivably be different from what it is at present, which would be a strictly necessitarian world in which process would come to an end. The distinction between past and future is the same as that between reality that is determined and reality that is determinable or yet to be determined. The present, on the processual account, is the becoming determinate of what was previously indeterminate. This processual view has clear implications for deity in that there is a need to distinguish between momentary divine actuality and the divine as a composite individual who is serially and sequentially ordered, in Hartshornian fashion. The series of divine occasions is characterized by universal relatedness to all actuality and all possibility (*DG*, 169–71).

Gamwell traces the inadequacies of classical theism to the influence of Plato and Aristotle on philosophers and theologians in the Abrahamic religions. I am not sure that this is accurate, at least in the case of Plato. Gamwell is correct that classical theism is riddled with contradictions, but I suspect that he is premature in thinking that classical theism is now merely of historical interest. This suspicion is due to the fact that many or most analytic (and other) theists are still classical theists. I would like to say a few things about Plato, leaving a more detailed criticism of classical theism until later. Gamwell has us realize, however, that we should shake ourselves loose of the widely held assumption that regarding metaphysics there are only two major options: some version of classical metaphysics and some version of skepticism regarding classical metaphysics that relies on Hume or Kant or both. At the very least, there is a third neoclassical alternative that relies on Hume and Kant and others for its criticisms of classical theism, but which thinks that these thinkers themselves prematurely closed the door to metaphysical thinking. Neoclassical metaphysics has not so much been refuted as ignored. That is, philosophy without metaphysics is usually the result of ignorance of the neoclassical alternative (*DG*, 175; *EG*, 3, 38).

Plato's thoughts on the concept of God have two facets, one static and the other dynamic, with the latter being largely forgotten by classical theists. The first facet has a distinction between the immutable and the mutable or between the formal and the material. Both soul and God are put into the former elements in each of these pairs, in monopolar fashion. However, in the second facet of Plato's thought on God, motion is granted to soul, including God as the World Soul. Reality, including divine reality, is one, but this unity can only be discursively or metaphysically understood in terms of these two facets. In the first, and more famous, facet of Plato's concept of God he favors "ontolatry," the worship of being. Several Platonic texts come to mind in this regard (e.g., *Phaedo* 80a–b; *Republic* 380e, 381b–c, 381e, 382e; *Laws* 797d; *Epinomis* 982d–e, 985a). This facet sees something inherently perilous about change from the perspective of divine fixity. In this facet of Plato's thought about God there is no need for God to change in that if such a change were to occur, it would indicate something imperfect about God in that a perfect being would have no need to change. The second facet of Plato's concept of God flirts with "gignolatry," the worship of becoming. Here soul, including God as the World Soul, is defined as self-motion and vitality. That is, soul, including God as the World Soul, is anything but reified substance, but rather has the power or *dynamis* of self-motion (e.g., *Phaedrus* 245–46; book 10 of the *Laws*). But not even in this second facet does Plato fully succumb to gignolatry in that even in this facet God *always* exhibits self-motion, indicating a consistency to divine *dynamis*.

There is an ironic shift that occurs in the transition from Plato to Aristotle, a shift that is crucial to the development of classical theism via the mediation of the neoplatonists (who were just as much neoaristotelians). Plato is famous for a dipolar categorical scheme, wherein form is contrasted to matter and being is contrasted to becoming, but he ends up with a sort of cosmological monism wherein the divine animal (the World Soul) includes all. Aristotle, conversely, is famous for a monopolar categorical scheme of embodied form, yet he ends up with a cosmological dualism more severe than anything found in Plato's dialogues. That is, the mistaken *identification* of Plato's view with the first facet of his thought on God is problematic because, like a child begging for both, Plato declares through the Eleatic Stranger in the *Sophist* (249d) that reality as dynamic power involves abstract continuity through change. The second facet of Plato's concept of God drops out altogether in Aristotle and in the classical theists he influenced, whether directly or indirectly.

It should now be clear why the aforementioned claim on the part of Gamwell (*DG*, 175), that the defects in classical theists in the Abrahamic traditions are due to what they inherited from Plato and Aristotle, needs to be nuanced. The problem does not lie in the assumption found in the *Republic* (381b) that God is in every way the best possible, but rather with the assumption that the best possible would be changeless in every respect. Although Plato himself is partly to blame for traveling as far as he did down the road to ontolatry, he took other journeys in his dialogues that are worth revisiting. It is Aristotle, not Plato, who is most responsible for the metaphysical problems found in classical theism (again via the mediation of the neoplatonists), hence it would serve us well to notice the historical contingency of what exactly classical theists borrowed from the Greeks and what they ignored. There is nothing objectionable in itself about the view of divine perfection found in the *Republic*, wherein a perfect being is assumed not to change, as long as this view is seen as applying to abstract divine existence, rather than to concrete divine actuality. God *always changes* and both words are needed.

In the next chapter I will continue the effort, initiated here in this chapter, to avoid the widespread false dilemma between classical theistic metaphysics and skepticism regarding metaphysical thinking, in general. A consideration of Plato in this regard helps us to realize that the historical sedimentation of principles in theistic metaphysics is not nearly as simple as many suppose. Process theistic metaphysics is especially intent on revitalizing and slightly modifying Plato's definition of being in the *Sophist* (247e) as power (*dynamis*), both the power to influence others and the power to be influenced by others, in however slight a manner. It is this view of reality—from the subatomic to the human to the divine levels—as composed of dynamic pulses of energy that animates process thinkers, in general, including Gamwell.

One should always be cognizant, however, of Gamwell's joint interest in both theistic metaphysics and the ultimate grounding of moral-political thought. For example, in response to the amoralists mentioned above, a Gamwellian syllogism might go as follows: If God does not exist, then objective moral values do not exist (as atheists themselves like Jean-Paul Sartre are more than willing to grant). But objective moral values do exist (as is presupposed in our daily moral activities, especially when we are mistreated). Therefore, God exists. This brief argument provides a smooth segue to one of the two major metaphysical claims explicated in the next chapter.

In the present chapter I have been examining the metaphysical outline sketched by Gamwell in light of the thought of Whitehead and especially Hartshorne. True metaphysical statements are coherent such that if "something exists" is true, this implies that "something that is temporal exists" and "something that is related to other things exists." In contrast to the philosophical tradition that identifies the metaphysical final things as substances that need nothing other than themselves in order to exist, the process view is that the final real things are actual occasions or events. Another distinctive feature of this view of metaphysics is that it includes as the universal character of actual occasions the idea that not only concrete things are real but also possibilities. This is a far cry from the dualist view that has haunted the history of metaphysics that there are ultimately two sorts of reality, both of them substances: physical and nonphysical. Metaphysical dualism is incoherent in that metaphysics deals with *universal* characteristics of the real and, on the dualist hypothesis, there are no ultimate characteristics of the real but two sets of characteristics that are in conflict with each other. Each actual occasion, on the process view, has internal relations to the past but is largely externally related to the future. Further, each actual occasion has *some* measure of subjective self-determination or self-creation in the present as it decides (literally) which past influences will be cut off and left behind and which will exert additional causal influence on the future. Subject and object are not so much separate substances but different phases in the history of actual occasions and the historical routes of such (*EG*, 59–65).

Time as a succession of presents consists in a series of actual occasions wherein past actualities are grasped by present subjective occasions under the pressure of choosing among future possibilities. Because inclusion of the past can be only partial, determinism is ruled out. That is, becoming cannot completely reenact what has happened before. That the differences among past, present, and future are relative is itself nonrelative, which is quite different from the claim that all objectively true sentences are eternally true. Only the very abstract can be true necessarily, not any concrete decisions that are made in time. In speaking of things that exist, we frequently talk not of actual occasions but of societies of such as they occur in a series or in a line of inheritance. A human being, for example, is a complex society of societies of societies. This is true of God as well, but the divine cosmic society is nonfragmentary, in contrast to human and subhuman fragmentariness. Fragmentary relatedness is quite different from all-inclusive relatedness (*EG*, 66–73).

There is also quite a difference between claiming that there has to be something or other and claiming that there has to be some particular being. Analogously, there is quite a difference between claiming that God has to have *some* actual state in the future and claiming what the particular actual state will be. Concepts can designate abstracts or indeterminates, but not concrete actuality. Gamwell endorses Whitehead's doctrine that "the many become one and are increased by one," which applies to all actual occasions. It is a metaphysical doctrine because it applies to the character of existence as such. This Whiteheadian dictum, however, may be in conflict with Whitehead's own doctrine of God, as many commentators have noticed. In this regard it is important to notice that Gamwell resolves any conflict that might occur between the Whiteheadian and Hartshornian views of God in favor of the latter. God is an everlasting series of divine experiences that are strung together with a line of inheritance that exhibits the supreme, greatest conceivable divine character (*EG*, 74–88).

Because the complete absence of existence is impossible, as we will see in the following chapter, each worldly actual occasion exemplifies metaphysical characteristics. Each of these actual occasions partially reenacts previous actual occasions that have influenced it, but present relations with the past cannot engage in a *complete* reenactment if the present actual occasion is a novel event (which it is), whether the event in question is an occasion in the divine life or one in the life of a nondivine being. All of the abstracts or the inconcretia in reality are emergent, except for those that are truly universal in the sense that they characterize either existence as such or subjectivity as such. One of these very abstract features that operates transcendentally is the temporal structure of existence, which is constituted by determinate realities from the past, future determinables, and the present process by which determinables are made determinate (*EG*, 184).

The Hartshornian influence on Gamwell is especially in evidence when Gamwell sees philosophy (specifically metaphysics) as critical reflection that asks about the most general features of reality and of human experience. Gamwell is skeptical as to whether Whitehead affirmed the transcendental character of metaphysics in its two senses, although he thinks that such affirmation may be implicit in Whitehead. It is certainly explicit in Hartshorne and Gamwell. As an example, the very distinction between necessary and contingent features of reality or of human experience *is itself* a necessary or transcendental or metaphysical feature of every possible something that exists. Another way to put the point is to say that every actual occasion may be understood as a localization of the divine (*MN*, 225, 233).

The connection between metaphysics and political philosophy in Gamwell is similar to that in Whitehead: The humanitarian ideal is threatened by modern renunciation of metaphysics (see Petek 2022). Even democracy loses its security when it is untethered to both its ultimate intellectual justification and the appeal to final causes. Whitehead's formulation of what he calls "speculative philosophy" (rather than "metaphysics") is in terms of a coherent, logical, necessary system of general ideas in terms of which every element of our experience can be interpreted. We will see that it is precisely because of this necessary character that metaphysical concepts are universally applicable, even in politics. Concepts that are maximally abstract have application to all concrete experiences *precisely because* they are so abstract. In a way, it is futile to try to separate oneself from metaphysical truths in that this very effort would require that we alienate ourselves from the rest of the real world, both actual and potential (*DP*, 5; *EG*, 31–35, 171; also see Whitehead 1967a, 33, 36; 1978, 3).

The classical concept of God as completely changeless cannot be redeemed by argument; it cannot be a defensible metaphysical concept, in that it designates only by negation, as we will see in the next chapter. But this does not mean that adequate metaphysical knowledge transcends reason, only that the classical concept of God is defective. The alternative process or neoclassical concept of God defended by Gamwell is one that is not only defensible theoretically; it is also more adequate than the classical concept of God in explicating religious experience (*PCV*, 66–69).

Gamwell's neoclassical theism informs his criticisms of several thinkers, including Friedrich Schleiermacher. In the following chapter we will see the problems associated with designation by complete negation. A supposed thought whose content is completely negative is meaningless. Despite Schleiermacher's accomplishments in other areas, Gamwell sees him as continuing the problems found in Thomas Aquinas in suggesting that all positive language about God is at best symbolic or analogical. The problem here is that if positive designation can in no sense be literal, then the very basis for symbolic or analogical discourse is destroyed. If analogy involves comparisons between two things that are somewhat similar and somewhat different, then the literal similarities must be secured in order to secure in turn the analogy. As Gamwell puts the issue:

> Contrary to Schleiermacher, then, constitutive awareness of God includes metaphysical content, that is, content whose literal and positive representation by reflective consciousness has as its object existence as such. If we assume, with Schleiermacher, that every moment of human life is marked by a feeling of partial freedom, our immediate consciousness also includes moral content. . . . An understanding of God's character typically implies and is implied by a comprehensive good to which all human purposes ought to be directed. . . . The transformation of Schleiermacher I propose understands our common human experience to be an implicit understanding of self in relation to God and the world that defines the self in terms of a divine telos. As a condition of subjectivity as such, this self-understanding is a transcendental condition in the broad sense, and it includes the transcendental character, in the strict sense, of God and the world. (*MN*, 84)

Further, Gamwell argues that it is Schleiermacher's classical theistic assumptions regarding the concept of God that cause his intellectual problems. It is only when God is conceived as temporal (indeed as eminently temporal) that literal and positive designation is possible. Schleiermacher, by contrast, speaks of an eternal God outside of time in a way similar to the manner in which Kant refers to noumena only as nonphenomena. On this mistaken basis, we cannot have an intuition of either noumena or God.

CHAPTER THREE

Two Metaphysical Claims

In this chapter I will offer a defense of two Hartshornian and Gamwellian claims: "something exists" and "God exists." These claims are based on the view that metaphysics is the study of nonrestrictive existential statements. It is generally agreed that ordinary factual statements are at least *partially restrictive* of existential possibilities. That is, if they are affirmative, they at least implicitly deny something; further, if they are negative, they at least implicitly affirm something. For example, if I say that the corkscrew is in the drawer, I am denying that the drawer is filled with things other than corkscrews. Or if I say that there is no corkscrew in the drawer, I am affirming that everything in the drawer is something other than a corkscrew.

The above statements are partially restrictive, in contrast to those that are either *completely restrictive* or *completely nonrestrictive*. A completely restrictive statement is one that denies that *any* existential possibility is realized. An example would be saying that "absolutely nothing exists." A completely nonrestrictive statement is exemplified in the claim that "something exists." This latter claim is the contradictory of the wholly restrictive statement that "absolutely nothing exists." I will argue that the claim that "absolutely nothing exists" expresses an impossibility rather than a conceivable but unrealized fact (as in the possibility that there could be a corkscrew in the drawer even if there is no corkscrew there at present). A contradictory of an impossible statement is necessarily true; hence it will be no surprise to learn that I will also argue that the statement that "something exists" is necessarily true.

The humility of the metaphysician (on this account of metaphysics) is in evidence when it is realized that the vast majority of knowledge claims, as found in either common sense or science, involve partially restrictive statements that are contingent. In addition, metaphysics also differs from mathematics, which admittedly also studies nonrestrictive statements, but those that are in a way nonexistential. That is, metaphysics on the view I will defend is a very narrow discipline in contrast to the expansiveness of common sense, science, and mathematics.

Critics might object that, by viewing metaphysics as the study of nonrestrictive existential statements, hubris has indeed been avoided, but the significance of metaphysics has been reduced to the vanishing point. My reply involves at least two points. First, escaping from the still pervasive Humean view that all existential statements are contingent is no small accomplishment if only partially restrictive existential statements are contingent. That is, some existential statements (e.g., "something exists") are necessary and some are impossible (e.g., square-circles exist). Second, the real excitement in metaphysics starts with the effort to show that there are other interesting results in the search for nonrestrictive existential statements that are necessarily true.

I will gesture toward what some of these results might be on the assumption that "something exists" embraces within its meaning all of the metaphysical truths, albeit not in any immediately obvious way. To the bare assertion that "something exists" we can add "experience occurs" and "divine experience occurs." In each case, I will allege, denial of any of these necessarily true claims involves a contradiction.

The view to be defended, held by both Hartshorne and Gamwell, can be called "neoclassical metaphysics." It is "classical" in the sense that the old phrase "being qua being" is still relevant in that metaphysics does not study this or that particular fact, but the strictly universal features of existential possibility, those that cannot be unexemplified. But it is also "neo" in the sense that it is cast in terms of an event ontology, in contrast to the traditional substance-based view.

To use different language from Karl Popper in defense of the neoclassical stance, knowledge is of two kinds: empirical and a priori. Empirical truths are those that some conceivable experience could *falsify*. Although they cannot be *verified* by experience, they can be *supported or corroborated* by actual experience. Truths in mathematics, logic, and metaphysics, however, are not of this sort. These disciplines deal with nonempirical and noncontingent truth. That is, there is no empirical metaphysics on the controversial view I am defending or on the use of the term "metaphysics" as I am defining it. Hartshorne agrees and I think Gamwell does as well. The reason is that metaphysical truths are not vulnerable to observational tests in that they claim to harmonize not simply with actual but with conceivable experience. Metaphysical truths *can* be tested, but by imaginative or intellectual experimentation rather than by perception or physical experimentation.

In metaphysics, as I am conceiving it, there can be falsity, but falsity is shown either by contradiction or by a lack of any coherent meaning. This means that it makes more sense to refer to truth by coherence in metaphysics than it does to refer to truth by coherence in science. Observations of the actual world alone cannot establish metaphysical principles, even if such observations are the lifeblood of empirical disciplines. Both metaphysics and empirical disciplines deal with reality, but empirical disciplines do not study reality as such or the necessary features of the real. They study *particular* realities in their very contingency.

On the Hartshornian and Gamwellian view I am defending, metaphysics studies the necessary character of all existence. This position is part of an effort to offer a philosophical alternative to classical metaphysics, on the one hand, and to contemporary efforts (largely derived from Hume and Kant and others) to discredit metaphysics, on the other. The latter are usually offered without any awareness of the neoclassical alternative.

A putative thought whose content is completely negative is, as I see things, contradictory. One may utter the words "a colorless blue thing" or "the existence of absolutely nothing," but there is something contradictory in each case. The propositional content of a metaphysical statement (e.g., "something exists"), however, is such that its *denial* is self-contradictory or meaningless. Further, if one denies (a la Hume or Kant) that *any* understanding of existence can be necessarily true, then one is, in effect, suggesting that "absolutely nothing exists" is possibly true, and hence opening oneself to the charges of (both semantic and pragmatic) self-contradiction or meaninglessness. To say that "absolutely nothing exists" is to imply what one also precludes (*DG*, 110–12, 159–62, 172–73).

Gamwell goes so far as to claim that "no decision in philosophical thought is more fundamental than whether or not 'something exists' is necessarily true" (*EG*, 29). There is nothing hyperbolic in Gamwell's claim if it has the remarkable consequence of destabilizing the distinction (held as dogma by many philosophers) between *de dicto* and *de re* necessity and the claim that only the former is defensible. That is, this widely defended distinction along with the denial of *de re* necessity relies at least implicitly on the possibility that "absolutely nothing exists" is true. The sheer absence of what is ontologically necessary is assumed by these thinkers to be logically possible. It is precisely this assumption and thus the distinction in question that I view as illicit (*EG*, 22–31).

Of course, one might claim that "something exists" is necessary and then conclude that little, if anything, follows from this claim. But seeing "something exists" as necessarily true is to provide a template for other metaphysical truths, hence Gamwell's aforementioned (only apparent) hyperbole. Metaphysical necessity refers to those conditions or characteristics of existence that cannot fail to obtain or that cannot fail to be exemplified. Their denials are not possibly true. Metaphysical claims are nonetheless criticizable if one or more of the concepts found in the claim are vague or incoherent. They are also criticizable if there are implications of metaphysical claims that are not yet formulated that may in the future prove to be incoherent. Seen in this light, metaphysics is an attempt to formulate more and more defensible schemes than those proposed in the past regarding unrestrictive claims about existence. As before, metaphysical claims are not only criticizable, but they can also be corroborated (if not verified) by showing that efforts to demonstrate that their denial could be true have thus far proved to be unsuccessful (*MN*, 222–23).

Some scholars restrict their attempts to generalize about possibilities and actualities to contingent or empirical features of reality. Neither Gamwell nor I have a quarrel with these thinkers so long as the excellent work that they do in science or even cosmology (which they might refer to as a sort of "empirical metaphysics") is not meant to restrict study of the truly metaphysical characteristics of *all* items of experience, both possible and actual. The term "generic" can indeed mean "most general" in the sense of empirical generalization, but the term can also refer to the necessarily true features of the real. Not only is it obviously true that something exists; it is true a priori. No possible experience could show that nothing at all existed because the experience itself would exist. "Something exists" is a necessary, metaphysical truth and to claim that "there might have been absolutely nothing" is to have language idling, to put the point in Wittgensteinian terms.

It is common to view the sort of argument offered here as "transcendental." In addition to the medieval transcendentals (being, one, true, good, and beautiful) there is a disjunctive transcendental: necessary or contingent. Anything real can be said to be either necessary or contingent and it would be a mistake to think that only the latter characterizes the real. Transcendental metaphysics is actually a type of logic, in contrast to a contingently true or false statement. Or at least such a view can be called transcendental if we replace "being" with "becoming" as characterizing the basic character of reality. A statement such as "something that is *x* exists" is necessarily true when it is a feature or condition of the possible as such. In this regard it should be noted that all contingent meanings imply the metaphysical ones, as when we say that "kangaroos exist" implies that "something exists." Statements about existential necessities designate features of the real exemplified in both the infinite past and future, in contrast to a contingent feature of the real that is necessarily finite. It is finite by virtue of what it excludes (*MN*, 3–17).

The significance of transcendental metaphysics is evidenced in its bold (in Popper's sense of "boldness") rejection of what Gamwell sees as *the* most widely accepted assumption in contemporary philosophy: that all existential statements can be denied without self-contradiction. Thus, on the basis of this assumption, every true existential statement *has to be* true contingently (see *MN*, 13, regarding this glaring example of pragmatic self-contradiction). The claim that all existential statements can be denied without self-contradiction, or that all existential statements are logically contingent, at the very least reflects a *dominant* consensus in contemporary philosophy, if Gamwell's once again quite defensible view that it is *the* most widely accepted assumption is seen as hyperbolic.

In addition to being explicit about the transcendental character of metaphysics, I should be clear about the sorts of self-contradiction to which I am calling attention. The self-contradiction referred to here is *semantic* and thus designates a self-contradiction that occurs within the *meaning* of a statement, as in the aforementioned reference to a colorless object that is blue. This is in contrast to a self-contradiction that is *syntactic* and that occurs in the *structure* of a statement's signs independent of meaning, as in "*x* is *p* and *not-p*." Both of these are to be distinguished from *pragmatic* self-contradiction or self-refutation where what one says is at odds with the requirements of our *activity in the world*. On the consensus view, by contrast, "absolutely nothing exists" is possibly true and hence this view is liable to the charges of semantic and pragmatic self-contradiction. "Absolutely nothing exists" is a pragmatic self-contradiction because any subject who asserts it simultaneously is giving evidence of its own existence (*MN*, 21–37).

Hartshorne, Gamwell, and I are modal egalitarians who find a role for all three of the following: some (even most) existence claims are indeed contingent, but some are impossible, and some are necessary. For example, "absolutely nothing exists," I argue, is impossible and "something exists" is necessary. It is a difficult question whether Kant deserves additional criticism here in that, on the one hand, he seems to say that noumenal presence can *only* be designated by negation, but on the other he seems to say that this presence *is*. It is not often noticed that one pays a price for modal parsimony. Something *completely* negative cannot be distinguished from the supposed absence of all things (*MN*, 39–45).

It might be objected that "absolutely nothing exists" might be true because, were *all* things absent, there would be no subjects like us and hence no pragmatic self-refutation. But this objection itself, it should be noted, implies that something that understands exists in the very articulation of the argument. A subject does, in fact, exist in order to assert "absolutely nothing exists." To define metaphysics as the explication of what must be the case if "absolutely nothing exists" is impossible, is to assert that to designate only by negation is not really to designate. A possibly true statement "something that is *x* exists" can be consistently denied only if the negation implies some other positive statement. Our awareness of absence depends on our awareness of presence, as Plato realized long ago in the *Sophist* (241d) when he committed parricide on "Father Parmenides" by showing the necessity of *relative* nonbeing or otherness (*me on*), but who nonetheless denied even the possibility of *absolute* nonbeing (*ouk on*). As before, metaphysics so defined is transcendental and explicates the semantic logic of existence, which requires "meontic" negativity, but not the "oukontic" sort. This is related to Gamwell's claim that the origin of (meontic) negation is the fact of plurality (*EG*, 54).

I would now like to address the aforementioned concern that the conception of metaphysics I am defending leads to very slim results if all that I can show is that "something exists." But there are several other defensible metaphysical claims, one of which is that "God exists." This is the second metaphysical claim mentioned in the title of this chapter. I will examine this claim via a modal version of the ontological argument, not with the hope that I will actually convince anyone who is not already convinced of the soundness of the argument (even if hope *does* spring eternal), but rather to further illustrate the cogency of metaphysics when seen as the discipline that deals with nonrestrictive claims regarding existence and that helps us to clarify in ordinary language the relations among three modal concepts: necessity, contingency, and impossibility. Consider the following version of the argument:

1. Modality of existence is a predicate (in that saying that *x* exists necessarily or contingently or impossibly, rather than merely saying that *x* exists, is surely to predicate something significant about *x*).

2. There are three (and only three) modes of existence: (a) impossible (cannot exist); (b) contingent (may or may not exist); and (c) necessary (must exist).

3. Step 2b contradicts the logic of perfection (which is St. Anselm's great discovery in chapter 3 of *Proslogion*) because a being that existed only contingently in some circumstances, but not in others, would not be the greatest conceivable.

4. Therefore, the existence of God—the greatest conceivable being or a perfect being—is either impossible or necessary (preliminary conclusion).

5. The existence of God is not impossible (which is the conclusion from other theistic arguments and from mystical experience).

6. Therefore, the existence of God is necessary; or, at the very least, the nonexistence of God is inconceivable (ultimate conclusion).

One of the most common mistakes that occurs when interpreting the ontological argument is to assume that what must be inseparable from the concept of God is not only the bare *existence* of God (*that* God exists), but also God's full *actuality* (*how* God exists from moment to moment). In ordinary cases of existence, not only is the particular concrete actuality contingent, but also it is contingent whether there is any existence embodying the predicate. On the basis of the ontological argument, however, God's existence is necessary or inevitably actualized, although the particularities of God's actualization at any particular time are contingent and open to human (and other) influence. In different terms, in our case existence and actuality are contingent, whereas in the divine case only actuality is contingent in that God's necessary existence means that divine existence is always somehow actualized, the details being contingent. Nothing concretely actual can be necessary. One of the reasons why Kant and others think that existence is not a predicate is that they identify existence with actuality, but the concept of a thing never implies actuality as a predicate (see *EG*, 8, 29, 74–80, 186).

Of the three forms of modality, it is *contingency* that characterizes human experience of, or knowledge of, God. This is because such experience or knowing is, in our case, neither *necessary* nor *impossible*. Or better, the point to the ontological argument is that, although it is impossible to conceive the nonexistence of God, it *is* possible to conceive of the possible existence of God. Further, mystics claim to *experience* God, which is not surprising given the conclusion of the ontological argument to the effect that *if* God's existence is conceived, it has to be conceived as existent. Although having a *concept* of God and having *experience* of God are quite different things, the two are compatible. In neoclassical theism, a defense of the ontological argument makes it possible to understand the complementary roles of the conceptual and the experiential (*MN*, 221–22).

The idea that the divine existence is entirely extraconceptual and must be experienced, rather than conceived, is extreme, as is the opposite view that the divine actuality can be deduced via logical argumentation. Of course, some thinkers claim that one cannot have a concept of God without religious experience. If this claim were true, then we would all (theists, atheists, and agnostics) have to be mystics before we could discourse about the concept of God! This seems hyperbolic. In a different sense, however, an appreciation of the concept of God itself *is* an experience, say when one achieves the Anselmian realization that God's existence could not be contingent. Indeed, all thought about God is close to the ontological argument in that if we really are thinking about God, we could not be thinking about merely an additional empirical fact about the world. For example, there is an analogy between the ontological argument and morality in the sense that either some moral claims are valid or we are left with amoralism; but Kant refuted amoralism. This is much like the preliminary conclusion to the above argument at step 4 (*DG*, 176–78).

To grasp what the concept of God is one needs no special historical reference or special perceptual experience, only the intelligence to be able to understand the most universal aspects of any kind of experience. God is a datum for human thinking *and* feeling, with the former highlighted in the ontological argument, while the latter is the stuff of mystical experience. One of the advantages of Anselm's way of thinking is that it can liberate us from traditional ways of thinking about God. "Greatness" refers to whatever properties it would be better to have than not to have, and it is by no means clear that classical theistic thinkers in previous ages have avoided mistakes regarding what properties the greatest being would have. For example, process thinkers in general have spent a great deal of energy showing that classical theistic omnipotence is infamous for creating an insoluble version of the theodicy problem and classical theistic omniscience (in the sense of God allegedly knowing future possibilities or probabilities as already actualized) gets in the way of a defense of human freedom. Because a defensible concept of God had to wait for the development of neoclassical theism, it is understandable why some scholars might prefer to stop at step 4 in the above argument rather than risking the move to step 6. In several previous publications I have tried to ease this transition (*DG*, 43–44).

It is often objected to the ontological argument that we normally do not analyze our thoughts to find out what exists. But questions regarding existence are at least sometimes conceptual. For example, we can know by conceptual analysis that a round-square cannot exist, that Abraham Lincoln could not vote to impeach Donald Trump, et cetera. The objector is, however, correct that the effort to find out what exists contingently cannot be determined merely conceptually. Anything definitely conceivable is either contingent or necessary, and, if necessary, necessary positively or negatively (impossible). If contingency of existence is shown (a la Anselm) not to apply in the case of a perfect being, then the key question is whether the positively necessary existence is conceivable. It must be admitted, however, that disproving atheism does not itself establish the conceivability or logical possibility of God (*WTP*, 179, 189–93).

A monolithic version of empiricism popular today would discredit theistic metaphysics. The thesis Hartshorne, Gamwell, and I hold is that the intellectual approach to God found in the ontological argument and mystical experience mutually reinforce each other. These are two ways in which God can be "verified"—or better, corroborated—by finite (or better, fragmentary) human beings. It has long been noted that the different rational arguments for the existence of God mutually support each other in that where one is weak, the other is strong. But I am trying to accomplish something a bit different by urging the mutual reinforcement intellect and experience can give to each other, a neoclassical version of something attempted (only partially successfully) in the medieval synthesis on a classical theistic basis. Metaphysics and contingent experience can complement each other even if they are conceptually distinct (*PCV*, 67).

Of course, it might be objected that if we really did have a coherent insight into the nature of perfection, which is what the ontological argument requires, then we would have no need of the argument in that we would know that God exists as a result of the mystical experience that made the insight possible. This objection is tempting, but it should be emphasized that the conceivability of God that the ontological argument requires is a logical conceivability that avoids the contradictions found in classical theism. The argument does *not* require that we have an intuition into divine actuality such as that allegedly experienced by various mystics. That is, there is no need to beg the question in favor of the ontological argument by *requiring* the sort of experience mystics claim to have.

One advantage in thinking of the ontological argument and mystical experience together is that we can be free of the familiar misconception that this argument moves illegitimately from the abstract to the concrete. Nothing could be further from the truth. The necessary existence of God that is the result of the argument is itself very abstract. The argument tells us about the abstract divine existence (which is either necessary or impossible), but not about concrete actuality, which must be either felt in mystical experience or, in Wittgensteinian fashion, shown but not said. The divine existence discussed in the ontological argument is unspeakably less than God as actual. The more concrete can never follow from the evidence in the less concrete. Concrete actuality is always more than bare existence. *That* the divine nature exists is one thing; *how* this nature is concretely actualized is another. Granted, classical theists who defend the ontological argument conflate the move from God's perfection to God's necessary existence with the move from abstract existence to concrete actuality, but there is no good reason for such conflation, from a neoclassical point of view.

The doctrine of *haecceity* from the middle ages (especially in Duns Scotus) points toward an important truth about concrete actuality: its idiosyncratic, unique, very particular quality, in contrast to abstract truths discussed in mathematics and physics and metaphysics. God is abstractly perfect *and* perfect in concrete details, which are experienced by mystics. The great achievement of the ontological argument is the conclusion that we cannot conceive perfection as nonexistent, but this conclusion does not tell us *how* a perfect being reacts at any particular moment to the current actual occasions in their own concreteness.

The point to the modal version of the ontological argument is not that existing is better than not existing, hence the unsurpassable being must exist. It is rather that a being who cannot be conceived not to exist is better than one who can be conceived not to exist. Of course, this argument assumes that we *can* develop a concept of God that is possible, in contrast to the classical theistic view wherein there are contradictions at every turn. Do we really know what we mean when we talk about "God"? The debate between classical theism and neoclassical theism is an attempt to clarify such meaning so that we can also understand what it would mean to *experience* such a being. Or again, although the ontological argument deals with the *concept* of God as a formal, necessary, metaphysical truth, the concept of God used by classical theists is quite different from that used by neoclassical theists in the effort to accommodate both divine concrete actuality and human experience of such.

To suppose that belief in God's existence is empirical is to suppose that, while some actual observations might be compatible with the existence of God, there might also be conceivable observations that might not be and as a result would falsify divine existence. The most likely location for these latter observations is in the theodicy problem, hence the importance of the critique of the concept of omnipotence in the development of the process or neoclassical concept of God. That is, some concepts of God *are* problematic, either because they involve contradiction or they lack coherent meaning, on the one hand, or they are insufficiently metaphysical because they are allied with the contingent truths/falsities of empirical reality, on the other.

There can be no possibility of the nonexistence of God *unless* the very concept of God is contradictory or incoherent. On the view of metaphysics Hartshorne, Gamwell, and I are presenting, the existence of God is a matter of concepts and not of observational facts. It must nonetheless be admitted that there is *some* empirical component in religious belief (if not in metaphysics) if the experiences of the mystics are to be trusted. But the argument from religious experience is not "metaphysics," as I am using the term. Mystical experience, if there is such, informs us more about divine *actuality* (or *how* God interacts with creatures) than about how to argue philosophically, indeed how to argue metaphysically, regarding the very *existence* of God. For those of us who are not mystics, God must be identified conceptually.

Although God's *existence* is either necessary or impossible, God's *actuality* (or *how* God exists from moment to moment) must be characterized by contingency *if* God knows and loves contingent creatures. By partial contrast with two famous metaphysicians, Aristotle thought that God was necessary in every respect, and hence he denied that God could know or care for contingent creatures; Spinoza also thought that God was strictly necessary, but Spinoza's God could nonetheless know the creatures because these latter were themselves strictly necessary. All three of these positions, however, are dealing with the same metaphysical problem of trying to articulate the proper relationship between necessity and contingency in the divine case. And all three (Aristotelian theism, Spinozistic theism, and neoclassical theism) are in opposition to the classical theistic belief in many thinkers in the Abrahamic religions that God is strictly necessary and immutable yet is mysteriously (in the pejorative sense of "mystery") able to know and love contingent and constantly changing creatures.

The ontological argument can clearly be formulated in a valid form where the conclusion follows logically from the premises, but its soundness depends on our having a consistent and coherent concept of God. *If* we can develop such a concept, then the argument implies that the necessity of God be actualized somehow, the details of which are contingent, just as "something exists" is necessary, the details of which are contingent. (Here we can see the connection between the two claims defended in the present chapter.) The difficulty of this task of developing a coherent concept of God is highlighted by the fact that historically there have been many concepts of God proposed that are either lacking clarity or are notoriously inconsistent. That is, our coming to know the metaphysical claim that God exists necessarily is itself highly contingent.

The neoclassical concept of God, a concept that involves dual transcendence of necessary existence as well as preeminent responses to creaturely contingencies, is, in one sense, based on the insights of several classical authors, but in another sense it is a radical revision of classical theism. Hence it is both "classical" and "neo." Hartshorne's striking way to put the point is to say that "if theism cannot be improved upon *profoundly*, then I for one have little desire to see it survive" (Hartshorne 1934a, 92).

The point I am trying to emphasize here is that the decisive metaphysical question regarding the ontological argument is whether the concept of God is genuinely conceivable. The nature of the question is nonempirical. In fact, an empirical premise is not only not needed, it would be an inappropriate category mistake to add one. To put the point in terms of the philosophically popular language of possible worlds, the concept of God is metaphysical in the sense that God either exists in all possible worlds or in none of them. By putting the point in this manner we are led counterintuitively to consider the *rhetorical* component even in an abstract discipline like metaphysics as I conceive it. That is, the burden of proof is on the opponent to the argument to indicate not merely reasons in opposition to the argument, but to show why the concept of God is *impossible* like a square-circle. This burden is heavier than many suppose.

When the arguments in the present chapter are linked with the discussion of process thinking in the previous chapter, one can conclude, along with Gamwell, that the "something" that exists is always characterized by temporality. Of course, the *abstract* characteristic "temporality" or "creativity" is, in a sense, *itself* nontemporal and noncreative. As the universal of universals, temporality or creativity, as the greatest abstraction, is, in a way, *not* something that is characterized by the difference between an actual past and a possible future. But all *actual* occasions are so characterized. We have seen that this view contradicts classical theism, with its belief in God as a nontemporal reality that is in all respects eternal. It is no wonder that, in this traditional view, one can speak of God in literal terms only if the terms are completely negative. But such terms, if *completely* negative, cannot be understood. The eminently temporal God of neoclassical theism stands in sharp contrast to the classical theistic stance, which is ultimately a sort of dualism in that there is no common character to temporal and (allegedly) nontemporal actualities. Gamwell uses "actuality" to refer to the fundamental class of things, while acknowledging that some things are real that are not actual (as in aggregates of actualities or as in very abstract realities). Strictly speaking, only actualities exemplify characteristics, with other realities doing so only in the sense that is reducible to exemplification by their member actualities (*DP*, 107–14).

It is a commonplace of modern science that the objects of everyday experience are composites or aggregates (composed of molecules, atoms, etc.). These composites or aggregates are real if not fundamental. Thus, there is nothing odd about Gamwell's view in terms of basic actualities and nonetheless real aggregates. Metaphysics seeks the common processual character of all actualities. Every actuality has internal relations to past actualities by which it is partially determined and external relations to the future that it helps to determine. No actuality can be completely determined by other things, even if self-conscious freedom is likely to occur only at the human level. Actualities (or better, actual occasions) are activities, even in the somewhat passive reception (prehension) of the past. Decision in a metaphysical sense involves cutting off some causal inheritances from the past so that others can live on, but it is only in the high-grade decisions by rational beings that self-understanding is involved. A human individual is a temporally ordered series of activities, all of which share a set of characteristics that individuate that particular human. A metaphysics of activities necessarily involves the rejection of the idea that time itself is created. It seems impossible to engage in self-understanding without a present that starts in relation to the past and is completed in pursuit of some future (*DP*, 115–19).

That is, one cannot conceive of a rational being for whom objects are not temporally ordered. The inescapable temporality of human (and other) activity means that time is the common character of all possible actualities. Gamwell notes that the two most prominent alternatives to this view require an object of understanding that is completely negative, which, as detailed above, is impossible. These alternatives are Thomas Aquinas's affirmation of a completely *non*temporal creator and Kant's distinction between temporal phenomena and completely *non*phenomenal reality (*DP*, 120–22).

I am arguing that we should agree with Gamwell that it is a mistake to cast moral and political good adrift without metaphysical backing. Such a backing, I claim, includes theism. *The* good is the maximal unity-in-diversity and richness of everyone's experiences. Although suspicion of universal truth is somewhat understandable in light of greater familiarity with cultures other than one's own, this circumstance often leads to skepticism of metaphysical claims in ignorance of the metaphysics offered by thinkers like Whitehead, Hartshorne, and Gamwell. Once again, traditional metaphysics and its Kantian denial do not, as many thinkers assume, exhaust the conceptually available alternatives. The neoclassical alternative posits a metaphysical structure of actualities and possibilities that is independent of historically situated contexts of meaning. Metaphysics is transcendental, on this view, in the sense that the denial of a truly metaphysical statement is pragmatically self-contradictory, as we have seen. Because of the two senses of metaphysics, there are at least two implications of metaphysics for moral/political thought: (1) there is a comprehensive purpose or good that implies a telos for all things, which is *the* good mentioned earlier in this paragraph; and (2) there is a comprehensive *moral* purpose which is a transcendental feature of subjective beings with rationality (*EG*, 1–7).

Although the divine is the eminently temporal individual, all actual occasions are microunits of process, each unifying its internal relations to others already unified and becoming something to which others in the future will internally relate. The fact that these actual occasions are oriented toward a comprehensive good is part of what Gamwell calls an "original decision," which includes the deepest motivation for more specific choices. Nonteleological theories of the good commit what we have seen Gamwell call the partialist fallacy by assuming what they also deny: a general evaluation of purposes themselves. For example, if one assumes that *all* alternatives for choice are morally indifferent, this assumption itself involves an evaluation of possible purposes in their entirety. The divine good is in the background as a source of the obligation to pursue the maximal good in the future as such (*EG*, 8–12).

We will see that Gamwell's commitment to comprehensive purpose does *not* have the political consequence that those with secular convictions are disadvantaged in public life. In this regard he is much closer to Rawls's view than he realizes. The important thing is that all citizens adhere to a transcendental purpose of communicative respect, as we will see. Each citizen has the right to affirm any reasonable conviction (with "reasonable" to be defined later) about the ultimate terms of political assessment, about "religion" in an extended sense. Free and full discourse regarding this comprehensive purpose requires, however, as Gamwell and I see things, an examination of the (limited albeit crucial) extent of transcendental argument and metaphysical necessity (*EG*, 13–15).

One of the key conceptual issues confronted by Gamwell is how democratic politics can ultimately depend on divine purpose and yet be constitutionally neutral regarding the comprehensive doctrines that citizens affirm. Theistic metaphysics in its neoclassical sense in fact *authorizes* a democratic form of government. Such authorization involves both metaphysics as explication of reality or existence as such and metaphysics as explication of subjectivity as such. The latter is a specification of the former (*WTP*, ix–x). One of Gamwell's favorite quotations is from Whitehead: democracy divorced from metaphysics "lost its security of intellectual justification" (Whitehead 1967a, 36). I will argue in a later chapter that this view is again closer to Rawls's view than Gamwell realizes in that Rawls expected citizens to turn to *some* comprehensive doctrine or metaphysical view to deal with questions that were not narrowly found in political justice or that dealt with metajustice issues. But which one? Rawls might ask. Gamwell turns to theistic metaphysics to support both democracy and the (Whiteheadian) "humanitarian ideal," but the abstract character of Gamwell's metaphysics provides sufficient elbow room for all reasonable political views (again, with "reasonable" to be defined in due course). That is, although metaphysics provides the *backing* for the humanitarian ideal, it does not stipulate in any detail how this ideal will be exemplified. There are obvious differences between Gamwell and Rawls, most notably in relation to Kant. It should be noted that Kant's rejection of a comprehensive telos for human beings is related to his rejection of metaphysics in the sense of an explication of existence as such. Gamwell does not share Kant's skepticism in this regard. Moral ideals, on the Gamwellian view, cannot consistently be divorced from the rest of things, including the two metaphysical truths I defended earlier in this chapter (*WTP*, 121–31).

In neoclassical metaphysics, reality is prior to understanding, not temporally but in terms of being prior in the process of constituting the subject—the opposite of Kant's view. The final real things are constituted by relations, all-inclusive relations in the divine case and fragmentary relations in creaturely cases. These are epitomized by relations of successors to predecessors. God's internal relations with all of the past and God's ideal knowledge of future possibilities and probabilities is implied by the following consideration: In the absence of an all-inclusive reality, moral activity would be directed toward a multitude of fragmentary goods, in which case the general imperative to maximize would make no sense. But such an imperative *does* make sense, as the thought of any number of utilitarians who are religious skeptics would otherwise indicate (*WTP*, 132–38).

The aim at maximal creativity in the future involves God as the personification of the all-inclusive whole. As a result, the moral law can be restated as: act so as to maximize the divine good. If all worldly realization of value is in *some* sense good, then this good is a contribution to the divine relativity. The good as conceived in neoclassical metaphysics clearly involves deontological norms because without these the maximal good could not be achieved. *Both* a comprehensive telos *and* a deontological principle are necessary conditions for moral/political good, hence there is a well-deserved place for Kant's lasting contribution to moral and political theory. A good society is one where there is an inviolable obligation to respect basic rights, including the right to communicative respect regarding free speech and concerning the comprehensive doctrine one chooses to affirm (*WTP*, 139–41).

Being the recipient of political respect enables human flourishing. Further, human flourishing not only enhances the political world, but also makes a difference to the divine or metaphysical individual as discussed above regarding the ontological argument. It is obviously true that religious diversity (including the rise of modern atheism and agnosticism) could be seen as a challenge to Gamwellian metaphysics. But this is not the only way to view the matter, especially given Gamwell's rare and admirable willingness to submit philosophical and theological claims to the rigors of discursive rational assessment. Neoclassical theism offers a critical interpretation not only of our common humanity, but also of the humanitarian ideal or the way of reason, including its intellectual justification in theistic metaphysics (*WTP* 142–46).

CHAPTER FOUR

Contingency and Necessity

The purpose of the present chapter is to explore further the concept of contingency as it operates in neoclassical or process metaphysics and to explore the ways in which it limits or complements transcendental argumentation. In the course of these explorations, I will have occasion to summarize neoclassical or process metaphysics in general in that the metaphysical stance in question centers on the dipolar contrast and complementarity between the necessary and the contingent. Although eminent reality exists necessarily, it also necessarily has some contingent features or other. The label "neoclassical" is appropriate because, although process thought is not usually thought of as perennial philosophy, its metaphysics is worked out in intimate relation to the tradition.

Various ideas have been proposed as ultimate in the history of metaphysics. The neoclassical or process proposal is to see creativity as the basic concept that is applicable to all of reality. The term "creativity" refers to the unpredictable character of the real whereby causality from the past provides the necessary but not sufficient conditions for what happens in the present. Each event is an addition to the definiteness of reality seen as an emergent whole. That is, reality is predictable insofar as it is not creative, but rather mechanical or habitual. Metaphysics exists so as to restore a reticulative perspective whereby we can understand reality as both somewhat predictable *and* creative. Gamwell agrees.

Focus on the most exalted types of creativity should not hide from us its humbler contingent versions that are always there, like the character in Moliere who spoke prose all of his life without realizing it. There is nothing but creative experience, on this view, once the inadequacies of both dualism and reductionistic materialism are in full view. I will not detail these inadequacies here (see Dombrowski 2017, ch. 1), but rather assume the ultimacy of creativity and the cogency of panpsychism. I realize that for some thinkers this is quite an assumption to make. For the purposes of discussion here, however, I can only say that the panpsychist view I assume does not commit one to the implausible view that stones feel, only to the claim that there is some degree of self-motion in the microscopic constituents of the stone (see Dombrowski 2020).

On the view I am defending, with which I assume Gamwell would agree, it is contingent becoming or contingent creativity that is itself necessary, not any particular becoming or creative act. Here strictly speaking "metaphysics" refers to a priori statements regarding existence, with "a priori" referring not to the complete absence of experience (whatever that might be), but rather to a statement that contradicts no conceivable experience. It is observational falsifiability that distinguishes empirical from metaphysical statements. Metaphysical truths are those that are compatible with any experience in that they are noncontingent. The main difference between contingent and necessary truths is that the former conflict with at least some conceivable experiences. Of course, an *allegedly* metaphysical statement may really be empirical and hence contingent, but genuinely metaphysical statements are strictly necessary.

We have seen that the necessary truths that metaphysics seeks to clarify are highly abstract, but it would be incorrect to conclude from this that they have some sort of ultra-Platonic status devoid of concrete embodiment. Rather, the opposite is the case. Metaphysical truths are concretized in *every* conceivable experience. On the view I am defending, metaphysics is the study of the abstraction "concreteness"; it concerns necessary truths regarding "contingency" as such. Abstract reality is derivative from the ubiquitous world of concrete contingencies.

The task of metaphysics is to describe the necessarily nonempty universe of the common aspects of all states of affairs. Contingency as such could not be unexemplified. It is in this light that metaphysics can be seen as the theory of contingency as such. Gamwell is correct to insist that strict nominalism is quintessentially antimetaphysical because it denies the very distinction between necessity and contingency on which metaphysics is developed. Only unconditionally necessary truths are metaphysical in that in this discipline we are not looking for particular, contingent facts, but for the principle of factuality itself. There can be no alternative to contingent alternativeness itself. Once again, the a priori character of necessary, metaphysical truths means that they cannot be derived from special kinds of experience even if they can be derived from *any* experience that is accompanied by reflection.

It should be emphasized that "a priori" is not synonymous with "certain." Instead, it refers to the necessary, nonrestrictive aspect of reality, concerning which we might make mistakes. One way to avoid such mistakes is to keep in mind that a denial of a metaphysical truth (as in "something exists") is merely verbal and inevitably leads to contradiction, in contrast to contingent truths that can easily be denied without contradiction.

There is no implication here that necessary truth about reality leads to *all* truth about reality. The opposite is actually the case: to see all truth as metaphysical is not to take the unique contribution of metaphysics seriously. Granted, historically there was a tendency in some rationalist philosophers to hyperbolize the degree to which the world could be explained metaphysically. This was, quite frankly, a sort of intellectual imperialism. This does not mean, however, that we should move to the opposite sort of intellectual imperialism that is currently popular whereby the contingent truths discovered by scientists are seen as hegemonic. There is something unstable in both sorts of empire: metaphysics cannot long survive if it swallows up science, and the empirical method will soon falter if it tries to adjudicate metaphysical disputes. Metaphysical truth is only one small portion of all the truth there is, but its modest stature is nonetheless extremely valuable due to its rarity. There is no need to support an exaggerated empirical reaction to exaggerated rationalist pretension.

The position defended here tries to mediate between the rationalist tendency to overemphasize necessity and the empiricist tendency to hyperbolize regarding contingency in that there are both necessary and contingent aspects of reality. This mediation is related to the effort to adjudicate between complete determinism, on the one hand, and complete freedom, on the other. In this regard, causality should be seen as providing necessary but not sufficient conditions for what happens at the level of concrete singulars.

It is nonetheless understandable why some philosophers have tried to deny the necessary truth of "something exists." Once one gets used to denying the existence of this or that particular thing, one can then posit the nonexistence of a whole species of things, then whole genera, et cetera. Some thinkers unfortunately convince themselves that this process of denial can go on infinitely to the point where absolute nothingness . . . exists. Herein lies the rub. When we think or talk about *it* (absolute nothingness) we thereby contradict ourselves.

The unintelligibility of absolute nothingness has implications not only for cosmic beginnings, but also for cosmic endings. It might be asked, what keeps the creative advance of the world going on, instead of petering out, so that after a certain moment there would be nothing going on at all? There can be no first actual occasion for the reason that what it *means* to be an actual occasion is to receive influence from the past (to prehend it or grasp it, rather than intellectually apprehend it), and then to exhibit self-motion in de-cisive response to such influence so as to bequeath such a decision to future actual occasions. Hence, there cannot be a last actual occasion in that what it *means* to be an actual occasion is to be a subject that becomes an object (a superject) for future subjects, a contributor to what comes after. No moment can make itself the last moment in that such a feat would violate what it means to be a moment in the systole and diastole of the processual character of the universe.

These considerations have implications for the God-world relation. A merely creaturely or a merely divine process would explain nothing. The former has no principle of order, no direction to enable creative events to produce anything but meaningless chaos—but the cosmos is not a meaningless chaos. The latter has no content in the sense that God without creatures would be a power-to-do without any doing, as in an omnibenevolent being with no one to love. What could this possibly mean? The upshot here is that the necessary and the contingent are themselves necessary to each other. Or again, the necessity that there be *some* contingent things or other is entirely consistent with the genuine contingency of these things.

The reason why there is a tight connection between metaphysics and natural theology is that the existence of deity cannot be contingent. However, if much of what God would know *is* contingent, then the God in question would have to be quite different from the unmoved mover, pure actuality, changeless, utterly noncontingent God of classical theism. It is not my desire as a metaphysician (in partial contrast to my desire as a philosopher of religion) to get tangled in thorny and divisive religious questions. Instead, I am especially interested in the claim that when one is thinking metaphysically one is very close to explicit thinking about God.

From the above it should be clear that I think, along with Gamwell, that the God of classical theism is impossible for various reasons. I will cite two infamous ones. The classical theistic God (who is omnipotent, omniscient, and omnibenevolent) would be incompatible with the existence of evil in the world; but there *is* evil in the world; therefore, there is no classical theistic God. And second, the classical theistic God is omniscient in the sense that this God is said to know, with absolute assurance and in minute detail, the outcome of what are (at least from a human point of view) future contingencies; hence this sort of knowledge is in disequilibrium with both future contingency and the possibility of human freedom; but human freedom seems to be required for practical life, on the process/pragmatic view, as in holding people responsible for their actions, in contrast to the determinist view; therefore, there is no classical theistic God.

I realize that these two problems are notoriously difficult. My aim here is to indicate why I think it is understandable that neoclassical or process theists, along with many agnostics and atheists, hold that the God of classical theism is impossible; hence it is crucial to develop a concept of God that avoids the contradictions found in classical theism. Once the contingency of the existence of God is eliminated as a logical possibility, intellectual space is opened up for a careful consideration of a concept of God that is logically possible; and, if possible, then necessary, via the modal logic of the ontological argument.

The role of contingency in neoclassical or process metaphysics is very important. Very early in the history of philosophy a certain bias became entrenched wherein one pole of dipolar contrasts was favored at the expense of the other pole. To cite just two examples: being was favored over becoming and necessity was favored over contingency. These biases seem to have been due to at least two different factors. One was the discovery in ancient Greece of pure mathematics and the understandable enthusiasm for very abstract ideas that resulted from this discovery. The other was a certain fear and despair regarding the vagaries of concrete living. Because a human being's future is always uncertain, and because individual human beings and even human institutions are fragile and ultimately die, an attack on change and contingency resulted, as the following simple diagram indicates:

Being (good)　　　　　Becoming (evil)
Necessity (good)　　　　Contingency (evil)

The roots of this monopolar prejudice are complex, but it seems that one of the motives behind it is a sort of escapism. We have seen previously that becoming itself does not become and does not pass away, nor is contingency itself contingent. Here I am calling attention to the hegemonic monopolarity of the history of metaphysics that is best countered not by a competing monopolarity wherein change is seen as superior to stability and contingency is seen as better than necessity. If "necessity" is a term of laudation and "contingency" implies denigration, then certain crucial features of reality, in general, and divine reality, in particular, are lost. What is necessary is that contingency have instances; hence it makes sense to try to improve on traditional monopolarity by paying sufficient attention to *both* the necessary *and* the contingent, as the following more complex diagram indicates:

Being (either positive or negative)	Becoming (either positive or negative)
Necessity (either positive or negative)	Contingency (either positive or negative)

The terms on the right side of this diagram can, in fact, involve negative features like fickleness, fragility, or undependability. Monopolar metaphysicians thus commendably avoid these negative features, but they pay a price for their style of avoidance. They miss out on the positive features of becoming and contingency, like sensitivity, responsiveness, adaptability, sympathy, and the like. Likewise, monopolar metaphysicians rightly notice the positive features that are often associated with the terms on the left side of the diagram, like stability, dependability, solidity, et cetera, but they pay a price for failing to notice the negative features that can also be associated with the terms on the left side: wooden inflexibility, mulish stubbornness, inadaptability, unresponsiveness, and the like. The task when thinking carefully about the concept of God is to attribute all excellences to God (both left *and* right sides) and not attribute to God any inferiorities (both right *and* left sides).

It is no accident that there should be accidents and it is predictable that unpredictable, contingent events will never cease. These claims are true regarding reality generally, but also regarding the divine case. We have seen that there is a famous Hartshornian distinction in neoclassical or process metaphysics between *existence* and *actuality*. The former refers to the idea *that* God is necessarily, whereas the latter refers to *how* God exists from moment to moment. In short, God's actuality is contingent even if God's existence is necessary, as Gamwell and I see things (*DP*, 114–17; *EG*, 85–92). Whereas the ontological argument tries to establish that God's existence is necessary, on the neoclassical or process appropriation of the argument (in contrast to Anselm's classical theistic appropriation of it), God's actuality is contingent due to previous divine decisions, the decisions of creatures that affect God, chance mutations, and many other factors that cannot in principle be predicted beforehand due to ubiquitous partial creativity.

In a way, contingency includes necessity due to the asymmetrical character of temporal process, as Gamwell also sees things. It makes sense to say that I am causally affected by what happened to me yesterday, but several difficulties arise when I say that I am now causally affected by what might happen to me tomorrow. This is because the outcome of future contingencies is not here yet to exert causal influence. The term "necessary" in the usage favored here refers to the inevitability of some contingencies or other being decided at each instant, but which ones? God's existence is present in all possible worlds or in none of them, given the incompatibility between divine perfection and contingency of existence. But God's actuality is pervasively affected by the contingent; otherwise divine knowledge of creaturely contingencies and divine love for creatures whose lives are dominated by contingencies, like illness and premature death, would be unintelligible. The necessary refers to what all contingencies have in common (*EG*, 25–38).

The ancient saying *Deus est caritas* is obviously religiously rich, but it is also a metaphysical claim that is understandable only if divinity is the supreme instance of relational existence that is affected not by this or that case of sentient reality, but by all of them. The following triad points out the grave defects in the classical theistic God who is devoid of any contact with contingency or responsive love:

X loves Y.
Y, who previously did not suffer, starts to suffer.
X remains strictly unmoved by Y's suffering.

If X refers to God and Y refers to creatures, the need for a revised or neoclassical concept of God becomes apparent. It is one thing to claim that God's existence is necessary, but to claim that God is necessary in every respect is to create all of the contradictions and inadequacies for which classical theism has become infamous over the past three centuries.

God is both necessary and contingent. But these contrasting predicates apply to different aspects of the divine nature; hence the principle of noncontradiction has not been violated. This is the neoclassical or process metaphysical doctrine of dual transcendence. In effect, neither necessity nor contingency have been properly understood in the history of metaphysics, on the view Gamwell and I defend. The tendency in classical theistic metaphysics, once the importance of both necessity and contingency is noted, is to conclude to some version of cosmological dualism, as in the belief that God, or what is metaphysically primary, is necessary, whereas the creatures, or what is secondary, are contingent. But it is a mistake, I think, to say that the relationship between the contrasting poles necessary and contingent is a mere conjunction designated by "and." Rather, the contingent contains the necessary. This is a version of the Aristotelian principle that the concrete or contingent contains the abstract or necessary, respectively. Hartshorne calls this the *principle of inclusive contrast* (*MRF*, 232–33).

Ultimate or metaphysical contraries (not contradictories) consist in two poles that contrast with each other, but which nonetheless stand or fall together. One such contrast is that between necessity and contingency. Though these polar opposites are ultimate or metaphysical, they do not have an equal status. Contingency is the inclusive pole, necessity the included one. That is, to suggest that there are ultimate dualities is not to defend dual*ism* in that contingent, concrete occasions of experience (and abstraction away from these) constitutes the whole of what is. Likewise, being marks what is permanent in the flux of becoming. This is true even in the divine life where God *always changes*, with both words crucial, as we have seen.

The principal intellectual challenge to the view Gamwell and I are defending here is determinism, which tries to explain away temporal asymmetry by replacing it with biconditional necessity and an aggressive version of necessary *and sufficient* conditions for everything that happens. Granted, a cause is a *sine qua non* that is required for a later event, but in its full actuality or concreteness an event is at least partially contingent. This is why an event depends on antecedent events yet is largely independent of subsequent ones. This does not mean that the future cannot be predicted, but such prediction must take the character of statistical generalization rather than algorithmic assurance in minute detail. In principle we cannot know the future in detail, whereas if we are ignorant of the past such nescience is due to lack of epistemological industry or accidental lack of evidence. It is a vain hope to think that if we discovered the "real causes" of things we could explain and predict *everything*. Present creative experiencing is basic.

Regarding deity at least two mistakes plague monopolar classical theism. First, necessity has been given an honorific status not given to contingent, creative, synthetic experiencing wherein the many causal influences from the past are brought together in a novel way in the present. And relatedly, necessity *simpliciter* has been used to designate deity, in contrast to the dipolar effort to find the appropriate place for both necessity and contingency. There is no need to make pessimism a metaphysical axiom by insisting that causes have to be greater than their effects if reception of causal influences from the past and advancing beyond them itself is a creative, progressive effort. The contrasting deterministic view largely depends on confusing a difference in degree between high and low levels of experiencing with a difference in kind between mind and mindless, inert matter, the latter of which is amenable to mechanistic and deterministic explanation.

Necessity can only be discovered in what is always found in the contingent. Even in the divine case, necessary existence is an everlasting series of contingent, temporal states. There just is no dualism of necessary things versus contingent things, only necessary constituents of a series of contingent events. The class of this series cannot be empty. The principle of inclusive contrast is supported by the following consideration: if we assume that "X is necessary and Y is contingent" is true, then this truth itself is contingent rather than necessary due to the latter part of this claim. As before, the contingent contains the necessary, but not vice versa. Classical theistic worship of the necessary aspect of deity *as* deity was a type of idolatry allied with a similar mistake: etiolatry (worship of causes) in contrast to neoclassical or process thinkers' worship of *both* eminent activity *and* supreme passivity.

On the neoclassical or process view, modality is both temporal and ontological. This is related to the aforementioned discovery that theism either involves hopeless contradiction or it points to a necessary truth. That which is necessarily always is; that which is contingently happens at a particular time. The past is wholly fixed and is no longer open to decision; and the future is a mixture of the already settled (in very abstract terms) and of possibilities open for literal de-cision (where some are cut off and rejected, while others remain). Statements regarding contingent things must specify the temporal stage within which they are alleged to hold. The claim that neoclassical or process metaphysics involves ontological as well as merely verbal necessity, and also ontological as well as merely verbal contingency, positions us well to steer a moderate course between the claim that *everything* is necessary and the claim that strictly speaking nothing is necessary.

God's existing necessarily does not conflict with the idea that divine existence proceeds by way of a series of concrete states or experiences that in themselves are contingent. The necessity here is equivalent to the claim that the class of divine experiences could not be empty. By contrast, *we* are contingent both in terms of existence and actuality. We are contingent through and through. But even God's concrete experiences are contingent in that they involve feeling of (divine or creaturely) contingent feeling.

The idea that *all* existential statements are contingent is problematic for several reasons detailed by Gamwell (*MN*, ch. 1). One of these is that some existential statements are impossible if they contain contradictions. Existential contingency is a distinct way of existing (in contrast to existing necessarily) rather than a redundancy. The necessity of God's existence, as we have seen, does not have to apply to the entire divine reality. The necessity deals with the very abstract characteristics that all contingencies have in common, whereas the contingent deals with the most concrete truths or entities. Indeed, competitiveness is the key to contingency in that what it means to be a contingent truth is that it could have been otherwise if some other decision had been made or some other factor had gotten the upper hand.

From the above it should be clear why it is legitimate to claim that, despite the necessity of something existing and of deity existing, contingency is pervasive. This realization is crucial for several religious reasons, as in the fact that on a neoclassical or process view (wherein divine omnipotence is denied), widespread suffering in the world is an understandable result of widespread contingency and the inadvertent clash of conflicting freedoms. For example, if A chooses to go to point X at time Y and if B chooses to go to point X at time Y, the resultant crash at X at time Y might not be anyone's fault. In different terms, there is no exact or ultimate "why" for the contingent in its somewhat arbitrary and not strictly deducible character, contra the doctrine of sufficient reason.

From the pervasiveness of contingency, however, we should not go so far as to deny altogether the concept of necessity or attempts at rational demonstration. The contingent and the necessary are hardly like oil and water or attempts to bind contingent human emotions to the fetters of Euclid, or again, like the attempt to submit the waters of Grasmere Lake to mathematical analysis. Here we can notice that the thinker who has most influenced Gamwell and I, Hartshorne (especially his *Creative Synthesis and Philosophic Method*, but other works as well), was not only the person most responsible for the rediscovery of the ontological argument in its modal form, but also an author of two books in empirical science that emphasize the experiential and the contingent. One of these books is still consulted widely by ornithologists (see *Born to Sing* [Hartshorne 1973]; also see *The Philosophy and Psychology of Sensation* [Hartshorne 1934b). There is much that militates against the view that the formal or the necessary dominates Hartshorne's or Gamwell's philosophies, not least of which is the importance placed in their thought on religious experience. In fact, Hartshorne's major complaint against the British empiricists was that their thought was ironically insufficiently empirical.

The pervasiveness of contingency in neoclassical or process metaphysics is not meant to hide the crucial role for the formal/necessary. Three alternatives should be considered: (1) there are no necessary truths; (2) there are necessary truths, but we cannot in principle know them; and (3) there are necessary truths and it makes sense for us to try to know them. A major problem with the first alternative is that on its basis not only does "necessary" have no application, but "contingent" also loses its meaning. The two terms are correlative and can only be defined in terms of each other. Likewise, if the second alternative were correct then when we speak not only of necessary truths, but also of contingent ones, we would not know what we were talking about, once again due to the fact that "necessary" and "contingent" are correlative terms. The most defensible alternative is the third one. This option points us toward those features that would have to be found in any possible world (necessary truths); it also helps us to secure an understanding of the contingent.

Necessary truths have developed a bad name because of certain historical mistakes, as in the assumption that necessary truths have to concern *eternal* realities that are beyond time altogether, rather than being concerned with *everlasting* realities that endure through all of time. The eternal is so abstract that it cannot have internal relations with that which becomes. Another mistake that has given necessary truths a bad name concerns confusion between the necessity of a proposition and our knowledge of it. Our knowledge of a necessary truth, if we have such, is not itself necessary but contingent. A third mistake is the dangerous assumption that if one does know a necessary truth one can then deduce contingent truths from the necessary ones. But this would end not only creaturely creativity, but also process itself. Even with knowledge of necessary truths under one's belt, one would still have to await the outcome of contingent events. It is one thing to know *that* a decision must be made, another to know which decision.

If God's knowledge of creatures is a type of prehension, a feeling of the creature's feelings, then it would not be possible for God to know the future feelings of creatures if they depend on at least partially free decisions not yet made. The ancient view of the issue in the famous sea-battle example from Aristotle seems to be that propositions regarding future contingents are neither true nor false, but indeterminate. The main alleged problem with this view is that it violates the law of excluded middle. But this law need not be violated. The indeterminacy of the future is to be represented not in the truth-value of propositions, but in three different predicates relating to the future itself (*de re* modality rather than *de dicto*). For example, for any event causal conditions either require it (will be), exclude it (will not be), or leave it undecided (may or may not be). These three alternatives exhaust the logical possibilities. If any one of these is true of the event, the other two are false, thus preserving the law of excluded middle. The region of "may or may not be" is quite large, even for God, and cannot be reduced to "will be" or "will not be" merely by virtue of knowledge of *some* truths that are necessary (see Shields and Viney 2003).

To altogether abandon the effort to discover the necessary aspects of reality is also to give up on the effort to understand the contingent and emergent aspects of reality, which have their full sense and definition only in relation to the necessary. But because universal agreement is not possible within any area of philosophy, including metaphysics, our very efforts to persuade each other of what we take to be necessary truths have a contingent character. That is, the effort to defend belief in necessary truths is not to be equated with the quest for dogmatic certainty in epistemology or with essentialism. We ought not confuse logical certainty (or necessary truth) with epistemic certainty (or beliefs immune to contestation). Claims to necessary truth themselves can be epistemically fallible such that the arena of fallible claims includes both metaphysical and nonmetaphysical statements. In addition (and this point is rarely noticed), the criticism that pursuit of metaphysical universality—when equated with the quest for certainty—is inconsistent with human fallibility *makes its own* claim to logical certainty by saying that human fallibility implies the *impossibility* of metaphysical necessity (*EG*, 181).

The twin evils of ontolatry (worship of being) and gignolatry (worship of becoming) can be avoided in a judicious theory of being and necessity as aspects of becoming and contingency, respectively. The aforementioned distinction between eternity and everlastingness is an attempt to avoid monopolarity. Indeed, being and necessity have been more insightfully explored in the history of metaphysics than the correlative concepts becoming and contingency. My hope is that the present chapter, in which God is seen as immutably mutable and as the greatest conceivable being who everlastingly becomes, helps to remedy this imbalance in a Gamwellian manner.

Pervasive contingency is opposed not only by those who explicitly defend necessitarian determinism, but also by classical theists who nominally admit contingency, yet who implicitly affirm determinism or who should be determinists given their muscular version of omniscience. To claim that God knows *everything* that will occur in the future with absolute assurance and in minute detail is to fall into predeterminism. A more defensible version of omniscience would claim that the greatest knower would know past actualities as already actualized, present realities in their presentness (subject to the laws of physics), and future contingencies *as contingent.* To claim to know a future contingency as already actualized is not an exhibition of the greatest knowledge. In this regard, the neoclassical or process God is not "ignorant" of the future if future contingencies are not here yet to be logically known. Or again, the tyrant God of classical theism is at odds with chance in reality in that all supposedly chance events would ultimately be the result of God's omnipotent will. But there *are* chance events in reality (as detailed in quantum physics and evolutionary biology); hence there are good grounds to doubt the existence of the classical theistic God.

I would like to close this chapter by noting a certain irony in the project I have presented. On the one hand, I have characterized the Gamwellian contribution of metaphysics as "modest" and "unique" in that it deals with only a "small portion" of all the truth there is. This *deflationary* tendency is due to the facts that metaphysical truth is necessary truth and most of what is true deals with the enormity of, indeed with the sublimity of, the contingent. On the other hand, although I have concentrated thus far on only two metaphysical claims, they each have far-reaching consequences, which my critics will no doubt see as *inflationary.*

First, if the claim "something exists" is, as I allege, necessarily true, then we are rescued from a worldview in which *everything* is contingent. In this regard we are in a position to reach rapprochement with several other implicitly metaphysical traditions from around the world, as in the undying and ungenerated in Buddhism. These views are metaphysically incompatible with absolute or "oukontic" nothingness and each seems to logically entail the claim that necessarily something exists. There is an infinite power of existence in the depth of things, a metaphysical backbone for a global *philosophia perennis.* This widespread agreement obviously does not in itself justify the claim that "something exists" is necessarily true, but it does help to counteract the widely held thesis that metaphysicians are all over the map and that no general agreement can be found in this discipline. Sheer nonbeing (in Greek, *ouk on*) is unintelligible such that any logical system presupposes nonemptiness in its universe of discourse. Indeed, nonemptiness is a requirement of logical coherence. Another way to put the point is that "there is something" is not one thesis among other happenstance theses, but a presupposition for having theses at all. Or again, without the realist assumption of a primary icon, we fall hopelessly into solipsism. The world of *esti* or "it is" is always instantiated, but it is instantiated by contingent natural entities of various kinds. "The world is" is not contradicted by the claim that there are mutable and contingent entities within the world that is. The idea that absolute nothingness exists is thus incoherent even as the description of a possible world in that there is no way this claim could possibly be known. The insight here is not refuted by some (but not all) contemporary physicists who argue that the natural world came from "absolute nothingness" through a quantum tunneling event in that a quantum vacuum is *not* absolute nothingness, but a very unusual somethingness.

Second, of course none of these considerations in themselves entail theism or the deification of necessarily existing reality, hence the need for the ontological or some other theistic argument or for fideistic commitment in order to defend the reasonableness of theistic belief. On the basis of a neoclassical use of a modal version of the ontological argument, however, the necessity of *some* world existing and God's necessary existence do not really differ; the contingencies of this particular world need not exist, but *some* world contributing to a dipolar God has to exist. I would like to dissuade those who are skeptical of, or perhaps even hostile to, theism that my purpose here (likewise Gamwell's purpose) is not to offer the supposed consolation dispensed by classical theism, as in the promise of personal immortality or the anodyne contained in the alleged assurance that everything will turn out well in the end. Due to pervasive contingency, life is tragic both for us and for God. No doubt the classical theistic objection will be that the neoclassical or process view is problematic because it leaves human existence in too fragile a state. The proper response should be to admit that human existence *is* fragile, once again due to pervasive contingency; therefore there is nothing wrong with noting this fragility. That is, human existence is not *too* fragile but fragile and hence very often tragic.

Nonetheless there is *some* consolation that comes from neoclassical or process metaphysics, in addition to the intrinsic value found in an accurate description of the real in its most abstract aspects, in its necessary and contingent features properly understood. This consolation is located against the backdrop provided by the process commonplace that the real root of tragedy is not found in the conflict between good and evil (although this conflict is real enough and the source of much grief), but in the transitoriness of contingent good (see Odin 2016). Momentary pleasure or virtue is gone almost as soon as it arrives, unless, of course, there is someone with an accurate memory and moral sensitivity to vicariously keep it alive. Human memory, however, is notoriously attenuated and sievelike, in contrast to divine memory. God lives on even when we are gone; hence any immortality that might be available consists in being remembered by such an omnibenevolent being. Some of us do not wish for more than this.

CHAPTER FIVE

Aristotle, Kant, and Modern Moral Theory

Whereas the previous two chapters dealt with metaphysics in the *strict* sense,
I am at pains in the present book to also highlight Gamwell's treatment
of metaphysics in the *restricted* sense (Gamwell misleadingly calls it the
broad sense) regarding the necessary character of subjective experience and
regarding the relationship between metaphysics and moral/political philosophy. The present chapter is devoted to the latter effort. One might claim
that the two major options in the history of Western philosophical ethics
are Aristotle and Kant, one the quintessential teleologist and the other the
greatest nonteleologist. Gamwell is astute to suggest that an appropriation
and integration of both is required.

What Gamwell finds most interesting in Aristotle's ethics is the complex
relationship between desire and reason. The intellect itself moves nothing in
Aristotle's ethics (*Nicomachean Ethics* 1139c), but this does not mean that
good action can be identified solely by desire. Moral virtue, in Aristotle,
consists in *excellence* of desire, the latter of which is the principle of motion
in living beings. Desire implies a telos in terms of *some* future possibility,
but the good is that at which *all* things aim (1094a), as Aristotle famously
maintained. Of course, there are difficulties that must be faced when determining which steps lead to the good. Dialectic (or reflective equilibrium) is
our best tool in attempting to resolve these difficulties. Dialectic starts with
received views or common sense and then moves on from there as objections
are raised and thorny ethical issues are encountered. There is partial truth
in each criticized opinion, including criticized opinions regarding the telos
of the good life: happiness. For example, there is the big issue regarding
the relationship between pleasure (*hedone*) and happiness (*eudaimonia*). But
certain components are essential, as in the aforementioned nutritive, sentient,

and rational requirements for beings like us. Desire is good when it accords with reason; hence it is appropriate for Aristotle to speak of "rational desire." Although some people appear to be naturally good, it is also clear that desire can potentially lead to chaos, hence the need for moral education through habituation. That is, there need be no huge conflict, as there might be in Kant, between pursuit of pleasure and moral duty. The continent person can control desires that are not virtuous and the genuinely virtuous person actually derives pleasure from doing the good. Reason is thus involved in ethics in two ways: in the education of desire and in the deliberation that occurs in making choices (*DG*, 19–23).

Although there is much with which to agree in Aristotle, Gamwell nonetheless thinks that there are problems with ethical inquiry relying too heavily on generalizations from particular examples, which occur quite frequently in Aristotle: dialectic starts from commonplaces in the culture, determination of the mean relies on items relative to us in particular contexts, virtuous activity is identified by appeal to virtuous individuals, et cetera. Granted, we should expect only as much precision in Aristotle as the subject matter will permit (1094b), but there is nonetheless a failure on Aristotle's part to even consider the position that there is a universal element in ethics if it is the case that some characteristic is presupposed by human action as such. Gamwell finds Aristotle generalizing from certain people or actions that are *already accepted* as examples of the good. In effect, Aristotle begs the question in ethics by defining virtue by assuming to know who the virtuous persons are. In this regard, Gamwell's criticism is like Kant's. On Gamwell's contrasting view, there is an a priori character to ethics, just as we saw in the previous two chapters that there is an a priori character to metaphysics in the strict sense (*DG*, 24–29, 42, 59).

The transition from Aristotle to Kant enables us to see better the possible strengths and weaknesses of each. But this transition also enables us to see Gamwell's love-hate relationship with modern moral theory, with Kant being most responsible for the consensus built up around modern moral theory. One prominent feature of this consensus is the independence of morality from theism, the latter of which is assumed to be incurably authoritarian. Almost all subsequent moral theory insists that the redemption of moral claims must be independent of theistic beliefs. Kant's own postulation of God's existence is itself independent of the justification of the moral law. That is, the categorical imperative does not assume or imply theism. (The point is debatable in that Marxist critics like Lucien Goldmann have traditionally viewed Kantian ethics as an intellectualized version of Christianity.) Further,

Kant's denial of any theoretical knowledge of God is one of the most influential arguments in the history of thought. Also influential is the argument that theistic belief is inherently heteronomous. Although Gamwell does not blame Kant for this, he nonetheless thinks that modern and postmodern amoralism is one possible implication of the conviction that theistic claims cannot be redeemed by reason. The implication is ironic given Kant's own commendable opposition to amoralism. The amoralist (or moral emotivist) engages in a denial of rational ethics that nonetheless purports to be the moral law (*DG*, 8–10; *MN*, 125).

The fact that many scholars are surprised by the label "Kantian metaphysics" is itself surprising. But by "metaphysics" Kant does not refer to inquiry into reality as such or being qua being, but rather to the a priori characteristics of human subjectivity. Indeed, Kant's famous first book devoted to ethics deals with the fundamental principles of the *metaphysics* of morals. Kantian metaphysical claims identify the nature of *practical* reason. Subsequent philosophers have tended to agree with Kant regarding the rejection of the attempt to understand reality as such on the basis of *theoretical* reason, an attempt that is often assumed to be integrally connected to classical theism (*DG*, 14–17).

In addition to their disagreement regarding the role of teleology in ethics, Aristotle and Kant differ considerably on the role of desire. Gamwell largely sides with Aristotle regarding desire and with Kant regarding the a priori characteristics that must be accounted for in ethics. But Kantian metaphysics or the a priori character of Kantian ethics consists in an attenuated version of metaphysics that refers only to the characteristics ethical reasoning must exhibit in order to be experienced by a sensible subject. Moral objectivity cannot be derived from strictly contingent conditions (as in Aristotle) because contingent affirmations can be denied without self-contradiction. Kant is also insightful, according to Gamwell, in asserting that the amoralist *always* chooses among ends arbitrarily, hence refuting the amoralist claim that there are no moral universals. For all it is worth, it is an empirical fact that most reflective human beings throughout most of history have worked on the beliefs that some ends are better than others, that some ends are actually required, and that ends are not to be chosen arbitrarily.

One of Gamwell's key technical terms is *constitutive choice*, which is a most general choice that informs the more particular choices that human beings make on a regular basis throughout life. The problem with amoralism as a constitutive choice is that adherence to amoralism itself is not seen by amoralists themselves as arbitrary. A defensible constitutive choice involves a consistent understanding. By contrast, if *all* choices among ends are arbitrary, then one *ought* to understand oneself as an arbitrary decision-maker in this way, hence the contradiction. Gamwell is like Kant in seeking a universal law. In Kant's case, this law is found in several versions of the categorical imperative. In Gamwell's case, it seems to refer to the following principle: act only in such a way that is consistent with the proper exercise of practical reason and that exemplifies the (Aristotelian) moral and intellectual virtues. This is at least compatible with, and in some ways is very close to, Kant's brilliant insight in the universalizability version of the categorical imperative (*DG*, 37, also 29–36).

Gamwell is also impressed with Kant's idea that autonomy is an important part of the a priori character of practical reason. But he does not think that autonomy is necessarily compromised by theism, although it may very well be compromised by certain forms of divine command theory. On Gamwell's account, amoralism is self-contradictory and we would be better served by following Aristotle's lead in thinking of a telos as a possible (i.e., future) state of affairs characterizing an exemplar to which an agent has a positive relation. Even Kant admits that there could be no human action without the pursuit of some end, but he thinks that the *morality* of a choice among purposes is not to be identified with any purpose, but rather with volition when an action is done from duty. The moral law must be purely formal, hence the nonteleological character of Kantian ethics. Another feature of the complex relationship between Aristotelian and Kantian ethics deals with happiness. Kant rejects the long tradition of thinking that the goal in ethics is happiness. He does not deny that human beings desire happiness; this is a result of their being sensuous as well as rational beings. But the point of morality is to be *worthy of* happiness, should it happen to you, rather than actually to be happy (*DG*, 37–41).

Whereas Kant affirms that the principle of good action is a priori, Aristotle would deny this. From the latter's perspective, such a principle can only be learned by generalizing from certain people and actions that are (independently) seen as good. We have seen that for Kant, on Gamwell's interpretation of Kant, this begs the question because it does not deal with practical reason or practical action as such. Despite the fact that Gamwell leans in Kant's direction here, he is nonetheless unwilling to accept the phenomenon-noumenon distinction and the two conceptions of "end" involved in this distinction. On one concept, ends do not identify good action as such because they are phenomenal, empirical, only apparent states of affairs; on the other concept, there is a noumenal end-in-itself.

But noumena can only be conceived negatively as nonphenomena, which reminds us of the problems detailed in the previous two chapters regarding runaway negativity (*DG*, 42–46).

There is also a problem with Kantian versions of liberalism both because the categorical imperative cannot help us chose between the libertarian and welfare versions of liberalism treated earlier—with Nozickian Kantians choosing one of these and Rawlsian Kantians choosing the other—and because it does not help us in the effort to criticize both versions of established liberalism due to their commitment to political freedom in terms of preference satisfaction. Although Kant tells us much about worthiness to be happy, he is not as informative about the highest good or ultimate purpose. For example, happiness is not the highest good for Kant because the only thing that is good without qualification is a good will, as is well known. Any positive concept of the highest good that involves a telos (which is inseparable from temporality) is inconsistent with Kant's ethics (*DG*, 47–53).

Here is the problem as Gamwell sees things: although Kant enjoins us to seek the highest good as the coincidence of happiness with morality, his concept of the highest good seems like a begrudged concession to the natural *desire* for happiness; but this project is defeated by Kant's understanding of the source of moral worth as *nonsensuous*. That is, on Gamwell's reading, there really is a wide gap in Kant between the phenomenal world that is theoretically knowable and the noumenal world that legislates practically. Kant is more successful when he notices the self-refutation that occurs in, say, false promising. But there can be no moral law without (Aristotelian) desire; hence the categorical imperative in one sense deserves to be indicted. The good life is one where desire is directed to the good. Aristotle is correct that morality is closely connected to desire, and Kant is right that morality must be identified a priori because practical reason itself implies an a priori character to reality, as detailed in the previous chapter. Morality is dependent on metaphysics. Against both Aristotle and Kant, there must be a metaphysical telos by which constitutive choice can be made (and not in the attenuated version of metaphysics found in Kant) (*DG*, 54–60).

To claim that Kant's moral law is empty (because it does not provide much guidance in distinguishing between moral and immoral choice, and this because he thinks that the moral law is identified independently of any telos) is admittedly a significant move on Gamwell's part. By contrast, the maximal human happiness prescribed by Gamwell reintroduces teleology into morality. Kant's mistake is the result of the conjunction of three beliefs on his part: that the moral law is a priori, that a moral telos is metaphysical, and that metaphysics in the strict sense is impossible. It is the third of these beliefs that is the source of difficulty. That is, the first two are acceptable to Gamwell, as is Kant's argument that amoralism is self-contradictory because the very character of practical reason is prescriptive. Metaphysical teleology is the logical contradictory of amoralism. And it is the amoralist claim that no moral claims are rationally defensible that underlies established liberalism's claim that human freedom is solely a matter of preference, as discussed in the first chapter (*DG*, 61–63, 157–58).

It should also be noted that Gamwell does not so much reject Kant's attenuated version of metaphysics as he incorporates it within a larger whole of metaphysics in the strict sense. This larger whole, however, does not so much signal a return to pre-Kantian metaphysics or to classical theism, but is rather an attempt to include it within a larger neoclassical whole where there is a role for being *and* becoming, permanence *and* change, et cetera. It is ironically Kant's thought that is captive to pre-Kantian metaphysics. Although Kant's view has radical implications for the *existence* of God, his *concept* of God is frustratingly traditional, from Gamwell's Hartshornian point of view. And it is precisely the classical concept of God, when linked with Kant's criticisms of theoretical arguments for the existence of God, that has led philosophers (and theologians!) away from theism. It is quite common to see thinkers criticizing classical theism and reaching the conclusion that they have criticized theism itself. It is Hartshorne, on Gamwell's view, who offers the best example of how to defend the evolving divine individual, whose abstract aspects remain permanent in the midst of divine becoming (*DG*, 163, 175–78).

The object of metaphysics on Kant's attenuated version of the discipline is the a priori character not of reality as such but of human reason or subjectivity. This trimmed version of the discipline was appropriate, Kant thought, to any future for metaphysics. This is because we simply cannot know things-in-themselves, including God. Gamwell's task is to restore reflection on the universal character of human subjectivity *as well as* the universal character of reality as such, but he wishes to bring about such a restoration without the substance-based assumptions of traditional metaphysics (*DP*, 106–7).

The present chapter's consideration of Aristotle and Kant, with the latter being a quintessential representative of the Enlightenment, provides an opportunity to isolate Gamwell's stance toward the Enlightenment and its association with "secularization." This term refers to the process by which various sectors of society are removed from domination by religious institutions and symbols. By contrast, premodern society was dominated by what Peter Berger calls "the sacred canopy." As is well known, economic activity was a key driver of the process of secularization in the modern period. But the process of secularization involved escape not only from religion, but also from metaphysical thinking, as emphasized by Jurgen Habermas. As is also well known, the vacuum created by the waning of religious institutions and symbols was filled by reason (*MRF*, 207–9).

At this point I would like to emphasize something that will help to prevent what could lead to a major misunderstanding of Gamwell's philosophy. Gamwell is an ardent *supporter* of Enlightenment rationality. Modern culture is distinguished by its affirmation that human understandings can be redeemed only by appeal to experience *and reason*, in contrast to premodern authoritarianism. Granted, there were pockets of rationality in the premodern period (as in Aristotle) and authoritarian tendencies can (unfortunately) be detected in the modern era. In general, however, the contrast stands. Gamwell is cognizant of the fact that the attempt to maintain religious adherence by authoritarian appeal becomes increasingly ineffective. What leads Gamwell to be critical of the Enlightenment is not its emphasis on reason, but rather its belief that religious truths cannot be supported by theoretical reason. Strange as this sounds, Gamwell is more of an Enlightenment thinker than Kant precisely because he expands the scope of rationality to include religious and metaphysical truths! (*MRF*, 210–12).

When Gamwell challenges modern moral theory, it is not due to modernity's emphasis on reason in morality, but rather to the dogmatic assumption that moral claims are independent of theistic affirmations. On Gamwell's view, religious affirmations are implied by the moral enterprise as such. In short, divine reality is the ground of moral claims. As we have seen and will continue to see, Gamwell *argues* against the discrediting of the transcendental project and supports the Whiteheadian appeal to the reason to which all authority must bow (Whitehead 1967a, 161). Of course, much depends on what one means by "reason" in that the shedding of speculative (yet fallible) rationality and overemphasis of merely instrumental rationality can lead to totalitarianism, as emphasized once again by Habermas as well as by Hannah Arendt. The conviction that human existence has no ultimate significance and that meaning is an arbitrary creation of human willfulness can have quite devastating consequences (*DG*, 1–8).

Some people might assume that, upon hearing that Gamwell would like to restore theistic metaphysics, he is also attempting to restore appeal to divine revelation, either in terms of divine command theory or natural law theory. This is not the case. Rather, he is reacting against the tendency on the part of modern moral theorists to either reject or deconstruct altogether the moral enterprise or pursue nontheistic moral theory. Gamwell *is* defending the modern commitment to autonomy. In fact, he thinks that resistance to autonomy is self-refuting. This is because one cannot avoid the modern presupposition of autonomy in the very questioning of it. In different terms, the *rational choice* between autonomy and heteronomy presupposes autonomy, which makes possible rational choice. The only real alternative to autonomy is authoritarianism, which Gamwell rejects. Once the modern affirmation of autonomy appears on the scene and is understood, we are irreversibly pushed into a future in which autonomy is presupposed (*MRF*, 10–14).

Gamwell is a defender of transcendental arguments at the very least because the assertion that the conditions of practical reason are entirely empirical cannot itself be redeemed empirically. Or again, the claim that practical reason has *no* a priori conditions itself can only be validated a priori. In these assertions no harm is done by replacing "a priori" with "transcendental." Transcendental reflection in the restricted sense refers to reflection on the presuppositions of any genuine act of cognition or understanding. It deals with the presuppositions of understanding as such. In this regard I am distinguishing Gamwell from other transcendental thinkers like Kant and Karl-Otto Apel, on the one hand, as well as from nontranscendental thinkers like Alasdair MacIntyre, Richard Rorty, and many others. Gamwell's argument is that one cannot consistently reject transcendental thought. This is because denials of the transcendental project are self-refuting (*DG*, 85–87).

On the basis of Gamwell's philosophy, although Kant's moral law is empty, this does not show that the Enlightenment in general can be discredited. At every turn Gamwell is careful to point out that matters are always more complicated than they seem initially. In addition to criticizing some transcendental and all nontranscendental moral philosophy, he is also opposed to amoralism or moral skepticism. Although the latter view might have an initial appeal as a response to authoritarianism, it falls victim to transcendental reasoning. Consider the following prescient distinction made by Gamwell: "So far as I can see . . . the undeniable historicity of every human individual and community does not in itself constitute a reason to reject transcendental thought. It is one thing to say that all human understanding is conditioned by its specific time and place and another thing to say that *only* historically specific conditions can be understood" (*DG*, 92; emphasis added). He is also insightful in noticing that the absence of complete success of previous cases of transcendental thinking is not the same as complete absence of success. Logical certainty is not the same as epistemological certainty in that the former can be present even if the latter is characterized by fallibility. That is, only epistemological certainty is out of reach. Further, the distinction that looms large in the present book between logically contingent and logically necessary claims itself lies within the realm of fallible thought (*DG*, 88–93).

The fact that transcendental thought seeks a certain sort of certainty does not in itself discredit the project in any obvious way, especially given the distinction above that includes the fallibility of claims to epistemological certainty. Nor do assertions that all thought is either historical or intralinguistic or theory-laden or occurs within a hermeneutical circle tear down the transcendental project, as I am arguing throughout the book. Transcendental claims in the restricted sense correspond to the reality of human subjectivity as such. This is because transcendental claims are those that are compatible with every other claim we take to be true or even could take to be true. We cannot speak at all without saying something at least implicitly about certain necessary conditions of any use of language. Hence, the meaning and truth of transcendental claims consists in their correspondence to the reality of human subjectivity *and* to their intralinguistic compatibility. The transcendental project defended by Gamwell includes the claim that skepticism (or amoralism) is self-contradictory in that there are necessary conditions that any use of language implicitly affirms or at least presupposes. Further, in a claim that echoes Popper's famous falsification principle, absent transcendental conditions we cannot make sense of any falsification of theories or claims. But we *do* falsify with assurance, as when I claim that scratching my head is *not* the cause of climate change. If one says that what we can conceive *never* exhausts what is conceivable, then *this* assertion itself must be fallible, in which case we should conclude that an alternative to it is conceivable (*DG*, 94–99, 107).

To claim that *every* instance of human knowing is strictly and without remainder intralinguistic, and hence contradicts the transcendental project, is a self-refuting proposal in that it consists in the very sort of claim about human understanding that it at the same time prohibits. In different terms, to say that *all* human understanding is dependent on the conceptual scheme that is arbitrarily adopted must, in spite of itself, be a transcendental "fact." This is because conceptual relativity itself cannot simultaneously be independent of a conceptual scheme and dependent on a conceptual scheme. Objections to the sort of philosophy done by Gamwell typically imply what they deny. A transcendental claim is one that is affirmed when its denial is self-refuting or self-contradictory.

I also think that we should pay needed attention to Gamwell's claim that human freedom or decision-making cannot be denied without self-contradiction. Transcendental arguments are successful when one understands the limits of what is conceivable and shows that there is no conceivable alternative. The fact that we can never consider and refute all competing views does not necessarily count against the transcendental project. Transcendental thought claims that all verbal alternatives have been *implicitly* refuted and asks any challengers to come up with an alternative that refutes the transcendental claim in question. As before, the claim that human fallibility shows the *impossibility* of transcendental thought is itself self-referentially contradictory (*DG*, 100–109, 113).

Although we cannot humanly consider and refute *all* competing views, we *can* in a very abstract way reduce the logical possibilities to a finite number, from which, by a similarly finite number of axioms or intuitions, we can then eliminate all but one defensible response to metaphysical questions. This sort of intellectual progress can occur so long as we adhere along the way to virtuous argumentation by showing openness to criticism, avoiding evasive or offensive *ad hominem* tactics, et cetera, that prevent fair and effective communication. The result of such Hartshornian and Gamwellian efforts is neoclassical metaphysics, efforts that are analogous to the move in physics away from classical sources, the latter of which are worthy of respect, but which are no longer sufficient. Transcendental philosophy is an attempt to understand argumentative discourse itself, the communicative character of subjectivity, and fallibility as a transcendental condition of human subjectivity. Further, at least some of the conditions of subjectivity as such are also characteristics of reality as such (*DG*, 132, 149, 153).

In contrast to modern moral theory, Gamwell's theory is metaphysical in both strict and restricted senses. An actual occasion is a unification of relations to the past by which a decision is made that makes it a single thing for the future. The metaphysical character of the final real things is summarized by the famous motto from Whitehead: "The many become one, and are increased by one" (Whitehead 1978, 21). The many effects of past actual occasions are synthesized so that a new actuality becomes part of the past to which future actual occasions then relate. These creative syntheses contribute greater (or lesser) *worth* to reality, both aesthetic and moral. Creativity is an aesthetic achievement whenever it occurs in the sense that *aisthesis* refers to achieved value or worth in every *experience*. The word "aesthetic" is appropriate because an excessive concern for unity seems to restrict relations and weakens a sense of contrast, whereas an excessive concern for diversity seems to overload experience and to deprive it of integrity. Both excesses lead to aesthetic disvalue: boredom or monotony, in one case, and disorientation or cacophony, in the other. Of course, *some* degree of harmonic dissonance can nonetheless contribute to aesthetic worth, as is noticed especially in jazz. In terms of moral worth, too little freedom cries out for emancipation, but too much freedom often leads to a dangerous desire for order at any cost. The comprehensive purpose involves moderation in both aesthetic and moral terms. Freedom here means both freedom *from* external constraints and freedom *for* the realization of creative pursuits. To be morally good is to maximize the unity-in-diversity of one's actions, given the possibilities presented by one's past (*DP*, 122–31).

To affirm justice as general emancipation also commits one to what Gamwell calls the way of reason. But reason does not necessarily point us, as it did several premodern thinkers, to the thesis that change is an indication of imperfection, and therefore God had to be changeless. That is, reason takes us to a somewhat different, neoclassical concept of God in which God is seen as all-embracing Love. God gives to us *and* receives from us. It is the life*less* things of the world (when seen as aggregates of active parts) that most closely approximate being changeless. The higher kinds of being, however, are those with *greater* openness to change. Of course, when speaking of God analogically there are *some* differences, one of which is that God is not subject to a kind of change that affects us: the change from life to death. But God is not only temporal, but supremely temporal in that God, as that than which no greater can be conceived, exists everlastingly, in contrast to our finite span of existence.

The contrast here to modern moral theory is striking in that it was typical of modern philosophers, especially Kant, to have a deflationary view of our ability to know the existence of God, but when they did talk of God, again especially Kant, the assumption was that by "God" was meant the God of classical theism. (Hume was an exception in that, whatever he thought about the *existence* of God, he was nonetheless open-minded regarding the *concept* of God.) *If* God is seen, in classical theistic fashion, as eternally complete, then nothing we could do or say would make any difference whatsoever to the divine being. On the contrasting neoclassical view, our actions are given everlasting significance in that they contribute to the ongoing and never-ending divine life. The difference we make is ultimately the difference we make to divine actuality. Present action thus passes into permanent significance for the universe. Otherwise, as Whitehead emphasized (Whitehead 1941, 698), our actions are merely passing whiffs of insignificance (*PCV*, 99–105).

There is obviously much more that could be said about the transition from premodern to modern moral theory. For example, thus far I might understandably be interpreted as downplaying the role of rationality in premodern thought. Thomas Aquinas, however, provided a robust role for rationality in that, even when speaking of God, he thought that kataphatic (positive) discourse is always analogical and analogical predication requires human reason. This is because reason is needed in analogical discourse to chart a mean between simple univocation and equivocation. It requires an independent understanding of the relations among things that allows them to be so named. Many or most truths in religion as well as in morality/politics can be demonstrated independently of special revelation, according to Thomas Aquinas. His favorite example of an analogical term is one that helps to explicate the moral views that he inherited from Aristotle: healthiness. This term, when applied to both human beings and nonhuman animals, is not exactly the same, but to say that a human being is healthy and a nonhuman animal is healthy is not exactly to equivocate, either. Gamwell largely departs from Thomas Aquinas's view of God not because it is analogical, but rather because it is insufficiently analogical. A being who is completely devoid of internal relations to the creatures, but who nonetheless loves them, is not even remotely analogous to human relations or to human love. The problem is not with calling God perfect, but in failing to notice that "perfection" is an analogical term and that there is such a thing as dynamic perfection as well as steadfast or enduring perfection (*MN*, 47–64).

Further, Thomas Aquinas's affirmation of the principle of prior actuality is an expression of the basic metaphysical recognition that existence as such cannot be completely absent. A complete negation of existence is senseless. This brings Thomas Aquinas closer to the two neoclassical metaphysical claims defended in a previous chapter than many suppose. This is not surprising when it is realized that the best insights in classical theism are included in, and are not rejected by, neoclassical theists. "There might have been absolutely nothing" or "existence as such might cease" are merely verbal statements that make no sense in that there cannot be a *completely* restrictive existential possibility, as we have seen. On the neoclassical view that Gamwell sees as the most promising option in contemporary metaphysics and philosophy of religion, an actuality is a creative synthesis or unification of real relations with other actualities as well as to possibilities. In the divine case these relations are all-inclusive, whereas in the human case they are fragmentary. It is the attenuated character of the latter that often leads to tragedy and disappointment in moral and political life (*MN*, 65–70, 228). It should also be emphasized that Thomas Aquinas offered the most systematic premodern statement of a comprehensive teleology wherein human life is properly directed to a telos defined by reality as such; in this regard Gamwell is very much like Thomas Aquinas, but on a neoclassical rather than on a classical theistic basis (*DP*, 1–2).

Gamwell's Enlightenment tendencies are compatible with the realization that there were thinkers who were profoundly committed to rationality in the premodern period, like Thomas Aquinas, and thinkers who attempted to undermine rationality in the modern (or postmodern) period, like Martin Heidegger. On Heidegger's account, every unconcealment is also a concealment, an account that is integral to Heidegger's indictment of metaphysics from the time of Plato to the present. However, Gamwell argues that if one embraces the essential connection between unconcealment and concealment, then the unconcealing/concealing event itself is circumscribed and implies (albeit inconsistently) the possibility of some other context of interpretation that does not involve concealment. That is, Heidegger's account is pragmatically self-contradictory in that he aims to *make clear* the history of metaphysics. Because Gamwell is interested in metaphysics in a twofold sense, including the effort to determine necessarily true statements about subjectivity as such, he can reach partial rapprochement with Heidegger's insistence in *Being and Time* that asking about Being is inseparable from practical engagement with *Dasein*. But Gamwell, unlike Heidegger, takes this point into the heart of morality: the claim that "something is bound by the moral law" is pragmatically necessary in that every subject who denies this claim nonetheless implies it (i.e., by implying that we *ought* to reject it) and thus engages in pragmatic self-contradiction (*EG*, 39–50).

Further, metaphysical statements regarding subjective existence imply those that deal with existence as such, but metaphysical statements regarding existence as such do not necessarily imply those that deal with subjectivity as such. In both senses of metaphysics, however, there are efforts to render explicit what was originally implicit. The biggest mistake made by traditional metaphysicians, according to Gamwell in partial distinction from Heidegger, was to assume that preeminent being was changeless (*EG*, 51–57; *MN*, 231). As Gamwell puts the point, "Every subject's projection into the future, we might say, includes an implicit understanding of the teleological character of beings as such without which no other meaning or understanding is possible" (*EG*, 58).

One thinker who operates as a bridge between what Gamwell takes to be the best in the premodern and the modern is Iris Murdoch. She was a reserved friend of theistic metaphysics, even if she was not herself a theist. Likewise, she asserted the fundamental importance of the ontological argument, even if she did not succumb to the soundness of the argument (see Burns 2013). She did, however, like Gamwell, insist on metaphysics as a guide to morals. The most general or abiding factors of the human condition are not irrelevant to practical moral concerns. And these most general (i.e., metaphysical) factors are not restricted to theories about human subjectivity. They also offer us a picture of the deep or fundamental character of reality. Like Plato (and like the contemporary philosopher Robert Neville), Murdoch sees the concept of goodness as integrally connected to reality. Indeed, she speaks of the omnipresence of value. This does not mean that everything is good *simpliciter*, but rather that the modern effort to completely sever fact from value is futile. That is, we experience things as valuable in themselves, quite apart from our evaluation of them. Valuing is not so much a specialized subjective act of will as it is an apprehension or cognition of the world. What Murdoch enables Gamwell to do is to expand on the metaphysical necessity of the claim that "something exists" so as to include the claims that goodness and value also exist of necessity, as in the haunting yet quite natural moral magnetism of the concept of truth. We notice this especially when we experience outrage when we are the recipients of a lie (*WTP*, 179–82).

Truthful cognition, in turn, is integrally connected to right action. But it is not easy to achieve truthful cognition, especially regarding the elusive goal of self-knowledge, which is often disturbed by the twin evils of self-abasement and self-aggrandizement. Surely Murdoch is correct that there is still much to be learned from the Greeks, including Sophocles, about the need for self-knowledge. And from the medievals we can still learn about the incurably *personal* character of the moral pilgrimage. Murdoch's moral realism implies an idea of perfection if only because of the familiar experience we have of imperfection in things, in certain ideas, and in institutions. By implication, we also experience, albeit at a distance, the reality of perfection or of *the* good. This is the abiding significance of the ontological argument mentioned above. If all of this sounds very premodern, it should also be emphasized that Murdoch is typically modern in her commitment to demythologization of religion. That is, modern religion must be *thoroughly* rational in order to be believable. From Gamwell's point of view, however, we ought not throw away theism with the demythologized bathwater. In a way, all true statements orient us to the good and, if one is a theist, to a God who cognizes in a preeminent way the concept of goodness (*WTP*, 183–87).

Gamwell's way of putting the matter is telling: "The absence of something ultimate at stake means only that ultimately there is nothing at stake in our decisions" (*WTP*, 188). But there *is* something at stake in our decisions. When we act deliberately, we assume that our actions in some sense *make a difference* that no turn of events in the future can annul. They pass into permanent significance for the universe, to put the point in Whitehead's terms. Otherwise, our actions are passing whiffs of insignificance (Whitehead 1941, 698), as we have seen. To be a neoclassical theist is to live with a certain degree of confidence that there is an unconditioned worth of our adventures. It is the very function of religion to offer a representation—or better, a concept—of perfection that cultivates our pilgrimage from appearance to reality. Successful arguments for God's existence like the ontological one are not, however, meant to create an experience of God that was not already present. Moral realism presents us with a view of perfection (often indirectly by way of imperfection) that is evidence of the integral connection between our practical concern to live well and theistic metaphysics (*WTP*, 188–93).

CHAPTER SIX

MacIntyre, Rorty, Apel, and Habermas

In the previous chapter, Gamwell's appropriation of Aristotle and Kant and his prehension and critique of modern moral theory were treated, a treatment that sets the stage for a consideration of four very influential and quite different contemporary moral theorists who philosophize in the wake of Aristotle and Kant. The first of these is Alasdair MacIntyre, whose book *After Virtue* and its sequel, *Whose Justice? Which Rationality?*, advance an understanding of the moral enterprise in an Aristotelian manner by seeing that enterprise as essentially empirical and non–a priori. MacIntyre is famous for characterizing the world in which we live in terms of a fragmented array of moral precepts that create utter cacophony. His indictment of modern moral thought is encapsulated in the choice he gives to us at the end of *After Virtue*: Nietzsche or Aristotle? Although MacIntyre chooses the latter philosopher in this forced choice, such an option is by no means easy to enact in a world where rational agreement about *common* ends or values seems a real longshot. As MacIntyre sees things, a loss of natural teleology prevents rational discussion of moral claims. Nonetheless, MacIntyre heroically tries to retrieve and strengthen the Aristotelian tradition, but as a result he ends up with a view that asserts the inescapable historicity of morality. Narrative history is essential, he thinks, and moral actions are always to be understood as related to a particular setting (*DG*, 64–67).

To ask "What is the good life for a human being?" is to seek a conception of *the* good, Gamwell thinks, but this use of a definite article is hampered in MacIntyre by a plurality of human practices that involve various internal goods as well as many entanglements with external goods. There are plenty of ends in MacIntyre but these are often in conflict. This pluralism understandably leads people to seek out an adequate sense of the traditions out of which arise the particular practices that help to define meaning in their lives. The good cannot be theoretically characterized in MacIntyre because the virtues cherished in one's tradition are historically constituted in communities through which people find their moral identities. *All* reasoning about the good takes place within the context of some traditional mode of thought. The sequel to *After Virtue* promised an account of human reason, but reason turned out to be just as much a product of historical context as moral value. It will be remembered that Aristotelian dialectic starts from received opinion and then tries to preserve the partial truth in each party to the dialectical conversation. The difficulties involved in this adjudication of principles within a tradition are magnified when it is realized that there is a need to adjudicate conceptions of rationality and moral value among various traditions as well. MacIntyre's own endorsement of the Aristotelian tradition seems to be the result of his own dialectical assessment of it in contrast to Enlightenment rationality (as well as in contrast to Icelandic mythology et al.). That is, his endorsement of the Aristotelian tradition is itself a part of a narrative quest, a historically embodied argument (*DG*, 68–74).

Gamwell's critique of MacIntyre's view starts with the observation that the distinction between moral *and immoral* states of character cannot, on the grounds of MacIntyre's theory, be identified in terms of a universal standard or a comprehensive good. *All* ends and theories regarding states of character are historically specific, on MacIntyre's view. Gamwell notices, however, that the principle to pursue the good specific to one's historical setting itself is purely formal. Further, not only is this principle purely formal, it implies that not all goods are historically specific. Saying that we *cannot* characterize actions independently of historical settings is to make a claim that is *not* historically specific. The contradictory of the concept that moral ends are in *no* respect universal is the concept that *some* of them are universal. This gives Gamwell elbow room to say that a universal good may very well have particular exemplifications (*DG*, 75–77).

Because theories of the virtues and theories of practical reason are integrally connected to each other, it makes sense from MacIntyre's point of view that they both be dependent on tradition. A particular tradition's virtues and reasonings can perhaps be vindicated dialectically by showing their superiority (but how?) to historically specific rivals. Gamwell's fear is that arbitrariness cannot be overcome in such dialectical judgments unless debate about rational standards itself is possible between traditions. Mac-Intyre seems to grant Gamwell's point here when he relies on the distinction between truth and warranted assertibility, with the latter having application only at some particular time and place and with truth having some sort of wider applicability (without necessarily subscribing to the thesis that truth is eternal). Gamwell wonders, however, how one could even know that one's thought is tradition-dependent if one did not have *some* sense of what it would mean to speak of necessary or universal truth. To formulate a question about inquiry that is tradition-dependent assumes a universal standard of theory assessment. In this sense, at least, Gamwell thinks that we should side with Kant in insisting on *some* a priori conditions for practical reason in that strictly empirical moral theory is rationally arbitrary or self-contradictory (*DG*, 78–84).

There is an influential contemporary version of empirical moral theory that is more extreme than MacIntyre's. Richard Rorty simply refuses to affirm or deny transcendental conditions for practical thought. Indeed, he wants to simply drop the vocabulary of necessary and contingent, abstract and concrete, objective and subjective, reality and appearance, et cetera. That is, he chooses to change the subject and the terms with which it has been discussed since the time of Plato. Whether he can do so consistently, however, is another matter. Although Rorty is surely correct that foundational philosophers from the past have sometimes been associated with dogmatism and authoritarian politics, these associations are not necessary, especially when the aforementioned point is considered that even falsification with assurance (quite apart from dogmatically stating the truth with assurance) requires intellectual foundations of a modest sort. The difficulty Rorty faces is that if he tries to advance a philosophical argument regarding the alleged negative historical consequences of previous foundational pursuits, then he will thereby enter into the very transcendental discussion that a neopragmatist like himself would otherwise want to avoid. Rorty tries to get off the hook here by claiming that he is only (modestly) doing philosophy rather than doing the foundational or transcendental activity engaged in by Gamwell, which Rorty would call Philosophy (with an uppercase "P"). But this is false modesty on Rorty's part in that he rather strenuously urges us to adopt his view, which, despite protests to the contrary, aims at more than merely muddling through and avoiding conflict with other statements human beings make that are doing the same (*DG*, 114–16).

One wonders what sort of claim Rorty is making when he says that moral truth, in particular, and truth, in general, *do not have* an essence. This seems to be a Philosophical claim on Rorty's part. Later we will see that Rorty's further claim that foundations or transcendental arguments make no pragmatic difference is suspect, but here I would like to emphasize Gamwell's position that Rorty (along with MacIntyre) does Philosophy in spite of himself. At times Rorty admits this in that he recognizes that commitment to democratic freedom, based as it is on the Socratic virtues of conversation, depends on something unhistorical and that explains why we should continue to converse in the manner of Socrates. Inauthentic understanding and mendacity will compromise both the moral enterprise and democratic freedom. Gamwell's project is, like Rorty's, pragmatic, but transcendentally so, as we will see. I mention this because Rorty thinks that Philosophy is not worth the trouble precisely because it is similar to Religion. Rorty does not so much argue against Philosophy or Religion. Rather, he chooses to affirm his own version of neopragmatism in place of these more ambitious disciplines. Neopragmatic refusal is simply a choice, according to Gamwell, which means that Rorty's philosophy is yet another version of preference satisfaction, as detailed above in the first chapter. When Rorty *does* seem to offer an argument in favor of his view, we have seen that he implies the very transcendental conditions that he refuses to affirm. The very choice between the transcendental project and its refusal presupposes the transcendental project. To put the point in Kantian terms, the *denial* of a transcendental law of practical reason is itself a (contradictory) law of practical reason. Kant's prescience regarding the transcendental conditions of morality (unfortunately without the backing of metaphysics in the strict sense) was not misguided; rather, it was a defensible response to the erosion of authoritarian or heteronomous understandings of the moral life (*DG*, 117–26).

A third contemporary thinker who is worthy of consideration from a Gamwellian point of view is Karl-Otto Apel, who in one important respect is much closer to Gamwell than MacIntyre and Rorty. This is due to the fact that Apel, unlike MacIntyre and Rorty, embraces transcendental arguments. But his transcendental project does not include metaphysical thinking in the strict sense; hence there remains a significant gap between his thought and Gamwell's. That is, Apel follows too closely Kant's rejection of metaphysics in the strict sense and settles for an attenuated or restricted version of metaphysics that applies only to human subjectivity. Transcendental reflection, for both Apel and Gamwell, is reflection upon presuppositions such that anyone who is interested in grounding basic moral norms is already engaging in transcendental reflection. Such reflection is intersubjective in Apel in that the task for philosophers is to determine the necessary conditions for cognition as such. To *deny* that there are such conditions is to contradict oneself in that the denial itself is an expression of a transcendental claim because the denial is said to have some force regarding all cognitive claims. If one says that *in principle* we cannot abstract away from the forces that condition us, we are claiming a sound insight into the limits of the possibility of the abstraction. This version of transcendental argument is intersubjective in the sense that making claims is in effect an offer to communicate to all potential subjects such that "solitary" thought consists in the internalization of dialogue in a potential community. Arguable claims are fallible claims and transcendental philosophy is an attempt to understand the nature of argumentative discourse as such (*DG*, 127–32).

Due to the communicative character of subjectivity, it makes sense to see Apel's thought as a type of transcendental hermeneutics or as a transcendental pragmatics of language because we cannot redeem our understandings by appeal to some prelinguistic apprehension of reality. But Apel, like Gamwell, is intent on avoiding epistemological relativism. Gamwell is unique in the way he ties this claim in with his critique of completely negative existential judgments discussed above in the third chapter. To say that another subject's (or culture's) understandings are in principle and completely incommensurable with one's own and hence lead to relativism is to say—incoherently—that inconceivable human understandings are possibly understood. Morality is possible only if there is some moral norm that subjectivity as such presupposes, as Kant also claimed. The main alternatives to this conclusion are positivism and existentialism, which agree to the claims that empirical facts are value-free and that morality is solely a matter of subjective, private, and ultimately irrational decisions. These characteristics play into the hands of established liberalism with its fetish for morality reduced to preference satisfaction. These alternatives also play into the hands of Weberian instrumental rationality (*DG*, 133–38).

Apel is helpful in the effort to articulate a metanorm for communicatively generating material norms that are more particular. One of these metanorms is that a public claim implies an offer to give reasons that command the assent of rational subjects, which involves a morality of reciprocal recognition of communication partners, a recognition that is violated when censorship occurs. In choosing any purpose at all one is presupposing norms with which conflicts of interest may be adjudicated. These norms ideally can be established consensually through argumentative discourse. Of course, this once again reminds us of Kant's universalizability version of the categorical imperative. One should acknowledge all of the claims of one's communicative partners that are compatible with the claims of all other members of the communicative community. This norm is presupposed in the establishment of material norms regarding, say, who gets to speak first and for how long, et cetera. Granted, any particular consensus that is reached can be the result of systematically distorted communication. This is due in part to the possibility of any particular communication partner acting immorally, say by lying. But the *regulative ideal* of progressively realizing a morality of consensual communication is the long-term goal. Practical reason as such presupposes commitment to the transcendental or ideal communication community (*DG*, 139–44).

For all of this Gamwell is appreciative. What divides Gamwell from Apel is the latter's Kantian severing of the moral law from metaphysics in the strict sense. On Gamwell's interpretation, theoretical reason in Kant does not include a positive concept of freedom. Further, the objects of theoretical reason are things-as-they-appear, while freedom would have to be a characteristic of things-in-themselves. This is why for Kant and Apel theoretical reason and practical reason are independent of each other. But Gamwell urges with a great deal of cogency that it is difficult to divorce theoretical and practical reason in that the claim that separates them is self-contradictory. The transcendental character of practical reason (admitted by Kant, Apel, and Gamwell alike) implies the transcendental character of theoretical reason (according to Gamwell). This is because the logical and rhetorical moves mentioned above in demonstrating the need for a priori conditions for practical reason as such are exactly the moves that can be used to establish the transcendental character of Gamwellian theoretical reason, as we saw above in the third chapter regarding the claims that something exists and that God exists (*DG*, 139, 144).

Apel's moral theory presupposes a comprehensive norm that is transcendental in character and that is required in making any moral claim at all. But he is skeptical of a truly comprehensive telos. To commit to a transcendental condition that identifies human subjectivity as such, and to simultaneously reject altogether metaphysics in the strict sense, however, is suspect because some of the transcendental conditions of subjectivity as such are also conditions of reality as such. If Apel is correct, along with Charles Sanders Peirce, that truth is the opinion that would ultimately be agreed upon by all conscientious investigators, then such convergence of opinion should occur as well regarding claims in metaphysics in the strict sense, as in the claim in the third chapter that "something exists" is necessarily true. True claims are those to which all rational subjects ought to give assent. In addition, fallible subjectivity presupposes a comprehensive and hence infallible Subjectivity; thus the other metaphysical claim defended in the third chapter regarding the necessary existence of God should also be on the table for rational discussion. Affirmations regarding reality as such (from subatomic reality to God) and human experience as such are often closely related. That is, the telos of a rational communication community can be, should be, included within a theistic telos (*DG*, 144–53).

At least one social practice is an implication of the metaethical character of every moral claim: the practice of respectful moral discourse in which claims are redeemed by the giving of reasons. Part of what is meant by "respectful" is opposition to treating people in a manner that denies contestation of controversial claims. People have a right to become participants in discourse and as participants they have a right to voice dissent. This is what is meant by saying that fair treatment of all potential participants in discourse is a metaethical presupposition of any moral claim. The price one has to pay to squash dissent is quite high, as in a situation of self-defense against speech that poses an immediate threat of violence. Gamwell is well aware of the fact, however, that there are subtle ways to coerce speakers or skewer discourse without outright censorship. These coercive tools frequently are related to money or the withholding of such (*DP*, 196–206).

Gamwell sees Apel's principle of communicative respect as part of a metaphysics of morals. The principle sees the defining purpose of discourse as the fair adjudication of moral claims in terms of the common pursuit of truth by way of equal freedom of all participants. This very general normative condition cannot be legitimately suspended by the internal norms of some specific practice but can only be criticized at the same very general level. Apel's (Kantian) transcendental account of subjectivity is defensible as far as it goes, but it runs into trouble when examined from the perspective of metaphysics in the strict sense. For example, if "absolutely nothing exists" is possibly true, then *all* existential statements can be called into question, including existential statements related to the transcendental character of subjects as members of an Apel-like communicative community (*EG*, 153–56; *MN*, 37–38).

Now that the major contours of Gamwell's metaphysical theism and reformed liberal theory are on the table, I would like to consider in more detail the connection between these two areas. Specifically, I would like to examine Gamwell's provocative claim that reformed liberal theory is implicit in neoclassical metaphysics. A common assumption in political liberalism is that human beings have a right to be treated as ends. What is distinctive about Gamwell's approach is that he joins this assumption with neoclassical theism: to pursue maximal divine creativity is to pursue the maximal creativity of all persons. To put the point in different Kantian language (although neither Kant nor his epigoni like Apel would agree with Gamwell's theistic metaphysics): so act as to treat creativity, whether one's own or that of other individuals, always as an end and never as a means only. Creativity is seen as intrinsically worthwhile; hence the use of the word "maximize" above might be replaced with the word "optimize" on the assumption that the claims of each are constrained by the claims of others in that conflict is inevitable. Because the creativity of actual occasions involves the creation of particularity, the divine telos includes the sort of historical specificity that MacIntyre is intent to protect. And because conflict of some sort seems inevitable, it would be unwise to seek out less abstract moral rules that are exceptionless. As Aristotle noticed, we should expect only as much precision as the subject matter will allow. Practical moral codes, as Whitehead also noticed, do not admit of as much precision as discourse at a more abstract level (Aristotle, *Nicomachean Ethics* 1094b; also Whitehead 1967a, 292). It should also be noted that maximal (or optimal) creativity is *always* related to one's setting, an admission that includes general principles (Apel agrees) as well as principles that are indexed to particular circumstance (as MacIntyre argues) (*DG*, 185–89).

To affirm a transcendental telos is also to admit that our reflection on it started with a view of ethics from the past that we inherit. As Gamwell urges: "But the fact that all human thought shares in the fallible particularity of human activity does not make a transcendental telos inaccessible, precisely because it is presupposed by and, therefore, is a condition of fallible particularity as such" (*DG*, 190). The transcendental telos can be expressed in any language, on the one hand, yet particular (MacIntyre-like) achievement cannot occur without the divine good, on the other. It is the divine good that permits discourse about an ideal standard or infallible measure, as evidenced in the everyday phrase "the way things *are*," in contrast to "the way things appear." The good as such and the true as such are ultimately theological terms. Another formulation of the moral law goes as follows: so act as to maximize (or optimize) our common humanity and thereby the creative life of God (*DG*, 190–94).

Of course, it might be asked if the very abstract character of Gamwell's transcendental telos has any practical import. In different terms, it might be asked whether there is any way to determine which purposes do and which do not conform to this telos. An initial reply is that this problem of specification arises for all moral theories because the particular or concrete is not entailed by the general or abstract. If we know there are monkeys, we also know that there are mammals, but the existence of mammals does not entail that there are monkeys. In fact, at one point in evolutionary history there were plenty of mammals but no monkeys. But a more basic reply to these questions consists in the claim that we appeal to the most general telos in order to respond adequately to our most general moral questions, not necessarily to respond adequately to very particular or concrete questions. To press too hard for practical advice from a transcendental telos is, in a way, to commit a category mistake. But this is not to say that there are *no* practical implications of a transcendental telos. For example, the comprehensive good points us in political philosophy toward democracy when seen as *an inclusive ideal* for the associative order of society, with the state being seen as a second-order association unifying both individuals and first-order associations (*DG*, 194–96).

We have seen some of the practical differences between libertarian and welfare liberalisms with respect to varying convictions regarding the proper distribution of social and economic resources with which preferential ends are pursued. The alternative democratic theory that Gamwell defends, reformed liberalism, is not based on preference satisfaction but on maximal (or optimal) common humanity. The reformed liberal ideal is thereby positioned to contribute to the maximal (or optimal) public world. It might be easier to see the contrast between Gamwell's version of liberalism and libertarianism than it is to see the contrast between Gamwell's view and welfare liberalism, but the latter contrast is nonetheless significant. This is because Gamwell is defending a view that emphasizes our capacity to be creative *in the sense that* we contribute to our common humanity (including one's own humanity), in contrast to the capacity to satisfy individual or associational preferences for their own sakes. Freedom of association in Gamwell's version of liberalism is not for the sake of preferential interests (or at least it is not solely for their sake), but for the sake of a maximal (or optimal) public world. We will see that this democratic ideal contains a prima facie prescription to foster equality, but there might be situations in which other considerations override this prescription. Once again, this discussion is theoretical and does not involve a judgment regarding any particular concrete situation (*DG*, 197–200).

Gamwell's stance here is close to that of Rawls, as we will see in more detail later, where a certain inequality might be needed so as to provide access to, say, medical education so that society as a whole can benefit from good doctors. But in the contemporary American context there is an obvious need for greater equality so as to provide the material resources on which abstract freedoms can have real meaning. That is, both egalitarian and inegalitarian components are required in order to further the telos of a common humanity. The *moral* meaning of democracy is integrally connected to the telos of a maximal (or optimal) public world. Religious communities need not be divisive in this regard but could foster the communal good of humanistic discourse regarding shared goods. We will see that, on Gamwell's interpretation, the moral point of the prohibition of any established religion in the state is ironically the very establishment of a noncoercive public world characterized by humane debate and religious-secular civility (*DG*, 201–9).

Aristotle was correct that the good life cannot be identified independently of desire in that desire is needed to develop a positive relation to *some* future possibility or telos. The most comprehensive telos requires us to develop the habit of an abiding disposition to act in accord with the divine good. Our very ability to deliberate presupposes an appetition for the highest good that cannot entirely be refused because its negation would also be the negation of the deliberative ability to flourish in the real world (*DG*, 209–11).

Rorty is more of a misologist than either MacIntyre or Apel (with Apel being more of a skeptic than MacIntyre), even if all three are skeptical of the role of rationality in religion. Gamwell's Enlightenment affirmation of reason even in the comprehensive order of reflection is meant to counteract all three, especially Rorty. Simply to refuse the comprehensive order of reflection, rather than to refute it, is insufficient on Rorty's part (see Rorty 1982, xiv). Further, Rorty endorses Rawls's alleged privatization of religion, although I will later cast doubt on the claim that Rawls does in fact fully privatize the comprehensive order of reflection. We have seen that Rorty's neopragmatism is misleading when it leads scholars to conclude that it is not metaphysical. The denial of Gamwell's view is as Philosophical or comprehensive or metaphysical as Gamwell's own view (even if Gamwell's view is more consistent than Rorty's), as is evidenced in the claims that *no* metaphysical claims are true, *all* theoretical claims are historically indexed, and *every* value judgment is (individually or culturally) relative. Moral relativism, in particular, asserts a *comparison* of all human activities and hence implies a response to the comprehensive question. Hence, it is self-refuting. The very designation "moral relativism" makes sense only when seen in contrast to "moral universalism." One can refuse the distinction between the two only if one also refuses the comprehensive order of reflection itself. In Gamwell's terms, a refusal is a denial (*MRF*, 135–40).

The denial of the rationality of all comprehensive convictions is expressed in several different forms: nihilism, logical positivism, existentialism, Rortyan neopragmatism, et cetera. But in all of its forms, such a denial involves the claim that a choice of purpose is *never* bound by a norm, which ironically is also to assert a norm, even a comprehensive one: human authenticity is *always* particular and/or relative. Or again, amoralism itself implies a moral principle because human beings may choose contrary to the view the amoralist asserts. If arbitrary choices among purposes is a disguised type of comprehensive purpose, however, one cannot consistently hold that the choices are arbitrary. As Kant noticed, it is self-contradictory to deny *all* moral claims. The idea that *all* comprehensive convictions are relative to historically specific conditions is, once again, self-refuting. On the assumption that self-consistency is a necessary condition for defensible comprehensive convictions, Gamwell's criticism of Rorty's view and of those who show a family resemblance to Rorty's view is on sound footing. Gamwell puts the point succinctly: "The denial of comprehensive reflection can only be represented as what in truth it is, namely, the comprehensive claim that human authenticity is always in all respects relative, either to given cultural [or] historical conditions or to the decision of each human activity" (*MRF*, 148, also 141–53).

A fourth contemporary philosopher should be mentioned, Jurgen Habermas, who enthusiastically endorses the transition to modernity from the religious and metaphysical worldviews of the medieval period. Such an endorsement in part relies on Habermas's belief that metaphysical views are immunized against criticism. This immunization, if it ever existed, is rejected by Gamwell, who, in turn, in contrast to Habermas, sees a mistake in modernity's pervasive assumption that liberation from (medieval) authority also liberates us in morality and politics from a comprehensive purpose. The real threat to democracy, in addition to authoritarianism, as Gamwell sees things, is to withdraw from discourse with respect to contested ends. A prominent example of such a withdrawal is provided by Habermas's post-metaphysical view that denies *even the possibility* of defending adequately a conception of common purpose. Strange as it sounds, Habermas's view is like MacIntyre's in assuming that conceptions of the good *cannot* transcend a particular lifeworld, with "cannot" signaling Habermas unwittingly succumbing to transcendental argument. A conception of the good can be defensible, on Habermas's reasoning, but only within a specific lifeworld. The problem here is not only the attenuated character of merely contextual soundness, but also the idea that conceptions of comprehensive good are *in all respects* historically specific cannot itself be specific to a historic lifeworld. That is, the claim that conceptions of the comprehensive good are "in all respects specific to historical conditions itself requires validation in universalist terms" (*DP*, 253). Further, Gamwell wonders how Habermas can defend justice as universal if conceptions of the good are *always* historically specific (*DP*, 2–4, 214, 237, 240–42, 253–55, 269).

There are some features of Habermas's intersubjective account of rationality that are convincing, especially his rejection of an individual preference view of moral and political life. Habermas is also to be commended for emphasizing, like Apel, communicative practice, especially regarding contested claims. The public sphere is the place for reasoned communicative exchange. As in Gamwell, practical reason is explicated in terms of discourse. In such discourse, Habermas (in partial contrast to Rawls) allows citizens to use untranslated religious reasons to support their view, but elected and other government officials in a pluralistic, democratic society should not be permitted to do this. In this way Habermas wants to affirm, even in the modern world, the presence and importance of religion, yet nonetheless retain an agnostic stance at the governmental level. Further, in this way Habermas hopes to allay the fears of thinkers like Gamwell who worry about what will happen when certain religious ideas—as in human beings being made in the image of God—are lost. Are we really willing to live with the view that human beings are merely accidental byproducts of evolutionary history and are of no more significance than any other protoplasmic stuff in the universe, as some secularists argue? That is, Habermas, although a committed modernist (or postmodernist), does not defend a modernism that has a tendency to spin out of control. There is still a place, indeed an essential place, for the religious idea of a common good (*WTP*, 91–100).

Gamwell clearly approves Habermas's admission of religious claims within political discourse, especially because of his commitment to democratic discourse that is equally open to all, including to theists. But he is also comfortable with Habermas's opposition to anyone who would insist on having "the last word" on any contested topic. Metaphysical conceptions of the good are neither "baggage" in the pejorative sense nor blank checks to run roughshod over opponents. Whereas Rawls requires of individual citizens that they meet the *translation proviso* that they make the terms of their comprehensive doctrines as they bear on the public sphere fit into language that any rational citizen could comprehend and possibly accept, Habermas does not do this. But he does require an *institutional translation proviso*. Both of these, Gamwell thinks, work on the erroneous assumption that religious comprehensive doctrines themselves are not amenable to rational discourse. Even Habermas's view seems to suggest that in order to adjudicate claims in the public square one must (temporarily?) cease to be religious. This is because Habermas claims that there is *no alternative to* the postmodern mode of doing philosophy. Here Gamwell suspects that there is not only hyperbole, but also a concealed sort of transcendental argument (*WTP*, 101–6).

A further word regarding the translation proviso, whether for (Rawlsian) individuals or for (Habermasian) government officials, is needed. The word "translation" can be misleading if what it suggests is that meaning can remain the same even when expressed in different languages. But in a political context, "translating" from a religious comprehensive doctrine to a secular one *does* change meaning. Going from a metaphysical to a postmetaphysical idiom resists any nimble transition. Perhaps "transformation" is a more accurate term than "translation," as Gamwell sees things (*WTP*, 212).

Gamwell's major disagreement with Habermas is the same as the one he has with Rawls. Both Habermas and Rawls assume modern (or postmodern) democracy and they assume that justice is *everywhere and always* circumscribed by historical and political context. That is, they ironically offer a comprehensive denial of the role of comprehensive doctrines in developing a conception of justice. Gamwell thinks that there is another alternative: "In contrast to Habermas and Rawls, democracy is not constituted by an overlapping consensus on freestanding principles or by an institutional threshold beyond which only secular reasons count—but, rather, constituted solely as politics by the way of full and free discourse" (*WTP*, 110). Arguing against one's competitors *is* a good thing, on Gamwell's view, even with respect to metaphysical and religious views (*WTP*, 107–19).

CHAPTER SEVEN

Politics as a Vocation

It might still be wondered how the two major foci of the present book—metaphysics and political philosophy—fit together. One of these is, along with mathematics and logic, the most abstract discipline, whereas the other deals with some of the most practical human affairs. But it should be noted that it is the most abstract features of political *philosophy* with which Gamwell is concerned. It is a metaphysics of political thought that primarily animates him, not the concrete details of party politics. His concerns overlap with the religion-politics debate as it has played out over the history of political liberalism. In fact, it can be said with a certain degree of confidence that political liberalism commenced with the effort to deal fairly with people in the wake of the wars of religion in the early modern period, as ably argued by John Rawls and others. In this chapter I will be treating metaphysics as an extension of religious thought at its best and when it is directed to the most abstract aspects of human endeavor.

Gamwell notes that the relationship between religion and politics has been a topic of debate throughout the history of Christianity, responses to which have ranged from the privatization of religion to its indispensable role in the pursuit of justice as part of one's religious (and/or metaphysical) vocation. The idea of "vocation" literally means a calling, which in medieval thought meant a specifically religious summons, especially to the priesthood. Following the Reformation, the concept was expanded to include occupational calling in general. The term has been further expanded through secularization to refer to any occupation or business. Gamwell insists on *politics* as a theistic vocation in that theists are citizens who have lives that should be oriented toward the common good. This vocation has as its locus democratic politics where citizens who bear the image of God engage in free political discourse by way of reason. Theists are called to democratic activity precisely because they are called to pursue a community of love (*PCV*, 1–6).

In the early centuries of Christianity, it was generally held that political powers were divinely ordained and hence should be obeyed. Political resistance risked the charge of resistance to divine will. This Pauline view contained the idea that active attention to the justice or injustice of the social order did not belong to the distinctive task of Christians. To the extent that social concern was taken seriously, it was the Christian community itself at the associational level that was the object of concern. Early Christians thought of themselves as *different* such that social concern was directed at common life *within* the new Christian community. No doubt this view was, in part, dictated by impotence in the face of the Roman Empire. Expectation of an apocalypse was also part of the story. One's purpose was to prepare for eternity *within* the Christian community. Early Christianity did not include politics as a vocation (*PCV*, 7–15).

Both historically and psychologically there is a certain appeal to this early view as noticed by Gamwell, especially at times when the political order seems especially odious. That is, Gamwell is cognizant of the fact that he is swimming against tradition in arguing for politics as a religious, indeed as a metaphysical, vocation. What complicates the early Christian view, according to Gamwell, is the fact that, on Augustinian and especially on Thomistic grounds, the *whole world* (including the political realm) is basically good because created by God, not just a parochial part of it. There is also Augustine's insight that the worst evil in the political world is civil disorder, strife, and war. These points lead to the conclusion that nonresistance to the governing authorities *is itself* a political act due to the fact that quiescence can facilitate civil disorder, strife, even war. It is possible to be political in spite of oneself; hence Gamwell thinks it crucial to explicate the underlying or transcendental characteristics of political life together. In different terms, quiescence is not consistent with love for a God who in turn loves the world (*PCV*, 16–27).

The modern emergence of rule by many has momentous consequences. The premodern tendency, for example, to think that political rule belongs to one or the few because of their uncommon virtue or wisdom (or divine appointment) is rejected. Thomas Aquinas did, however, unlike Augustine, allow a right to revolt against blatant tyranny. Various factors expanded on Thomas Aquinas's insight and contributed to the rise of modern democracy, as is well known: a growing belief in liberty of conscience facilitated government through discussion, the felt *practical* need for toleration was a result of the wars of religion, increasing admiration for reason was a result of the rise of modern science, increasing skepticism was exhibited regarding religious authority, the call for economic liberty was strong on the part of the rising middle class, et cetera. All of these factors contributed to solidifying the conclusions that the final political authority consists in the equal importance of each person's sovereign assessment and that the affirmation of religious toleration is based on *principled* necessity. Religious believers now generally affirm what may have been only implicit in earlier centuries: *all* individuals should be treated as beings loved by God. Further, given the aims of the present book, an important step toward joining metaphysics and political thought is taken when it is realized that a religious or metaphysical belief is distinguished from other kinds of belief by being an *explicit* response to the question: What is the ultimate ground of worth for a human being? (*PCV*, 28–36).

If someone holds that political assessments *cannot* appeal to universal principles, it should be emphasized that this stance itself indicates some understanding of the ultimate ground of worth. In Gamwell's terms, every political claim implies some sense of inclusive purpose. Or again, the separation of principles of justice from a theory regarding the comprehensive good (to be treated in more detail later in reference to Gamwell's analysis of Rawls's thought) is problematic when it is stipulated to apply to *all* citizens. It is unclear how we could affirm a truly *comprehensive* good that did not include principles of justice. The attempt to articulate principles of justice that are completely independent of the comprehensive good also fails to be self-democratizing, on Gamwell's view, in that such an attempt runs afoul of the sovereignty of individuals who *do* explicitly affirm a comprehensive good. Gamwell agrees with Habermas and Apel that making *any* political claim, including one that contests another political claim, is a communicative act in which one implies that one's claim can be validated or redeemed (or invalidated or rejected) by rational argument. But Gamwell (unlike Habermas or Apel) holds that this view makes sense only against a metaphysical background provided by a standard of truth (and of falsification with assurance). In this sense, politics is a vocation in that we are called to pursue the truth and justice in a communal setting conducive to discourse regarding the ultimate terms of political assessment. In fact, Gamwell holds that a claim is not properly political if it cannot be assessed through discourse (*PCV*, 37–45).

The vocation of which Gamwell speaks is given two roughly equivalent labels: the way of reason and the humanistic commitment. The commitment to reason is ironically an appeal to authority, but it is reason itself that is the ultimate judge to which all lesser authorities should bow. Once this affirmation of reason is accepted, there is no theoretical way to stop the drive to popular sovereignty. This is because the way of reason cannot justify ancestral privilege if the sole criterion is whether claims can be redeemed in discourse. That is, humanistic commitment is opposed to the idea of natural stratification. None of this is meant to undermine theistic metaphysics, as was assumed to be the implication of the way of reason both in many Enlightenment skeptics and in fideistic religious believers. Regarding the latter tradition, which goes back to Tertullian, Gamwell holds that to claim that reason is of no importance because religious belief requires God's special self-disclosure or revelatory *evidence*, is itself a response to a rational question. That is, fideism's conclusion is inconsistent with its concession to the need for justificatory warrant (*PCV*, 48–55).

The incisive cadences of Martin Luther King Jr. are testimony to the theses that metaphysical theism prescribes democracy and that the question of God is a rational one, despite the fact that since the eighteenth century there has been widespread doubt that religious or metaphysical claims can be assessed in discourse. Gamwell's transcendental style of argumentation is once again in evidence when he notices that to ask critically whether religious or metaphysical claims can be assessed through discourse is to seek *rational argument* for either a positive or a negative response. But a negative response to this question cannot be successfully defended by argument. This is because to dogmatically assert that religious or metaphysical truths go beyond what discourse can assess is to thereby withdraw from the debate. That is, raising the question critically regarding whether religious or metaphysical claims can be assessed through rational discourse commits one to a positive response to the question. Asking for *reasons* to affirm or deny the way of reason presupposes the way's credibility. Of course, Gamwell is not claiming that the assessment of religious or metaphysical claims is a simple process. The discussion, started by Plato, never ends (*PCV*, 56–60).

It may very well be the case that skepticism regarding the role of rationality in dealing with ultimate questions is the dominant tradition. Gamwell grants this point while nonetheless insisting that this tradition does not express the abiding content of either religion or metaphysics. His hope is that religion and metaphysics would come of age and make explicit what was implicit in the history of these disciplines. One reason historically for the popularity of Tertullian-like skepticism regarding the role of reason was the desire for religion to be accessible to the masses, in contrast to the esoteric skills necessary to engage in dialectic. In response to this understandable concern, it can be noticed that in a democratic age it is at least theoretically possible, and practically necessary in the long run, to have a literate population that could engage in rational discourse in an informed way. It is also possible to have philosophy return to an existential "way of life," as emphasized in the scholarship of Pierre Hadot, rather than be perceived as a barren intellectual activity restricted to academic conferences. Or more cautiously, if philosophy is not exactly an all-encompassing way of life, it *can* be a widespread argumentative practice (*PCV*, 61–65).

To be human is to choose among specific alternatives and sometimes these decisions are deep ones, say whether to understand oneself as a person who is enveloped by an all-embracing love such that authenticity involves service to this loving being. The concept of vocation might imply that this is a forced choice if one feels *compelled* to assent to divine love. Whether free or not, the decision in favor of metaphysical theism is what Gamwell means by the humanistic commitment wherein at the deepest level one cultivates the belief that one should live authentically. This belief involves the idea that religious or metaphysical views *can* be critically assessed, at least when they explicate what must be the case abstractly whenever life with understanding occurs. The affirmation of God's omnipresence implies the humanistic commitment with its way of reason in that, if omnipresent, God would be somehow present in the exercise of reason, indeed especially present in such exercise. One additional reason why many people are skeptical of the role of reason when dealing with ultimate questions—whether in religion or in metaphysics—is due to the inadequacies of classical theism. *If* God is seen as an eternal being in the sense of existing completely outside of time and embodiment, then it is no wonder that temporal and embodied reason seems impotent in the effort to understand such a being. *If* God is seen as omnipotent in the sense of being responsible for (or at least permitting) *everything* that occurs, including gratuitous suffering, then it is no wonder that reason seems unable to come up with a compelling account of theodicy. For these and other reasons, Gamwell adopts a neoclassical, rather than a classical, concept of God (*PCV*, 66–78).

Democratic government involves full and free discourse, according to Gamwell; hence it presupposes the humanistic commitment. Unfortunately, we live in a period in which commitment to the way of reason is at an (it is to be hoped temporary) ebb. The main difficulty with postmodern attenuated support of, or in some cases outright rejection of, rationality is that *critically* asking about it implies commitment to it. An *argument* cannot defend successfully a concept of nonrational validation. This is because success in doing so (if this were possible) would ironically indicate redemption by argument. If one rejects the humanistic commitment or the way of reason, such a rejection itself cannot (in order to be consistent) be established by argument. A variation on the postmodern critique is found when our capacity for rational argument is claimed to be circumscribed by our historicity, but such a claim itself cannot be circumscribed by any specific location. In effect, a critique of universal reason is itself a reasoned critique only if it violates the limits established by the critique. To live in an authentically human way requires a reasonable faith that life is worth living. It makes sense for us to respond to the call of reason. This is due to the fact that to ask if the humanistic commitment is credible itself presupposes that *reasons* can be presented so as to respond to the question. Once it is entertained, the way of reason cannot be consistently refuted because asking about it commits us to it (*PCV*, 165–69).

It should now be clear how the way of reason or the humanistic commitment supports Gamwell's argument against unreformed liberalisms that rely on preference satisfaction. If *all* moral and political claims are expressions of mere preference, then there is an unacknowledged or implied universalism or comprehensive good. Asking about an underlying ground of worth, as such occurs in religion or metaphysics, implies an affirmative response. Although (Descartes-like) belief in one's own existence seems clearer to us than the conviction that such existence is meaningful (hence the above admission that assessment of religious or metaphysical questions is by no means simple), this admission does not affect the firm logical status of the transcendental claims in religion or metaphysics as examined by Gamwell. In a way, every moment of human life implies an affirmation of one's worth (*PCV*, 170–71).

Gamwell is persuasive when he argues that if ultimate questions in religion and metaphysics are immune to argumentative assessment, then democracy *with religious freedom* becomes an alien imposition on views it claims to legitimize. The attempt to understand religious freedom will necessarily fail if religion and metaphysics are not seen as proper objects of reasoned assessment. Further, those who see religious or metaphysical convictions as either nonrational or suprarational must posit this very assumption nonrationally or suprarationally; thus they cannot be confident that they have it right. As before, defensible moral or political principles need metaphysical backing as clarified by neoclassical theism. One of these principles is that democracy is prescribed by the humanitarian commitment in the sense that our moral goal should be to maximize creativity in the future as such, which is nothing other than the future of God's actuality. Such creativity includes as an important component the aforementioned communicative respect, which facilitates, indeed empowers, human flourishing. In effect, these two assertions serve to bring together Gamwell's views of politics and metaphysics: religious freedom is part of the way of reason and neoclassical theism provides a more defensible path in relation to ultimate reality than either classical theism or religious skepticism. In addition, these two assertions are inseparable in that only a coherent theism secures the terms of political evaluation and democracy (including religious freedom) as part of the (divine) good for human beings (*WTP*, 195–200).

In recent years, when calls for (even the enactment of) censorship occur on both the political right and left, it is noteworthy that Gamwell thinks that when a citizen makes any claim in defense of a sound argument, this implies the right of any other citizen to contest the claim. He also thinks that both parties have an obligation to give reasons for their views when they are contested. This is because democracy itself should be (and often is) understood as politics by way of reason (*WTP*, 203, 208, 214).

At the very least, the separation of moral/political principles from comprehensive convictions requires argumentative support on the assumption that comprehensive convictions respond to a rational question. "Religious" freedom is meant to protect all explicit convictions about the ultimate terms of evaluation, even those that are not nominally religious. There is a strong sense in Gamwell that there is an encompassing Truth of which we are all (not only those who are explicitly religious) at least inchoately aware. Each activity in our lives individually or in the state generally should be consistent with this Truth. Without such a standard, and in light of the assumption that political contention is immune to reasoned adjudication, the only alternative is to settle differences of opinion through a prudential *modus vivendi*, at best, or through force, at worst. To be clear, the issue is not whether some people *claim* to have support for their views solely on the basis of authority or tradition or context (obviously they do), but whether these views can also be assessed in public discourse that is rational. The way of reason includes a *commitment* to debate or argument as the best way to adjudicate political claims. In different terms, the *pledge* to argumentative assessment is the one commitment that does not take sides in any political disagreement in a democracy. I assume that "commitment" and "pledge" have a family resemblance to "vocation" (*MN*, 173–78).

We have seen that there is a distinction in Gamwell between two different sorts of transcendental metaphysics: a strict sense, which deals with critical reflection on the necessary features of existence as such (where denial of a metaphysical statement is semantically and perhaps pragmatically self-contradictory), and a restricted sense that deals with critical reflection on the necessary features of subjectivity as such. There are further distinctions needed between moral agents and those who are not moral agents, on the one hand, and between moral and immoral decisions faced by moral agents, on the other. It has also been shown that if all existential statements can be denied without self-contradiction, then the statement "absolutely nothing exists" is possibly true; but this statement is not possibly true. This sort of transcendental metaphysics is possible, however, only if it is neoclassical (i.e., if becoming rather than being is the basic character of the real), as detailed not only by Gamwell, but also by Hartshorne, as well as by Whitehead and Schubert Ogden. It is to this sort of metaphysics that we are called, a claim that is not as odd as it might seem initially in light of the fact that one of the prime contributions of Hartshornian theism is the development of a concept of God compatible with divine love (in contrast to classical theism's difficulties in this area) (*MN*, 111–13).

Transcendental metaphysics in the strict sense leads us to the explication of an all-inclusive divine being, in contrast to ordinary beings who are fragmentarily related to the details of what is actual and possible. That there will be a future is necessary, in contrast to the details regarding the future, which are not here yet to be known in any detail. Actualization can occur only in the present, because the past has already been actualized and the future is yet to be actualized. Only the extraordinary actual occasions that comprise the divine life can be all-inclusive. Although the class of nondivine beings cannot be empty, each individual in this class is both contingent and fragmentary (*MN*, 114–18).

The topic of the present chapter is complicated by the realization that politics as a specifically Christian vocation involves both a highly exalted view of human nature as being made in the image of God *and* a sobering view of the human capacity for evil. St. Augustine's contribution to this realization in his work *On Free Choice of the Will* is that ultimately there is no cause for moral evil more important than the decisions that human beings themselves make. Later in his career Augustine became something of a theological determinist (due to an aggressive classical theistic approach to divine omniscience regarding the future), but at this earlier stage he was fully committed to free decisions on the part of human beings. But even at this earlier stage, what is most important is not so much free will or freedom of self-determination, but instead the freedom that is acquired when we perfect ourselves. It is not so much choosing itself as it is habitually choosing well that matters and that makes us truly free (*MN*, 87–94).

Gamwell's view of politics as a vocation is developed in dialogue with the thought of Reinhold Niebuhr in *Nature and the Destiny of Man*, who, in turn, is dependent on Augustine's views. Niebuhr, however, is thoroughly modern in the sense that he demythologizes human dependence on the depravity of Adam and he rejects ancient and medieval cosmologies. The occasion for moral evil in Niebuhr's thought is contemporary existential *anxiety*. In this regard, the Genesis story has (again, demythologized) relevance for every human decision. "Sin," to use Niebuhr's theological term for moral evil, is universal but not necessary. All human beings sin, but that is not all that they can do. Niebuhr goes so far as to suggest that "original" sin is the one empirically verifiable doctrine of Christianity. Gamwell ultimately rejects Niebuhr's account largely due to the mistakes found in classical theism that have a corrosive effect on Niebuhr's Augustinian view. On the one hand, Niebuhr asserts a belief in human freedom, but on the other hand he leans in the direction of the later, predestinarian Augustine in suggesting that human beings are free to choose *how*, but not *whether*, to sin (*MN*, 94–98).

Gamwell thinks that this contradiction calls into question the very credibility of theism; hence there is nothing trivial at stake in the effort to develop a rationally defensible theodicy. We have seen that in both cases (dealing with omniscience and human freedom as well as theodicy) Gamwell concludes that classical theism fails. Regarding omniscience, Gamwell's neoclassical view is that God knows everything that is logically knowable: past actualities as already actualized, present moments to the extent that they are knowable (subject to the laws of physics), and future possibilities or probabilities *as* possible or probable. The indeterminacy of how future possibilities will be actualized in detail leaves open the conceptual space to see human beings as (within the limits imposed by past actualities) robustly free and thus exempt from the conceptual problem Niebuhr inherited from Augustine. Regarding omnipotence, Gamwell's neoclassical (and Platonic) view is that if being *is* dynamic power, then no being, not even a divine one, could have *all* power; hence there is conceptual space to account intelligibly for evil in the world, given an infinite number of centers of power. Some of them have miniscule power, whereas some others can do a great deal of harm (*MN*, 99–107, 232–33).

If "God" is used to designate ultimate reality and the ground of worth, then there is something duplicitous about inauthentic self-understandings that do not accurately judge our worth. An overly deflationary self-understanding might lead to quietism of the sort mentioned above as exhibited by certain early Christians, on the assumption that we are not up to the task of creating a just society, whereas an overly inflationary self-understanding indicates a failure to come to grips with the darker aspects of human nature. Niebuhr is interesting in the way he tries to mediate between these two extremes by defending a conception of original sin that nonetheless makes sense in the contemporary world. Although anxiety is not a sin, it does indicate a sort of unease regarding the tension between exalted human freedom and debilitating finitude. Perhaps a rough synonym for "anxiety" is "temptation." More precisely, it is temptation that makes one anxious in the exercise of freedom. Even if it seems that sin is inevitable, this does not in any way diminish human responsibility, Niebuhr thinks. That is, it does not get in the way of politics as a vocation. Gamwell affirms Niebuhr's view that there is contemplation and action in almost every moment of life; hence the real danger is not the active life itself, but rather lack of virtue in one's contemplation-in-action. Some helpful success stories here are provided by the Jesuits, the Quakers, the Methodists, and others (*DP*, 59–71).

In addition to self-love, there is also group-pride to worry about in that there is a social aspect to temptation. Kant's (as well as Augustine's) influence on Niebuhr is apparent when he notices that human beings are rational as well as sensual beings, with social influences exerted on both rationality and our sensuous pursuits. The relation between fate and free-dom that runs through Augustine, Kant, and Niebuhr (all three of whom are classical theists) is challenged by Gamwell in a neoclassical manner. For example, Gamwell thinks that the human depravity discussed by Niebuhr might be largely accounted for instead through unjust social structures that encourage citizens to unduly devalue themselves and others, a devaluation that often leads to excessive self-sacrifice and self-denigration, as several feminist thinkers, including Judith Plaskow, have argued. Gamwell also wonders whether Niebuhr is correct that the really basic sin is pride or self-love. On Gamwell's account, this designation instead should be placed on duplicity, defined as a false understanding of (or facile rejection of) the comprehensive (divine) telos, which involves either an existential lie or a failure to come to terms with self-contradiction. This presupposes, of course, that a true understanding is possible. In this regard there is quite a difference of opinion between Niebuhr's conception of divine perfection as static and Gamwell's neoclassical view of the same in dynamic terms. The latter enables Gamwell to appreciate the fact that there is a difference between knowing the comprehensive dynamic divine telos, on the one hand,

and appreciating more concretely the equally dynamic immediate context of one's cultural and political institutions, on the other (*DP*, 72–104, 148).

Niebuhr's view of our political situation is, despite its defects, superior to the views of those who defend economic growth as the most important feature of our lives together. Gamwell's general emancipation involves much more than economic growth. The rough justice found in politically liberal societies is only a first approximation toward a common telos. Niebuhr is also correct to point out in an allusion to Homer's *Odyssey* that tyranny and anarchy are the Scylla and Charybdis through which the frail bark of justice must sail, contra the forces at work in society that aid and abet either tyranny or anarchy or both. Gamwell's commitment is to democracy within the reality of God, a commitment that evidences partial agreement with Niebuhrian realism (*DP*, 320–25).

Politics as a vocation is built on the belief that one cannot act without *some* presuppositions regarding the totality of things. Such action, to be effective, also presupposes mediation between "the foolish children of light" and "the cynical children of darkness," to use phrases from Niebuhr adopted by Gamwell. A quotation from Niebuhr's *Nature and the Destiny of Man* (1941–1943, xiii) that is a favorite of Gamwell holds that "man's [*sic*] capacity for justice makes democracy possible; but man's inclination to injustice makes democracy necessary." The aforementioned children of light include absolute pacifists, who fail to face the tragedy of human existence, according to Niebuhr and apparently according to Gamwell as well. Although world peace is an ideal or *concept* to be pursued, peace is not necessarily exemplified by a *conception* that involves a refusal under all circumstances to bear arms, given the fact that there are violent tyrants who too frequently appear in human history. Here Niebuhr and Gamwell are like Whitehead and Hartshorne (see Dombrowski 2017, ch. 4). Even if one rejects altogether Niebuhr's doctrine of original sin, there is ample historical evidence of the possibility of injustice and violence. Further, there is much to be said in favor of the view that an alternative to belief in original sin is the realization that human beings are pervasively characterized by fragmentariness, both temporally and spatially. Gamwell insightfully tries to refocus attention on "original freedom" in contrast to original sin, on a human being's ability to choose between authentic and duplicitous self-understanding. Or again, Gamwell directs us to an "original decision" to affirm our very basic relation to the good (*WTP*, 147–60; *MN*, 125; *DP*, 283; *EG*, 125).

Overall, Gamwell sees the problems in Niebuhr's political views as largely due to his classical theistic assumptions, even if Niebuhr did not spend a great deal of time dealing with the *concept* of God. Or better, it is the *implications* of classical theism that bring down Niebuhr. For example, because of a belief in divine omnipotence, there is a zero-sum game involved whenever human beings exert any effort at advancing self-interest. However, because human beings must, in certain circumstances, pursue self-interest (not to be confused with rightly denigrated selfishness), an overly negative view of human nature is the result: Niebuhr leans too far in the direction of the children of darkness. Further, because distinctions among past, present, and future are inapplicable to Niebuhr's classical view of deity, there is the familiar problem of how this eternal God outside of time and history could relate to the historical realities that are very much of concern to him. In some mysterious way (in the pejorative sense of "mystery") the eternal includes the temporal and historical. That is, Gamwell's view of politics as a vocation is very much a Niebuhrian one purged of classical theism. God is the eminently temporal whole that again and again unifies everything that has occurred in the world, in contrast to Niebuhr's classical theistic totality that eternally and unchangeably includes all change (but how?).

Gamwell even goes so far as to say that Niebuhr would have endorsed the neoclassical alternative if he had been presented with it. Gamwell ventures this opinion in light of Niebuhr's lifelong dissatisfaction with the concept of God with which he was familiar (*WTP*, 161–77).

CHAPTER EIGHT

Justice as Compound

It would be correct to conclude at this point that, despite the fact that transcendental arguments are at the core of Gamwell's philosophy, there are also limits to transcendental argumentation. But these limits are less restrictive in Gamwell than in almost all other contemporary thinkers. As a general rule, it can be stated with equanimity that transcendental arguments deal well with the most abstract issues in metaphysics (including the metaphysical aspects of political thought), but their applicability is attenuated as the issues become more and more concrete. For example, the aforementioned transcendental argument in favor of the maximal good or maximal creativity by and for the widest number of subjects does not tell us everything we need to know about the details of the moral/political life. We can know that the good to be realized cannot be forever postponed without self-contradiction, but the pace of our actions and the decisions regarding the minutiae of our actions are not the objects of transcendental argument. Our moral duty is to enhance greater capacity for experience that is intrinsically valuable. Much of the remaining work to be done in morality and politics requires habitual development of *virtue*, which helps to apply and to flesh out transcendental argumentation. A rough synonym for "virtue" frequently used by Gamwell is "emancipation," both in the sense of an original freedom possessed by human beings and an acquired freedom that comes when obstacles to flourishing are removed and when positive steps are taken that foster happiness (*DP*, 130–31).

The aim at the best possible future includes the idea that we make the most of our present selves as contributions to that future. As Aristotle argued, happiness requires not only virtue, but also a certain amount of good luck. Like Aristotle, Gamwell sees virtue as an *activity*, albeit an activity that is habituated over time and hence is cumulative. Like athletic success, Gamwell notes that the virtuous life requires extensive cultivation. In this regard we can notice the family resemblance between *ethos* (the Greek word for habit and hence for ethics) and *askesis* (the Greek word for athletic training, originally). It is sometimes suggested that a metaphysics of activity, including a morality based on activity, cannot make sense of responsibility for past actions if these were performed by a different subject from the one that exists in the present. But this fear is misguided, according to Gamwell. He thinks that persons in the present are *especially* accountable for their own past misdeeds both because they are their own—via causal prehension by which the past is included in the present but not vice versa—and because shirking one's responsibility in the present is a negative contribution to the future to be maximized. That is, to take special account of one's future requires that we take special responsibility for one's past in that (contra Hume) the past is included in the present. Further, special responsibility for one's past within the metaphysical context of time as both asymmetrical and cumulative is an integral part of the cultivation of virtue. There is a unique intimacy within the line of inheritance of actual occasions in a person's life that makes such cultivation possible. One's present self is, admittedly, *partially* different from a previous stage in one's life, but it is also somewhat the same due to prehensions (memories) of previous stages (*DP*, 132–39).

Another likely criticism, in addition to the claim that the process view of human identity cannot account for responsibility for past misdeeds, is the accusation that the very abstract view of teleological and metaphysical morality found in Gamwell can lead only to imperfect duties, not perfect ones, to use Kantian language. Perfect duties are those that one has to do (or not do) regarding actions of a specific kind, whatever the consequences, as in a duty not to break promises. Imperfect duties, by contrast, encourage actions that produce a general end, as in a duty to be beneficent. The charge is that the latter do not give us enough direction and can lead to a deleterious unpredictability. For example, the concern is that we could not depend on people keeping their promises if there were no perfect duties in that circumstances might dictate (or at least permit) breaking a promise if such would help to maximize the good. Gamwell admits that in themselves rules are helpful because similar cases tend to recur. The question is whether they need to be ironclad. His preferred view seems to be that moral rules offer genuine guidance, but the virtuous person sometimes judges it best to override them. Moral actors may abdicate their attachment to perfect duties by appeal to *in extremis* consequences (*DP*, 182–86).

It should not be concluded, however, that Gamwell's view is necessarily utilitarian, even if it is teleological. Tucked away in a footnote, Gamwell clarifies this important point (*EG*, 191). Utilitarianism is not the only plausible candidate for teleological morality. We will see momentarily that there is a difference between abstract formative principles and more concrete substantive principles, the two of them together constituting the compound character of justice. The formative principles that make up the comprehensive metaphysical purpose that Gamwell wishes to defend *might* be rendered more concrete by substantive utilitarian principles, but not necessarily. Utilitarian theory, which prescribes actions that maximize the *pleasure or utility* of all sentient beings, captures *some* of the things that should be maximized in a just society, but not all of them. This is why Gamwell is also indebted in different ways to Aristotle and Kant.

The rules of social practices can be seen as logically prior to specific cases in the sense that they provide a stage-setting for the individual cases. Gamwell takes an example regarding baseball from Rawls. One can swing a stick in the air three times in a row, but this does not constitute a strikeout outside of the rules of baseball. Likewise, one can post pictures of oneself in public places, but this does not constitute running for office outside of election laws. Gamwell's overall point regarding social practices, however, is that they require a supreme principle by which they are grounded. A comprehensive telos defines a principle in terms of which choices among more particular purposes can be made, including purposes in baseball or elections (*DP*, 186–91; Rawls 1999, 31).

Gamwell notes that the greatest commandment of the scriptures—to love God and to love your neighbor as yourself (Matthew 22:35–39)—expresses his principal philosophical conclusions. Human beings are called to understand themselves in relation to the maximal divine good and therefore to pursue the maximal good in the future as such. The two aspects of the great commandment imply each other in that to love God *is* to pursue the maximal good and vice versa. Another way to put the point is to say that the principles of justice depend on a comprehensive purpose that is the philosophical equivalent of the biblical great commandment. We have also seen that the comprehensive purpose needs democracy as a formative principle, otherwise the maximization of the good or of creativity cannot occur (*DP*, 179–81).

At this point I would like to turn to a crucial distinction in Gamwell regarding the concept of democracy as a formative principle. Justice has a compound character in Gamwell. It involves the distinction between abstract *formative* principles of a democratic constitution and more concrete *substantive* principles (often confusedly called *the* principles of justice) that ought to control what occurs throughout the democratic process. This distinction relies to a great extent on the thought of Habermas and Apel. An example of a formative principle is the aforementioned injunction to engage in communicative respect, which is a metaethical presupposition of discourse in a democratic society. Because it *is* formative, this principle is logically prior to substantive principles and norms at more concrete levels. The principle of communicative respect is a metanorm in the process of developing more material norms. The consequences are dire, Gamwell thinks, if this formative principle is not widely accepted: it is to be forever trapped in a Hobbesian state of nature. Of course, democratic discourse cannot be solely about the formative character of the discourse, given the concrete problems faced in any society, but such a formative principle is nonetheless a necessary condition for a just society. Any given moral claim in a democratic society includes, but is not exhausted by, its metaethical character. However, the assertion that justice specifies the divine good or that it specifies the metaethical character of the formative principles departs from most contemporary political philosophy, which as a result also denies the compound character of justice (*DP*, 181–82, 223–32).

A second example of a formative principle of justice, in addition to the principle of communicative respect, is the famous principle of religious freedom. By "religion" Gamwell means symbolic or figurative expressions about human life in relation to its ultimate context; or, in different terms, religion is the primary form of culture in which human beings ask explicitly and respond to the question of human authenticity as such. Therefore, any understanding of the comprehensive purpose is at least a possible religion. The principle of religious freedom will be discussed in more detail later in the book. Here I am only interested in how the principle of religious freedom helps explicate the compound character of justice. Formative philosophical conditions are those that characterize full and free political discourse and are strongly analogous to constitutional essentials in the legal realm, in contrast, say, to substantive principles and norms at a more concrete level that do not rise to the level of constitutional essentials. It is precisely because constitutional provisions have to be accepted by all participants that they can properly be called "formative." Although adherence to the constitution for moral reasons cannot be coerced, the state nonetheless has a right to teach commitment to discourse and commitment to religious freedom, especially due to the fact that more substantive norms are always subject to contestation (*DP*, 215–16, 233–34).

Of course, the exercise of any constitutional right, including the rights to free speech and freedom of religion, may be legally constrained when that exercise violates the equal rights of others. It is also clear that such constraint is subject to due process and equal protection of the law for all participants. Gamwell quite clearly defends the crucial liberal concept that the constitution should be explicitly neutral regarding all conceptions of human association so long as such conceptions themselves are consistent with the formative principle of communicative respect wherein contested claims are adjudicated through argumentation. This means that those who are unduly corrupted by the strategic assertion of their interests do not engage in genuine democratic discourse. Further, those who use financial advantage to have their point of view verge on the hegemonic also compromise genuine democratic discourse. It must be admitted that commitment to formative (or constitutional) principles often functions as a regulative ideal when it is realized that pursuit of the truth cannot be coerced. Because of this fact, and also due to the distinction between formative and substantive principles of justice, from the perspective of formative principles (or from a constitutional perspective) one can only anticipate or hope for just political discourse but not guarantee it (*DP*, 215–23).

The communicative right to participate in democratic politics is a specification of the transcendental obligation to maximize the good. As such it includes ad hoc discourse as well as the widest possible exchange of reasons compatible with morality, including the right to dissent. However, dissent brings with it the obligation to supply reasons for the dissent as part of the common aim at truth. We have seen that the right to free speech is religious when it deals with existence as such or with a comprehensive orientation to human life (*EG*, 156–57).

There is something amphibious about justice when it is considered that it both swims in the waters of the formative comprehensive order of reflection and walks on the substantive ground of practical reason. In due course I will examine in detail Gamwell's substantive principles of justice, but here I would like to treat once again the metaphysical definition of good as it relates to the compound character of justice. If Kant is correct that the good is to be defined solely in terms of a good will, such that anything that is pursued is neither moral nor immoral in itself, then nothing is needed in addition to adequate self-understanding. By contrast, Gamwell offers a metaphysical definition of the good, which functions as a formative principle. The idea that the good is nothing of importance in itself has been a popular one in the history of philosophy, as is evidenced by its presence in Hobbes and Hume and the early twentieth-century emotivists, to take just three examples. Gamwell and Kant are in a peculiar way alike in arguing against the emotivist view. The denial of all moral reasoning is self-refuting when it is realized that *every* theory or statement of practical reason, including those developed by Hobbes and Hume and the emotivists, implies a moral theory. The amoralist denial of moral reasoning cannot be solely a matter of description, as the amoralist supposes. This is because *with respect to choosing* some prescriptivity enters into the moral procedures found in Hobbes, Hume, and the emotivists themselves. One may deny universal theories of practical reason, say by claiming that the good is always and entirely relative to some historically specific situation, but this nonetheless implies that the good must still be defined *in this situation*. This is why moral relativism is also self-refuting in that it asserts the character of *all* practical reason and implies a comparison with respect to choosing. As before, relativism is, in spite of itself, a universal moral theory (*MN*, 123–25).

It counts in favor of the Kantian tradition, in general, including Habermas and Gewirth, to hold that *evaluative* understanding is bound by a universal principle in terms of which alternatives for purpose are compared. This is why even relativism or amoralism or emotivism offer a moral principle for *all* subjective decisions when they dip into prescriptivism in spite of themselves. However, a comparison with respect to choosing cannot, as Kantians typically think, be nonteleological. Moral reasoning certainly includes comparing specific alternative purposes. Sometimes we explicitly do this in light of a comprehensive or strictly metaphysical purpose. Even the conclusion that some things are without moral value is itself a moral conclusion that requires a moral comparison with things whose realization is good. The phrase "not good" is always a privation, as Augustine realized, in the sense that something that is good is not as good as it could or should be. This means that even if all things are good, they are clearly not equally good. That the comprehensive purpose is a moral *obligation* for moral agents is evidence of its transcendental character. Linking together metaphysics in the strict and restricted senses, Gamwell astutely notices that it is true not only that "something exists" is necessarily true, but also that "something that is good exists" is necessarily true. This is because the denial of each of these statements is semantically self-contradictory. The comprehensive purpose is transcendental to moral agents because such a purpose is presupposed even when we make judgments regarding something being immoral or amoral (*MN*, 126–30).

We have seen that the comprehensive moral law in Gamwell's philosophy can be stated as follows: act so as to maximize unity-in-diversity of experience in the future. This assumes that, even if reality is basically good, not all things are equally good. The final real things, actual occasions of experience, vary in the degree to which, and in the quality with which, they unify past influences in ways that yield present experiential value and contribute to future experiences of value. Maximizing creativity is *the* moral principle. We have also seen that a standard criticism of this view is that it offers only vague guidance subject to cancellation, only imperfect duties lacking the definiteness of deontological constraint. For example, the critic will say that Gamwell cannot give any principled defense of human rights, despite the fact that he is clearly a rights theorist. This is because rights are claimed to be morally controlling regardless of consequences.

But Gamwell does not think that this indictment can be sustained. The pursuit of maximal good rightly applied *can* make use of social practices defined by deontological norms, such as that promises should be kept and free speech should be protected. The pursuit of maximal creativity is a formative principle in need of further specification, as when it is suggested that maximal creativity requires democracy and that democracy requires communicative respect and freedom of religion, et cetera. Deontic norms can be part of this further specification, norms that can be eased under the pressure of *in extremis* conditions, as even many committed deontologists admit, as is well known. At times Gamwell puts the matter in even stronger terms: creativity cannot be maximized without deontological application. Or again, subjectivity as such implies a deontological principle. The comprehensive purpose and human rights actually mutually reinforce each other. Communicative rights as defended by Apel are especially noteworthy in Gamwell's own view. Failure to protect rights, including communicative rights, is to fail to obey the moral principles transcendental to subjects (*MN*, 134–39).

Gamwell's work is continuous with the emphasis on reason in the Enlightenment, despite several forces at work in the contemporary world that lead many to be suspicious of the Enlightenment. It is his belief that only if the comprehensive question is rational can an adequate defense of religious freedom be offered. The claim that human activities are entirely the products of efficient causation or determination by others, such that self-understandings are epiphenomenal, is contradictory. This is because our self-understandings imply distinctions among past, present, and future and imply as well the conclusions that we are conditioned by the past and we in turn condition the future. A present activity *is* the condition it imposes on the future. But complete determination by the past eliminates a distinction between past and present and *a fortiori* between past and future. To eliminate, again contra Robert Frost, the "alternatives" not chosen is to make the self that is determined the same self as the one that "determines" (*MRF*, 213–17).

Every particular activity is something new, as in (to use Gamwell's example) the moments in Abraham Lincoln's life from birth in Kentucky to the signing of the Emancipation Proclamation to his death in Ford's Theatre. These moments constitute a character that distinguished Lincoln from any other individual. But at any particular time his understandings were inter-subjective and depended on communication with others; they were implicit as well as explicit. Further, his understandings were always fragmentary and fallible. To the extent that these understandings were either veridical or mistaken, they implied a comprehensive understanding as a standard of comparison. The particular implies the general, even if the reverse does not follow. Human activity as such is, in part, constituted by responses to the comprehensive question. And the comprehensive question is as follows: What makes human activity as such authentic and devoid of duplicity? Although the question is ultimate, responses to it are always fallible, even if there are criteria that encourage us to think that we are not totally in the dark. One of these is coherence among our beliefs in many domains of discourse that on the surface appear to be quite different (*MRF*, 217–25).

It should be noted that "human activity as such is free (or unfree)" and "human activity as such is (or is not) bound by a moral norm" are comprehensive claims. Such claims, because of their formative character, require hermeneutical attention and/or analysis on our part. Gamwell is more than willing to offer such attention and analysis. Consider his claim that "human activity is free" is logically necessary *if* denial of this claim leads to contradiction. The denial *does* lead to contradiction on the basis of the foregoing analysis of past, present, and future: If the past completely determines the present, then there is no ultimate difference between the past and the present in that the present would be a reiteration of past reality. But the present clearly *is* different from the past on the evidence of widespread (inter)personal experience. "Human activity as such is free" is required by any act of *making* any claim at all. Further, "human activity as such is bound by a moral norm" is pragmatically necessary because denial of the claim indicates an appeal by way of negation to a moral norm. The metaphysical character of reality seems to be, as Gamwell and I see things, the best way to coherently account for the evidence (*MRF*, 226–31).

On the assumption that reality as such is temporal, the metaphysical claim that "something exists" leads us also to conclude that "something exists that is temporal." Further, if the ontological argument as defended earlier is sound, then we can also say that "something exists that is divine." Once again, coherence is the proper standard or criterion for assessment in metaphysics when there is a debate regarding proper responses to the comprehensive question. One reason why coherence *is* the proper criterion of the comprehensive order of reflection is that human authenticity involves a life of *integrity*. Whereas comprehensive purpose is a great gift, commitment to it is an inescapable demand. All of these formative principles lie behind the substantive principles at work at more concrete levels of engagement (*MRF*, 232–38).

It is the compound theory of justice, which means that the formative principles of a democratic constitution are different from the substantive principles that control political decisions by way of democratic discourse, that prevents the constitution from being used in a sort of legal overreach. The same applies to overreach at the level of the most concrete legislation. A "simple" theory of justice is one where the distinction between formative and substantive principles does not apply. But consider the following example, which supports the need for a distinction between formative and substantive principles: If two or more specific purposes are seen to be equally good, then a principle is implied in relation to which the purposes can be compared and determined to be equal. This implies an abstract, universal, formative principle of the good, as well as more concrete standards at the substantive level (*DP*, 250–52).

In process metaphysics, becomings are the final real things. Becomings at a certain level of sophistication are consciously aware of possibilities for future becoming. Gamwell is on firm ground when he insists that formative principles are presupposed by substantive principles, but he errs, I think, when he tries to express this point by saying that "totality is prior to meaning." The reason for my reticence here is that in a processual world totality is never reached, given the asymmetrical and cumulative character of the real. An actual occasion or sequence of actual occasions has the capacity to cumulate learning, sometimes in dramatic fashion. Further, it is common to have beings (i.e., personal sequences of actual occasions) be conscious of the fact that they have nonconscious relations to the past. Totality is never reached because every actual occasion arises as an effect from its past and ends as a cause facing its future, as Whitehead argued. In this regard, there is a tense relationship between Gamwell and two thinkers he otherwise views as friendly partners: Habermas and Apel. The processual view (heavily influenced by Peirce) is congenial to Habermas's and Apel's stance that a true understanding is one determined in relation to its possible effect on an ongoing ideal speech situation in which totality is never reached. At times Gamwell seems to agree with this view, but at other times he defines a true understanding as one with which the divine, on receiving it, agrees. Because the everlasting God in question is in flux, perhaps rapprochement between these two positions can be reached. It should also be noted that Gamwell's claim that totality is prior to meaning does make sense *if* what is intended is the idea, which has some backing in Gamwell's texts, that metaphysics in the strict sense is prior to metaphysics in the unrestricted (Gamwell says "broad") sense. That is, a subject is part of the whole and is related to the realm of possibility (*EG*, 52, 54, 93–98).

No doubt some thinkers with an antimetaphysics bias will wonder why we need formative principles at all if substantive principles—to be discussed in more detail later—are the ones that really matter at ground level. There are many ways to respond to this concern, one of which is that it is by no means a trivial point to learn that metaphysical statements are those that are pragmatically necessary in that whoever denies such statements lands in self-contradiction by implying what is denied. We have seen that the list of metaphysical statements includes "something exists," "something that is temporal exists," and "something that is divine exists." Because subjective activities necessarily affirm some understanding of the good, in which alternative ends are discriminated as better or worse, metaphysical statements can also be found in morality and more particularly in political philosophy. Opponents to this extension of metaphysics into morality/political philosophy often commit what was called in the first chapter "the partialist fallacy," which is basically Whitehead's fallacy of misplaced concreteness applied to moral theory. In the fallacy of misplaced concreteness, one equates a given thing or a given kind of thing with an abstract aspect or *part* of it. That is, this fallacy consists in mistaking a part of a thing for the whole thing. In the partialist fallacy, one analogously asserts that a comparison of alternative ends in some partial way is sufficient, when in reality there is a need for a standard of comparison that is comprehensive (*EG*, 99–103).

The partialist standards of comparison in moral/political philosophy are numerous: power, nationalism, egalitarianism, et cetera. By contrast,

Gamwell would have us develop substantive principles that are specifications, within given circumstances, of maximal goodness. Or again, the moral law is to maximize creativity in the future as such in terms of specifications of the Whiteheadian metaphysical principle that "the many become one, and are increased by one" (Whitehead 1978, 21). And creativity as the comprehensive good implies a belief in God, as I have argued. The very idea of a comprehensive good implies a universal individual who includes all actualities in a supreme memory. Without God, the maximal good to be pursued would be realized in a fragmentary way by isolated individuals or groups (*EG*, 104–7).

Gamwell distinguishes two sorts of freedom in moral agents. One can be called *self-determination* or free choice among alternatives made possible by one's past, whereas the other can be called *self-perfection*, where those with free choice habituate themselves to choose well, in contrast to merely having the ability to choose. In the former case one is emancipated from deterministic total control, and in the latter case one is emancipated from bad habits that get in the way of realization of the comprehensive good. A belief in comprehensive purpose is required in order to make sense of self-perfection. The comprehensive good is also necessary in order to understand self-determination in that such a standard is needed even to reach the conclusion that some purposes *are* better than others. The compound character of justice means that, in addition to decisions that are needed regarding the comprehensive good, there are also decisions to be made about what Gamwell calls "secondary" matters concerning morality and immorality in particular cases. Relying on Aristotle, Gamwell points out that one could perform a moral act in a secondary sense even if it does not express a decision for the comprehensive good, say if a promise were kept not to maximize the good, but rather to gain financially. Explicit decisions regarding specific alternatives are different from (often implicit) decisions to live authentically. Subjects are responsible for decisions regarding both original or formative principles as well as secondary or substantive principles (*EG*, 108–15).

On the process view, actual occasions are specifications of creativity, which is both descriptive and evaluative. The final real things just *are* instances of creativity, where the many become one and are influenced by one, but there are better or worse ways to unify influences from the past and to make a positive contribution to all who might benefit from such a contribution in the future. We have seen that "better" or "worse" are not unrelated to aesthetic categories in that felt unity among a greater number of parts is more aesthetically satisfying than unity among only a few elements. Such aesthetic experiences as they occur from moment to moment characterize not only creaturely life, but also divine life, on a Gamwellian basis (see Dombrowski 2004). Although the comprehensive purpose prescribes the pursuit of everyone's moral and aesthetic emancipation by trying to make the world more moral and beautiful, each *individual* decides what to make of the possibilities that are given to that individual. Justice can be seen as general emancipation: we should maximize the conditions of moral/aesthetic emancipation that are equally available to all. But substantive emancipation presupposes the right to formative equality in the discourse through which justice is pursued, hence the compound nature of justice (*EG*, 171–77).

A just political order is one where there is widespread commitment to argumentative practice, a practice that involves the distinction between constitutional or formative principles and substantive principles. The mark of a formative principle is that it is neutral with respect to substantive political disagreement *in the sense that* a formative principle prescribes nothing other than fair participation in a practice of political discourse regarding contested claims. Substantive principles deal with these contested claims and are often explicitly partisan. The principle of religious freedom is quintessentially formative. Analogously, Robert's Rules of Order are formative, in contrast to the substantive issues discussed in a meeting. The two sorts of principles are integrally connected, however, when it is realized that there is no point to Robert's Rules if there are no substantive issues discussed at meetings. But it is not the work of Robert's Rules or of the constitutional guarantee of religious freedom to dictate solutions to substantive problems or to determine which religion (or lack thereof) one will adopt (*PCV*, 46–47; *EG*, 149).

Of course, none of this is meant to imply that the formative principles cannot, at a higher level of abstraction, themselves be rationally debated. That is, we ought not be tempted by an alleged constitutional originalism or fixity of formative principles in that a political tradition identified with some abiding character is unavoidably entangled with efforts to clarify, interpret, and apply that character in circumstances that could not have been conceived by those who established the authority of the constitution in question. There is, for example, an enduring debate in United States politics between those for whom the union is the creation of previously sovereign states and those for whom the states were created along with the union. The former is known as the states' rights view and the latter as the national view. This debate erupted into violence at the time of the Civil War, with the states' rights view advocated by John C. Calhoun and the national view advanced by Abraham Lincoln (*WTP*, 204–5; *MN*, 194).

Gamwell argues that the states' rights view is defective because it implies subjectivism. It implies subjectivism because it holds, for example, that ratification of the US Constitution by nine or more states is *alone* the source of its authority. But the Constitution's authority also depends on something else, as Gamwell insightfully sees things. Gamwell does defend the principle of popular sovereignty, but what he means by "popular sovereignty" or "we the people" is not merely that a large number of people affirm X, but also that they affirm X for defensible moral reasons. This is precisely why Lincoln thought that the mere fact that the people of Kansas were opposed to the expansion of slavery into that territory was not grounds for rejoicing. If it were, then it might have been legitimate for the people of Nebraska to affirm such expansion. The "something else" that is required is the moral conviction articulated (albeit inadequately) in the US Declaration of Independence that all human persons deserve equal moral respect. In different terms, the states' rights view is perfectly compatible with moral relativism, but this view is, as Gamwell sees things, self-refuting, as we have seen. It implies, against itself, a comparison of *all* contexts (*MN*, 195–216). Gamwell's view of popular sovereignty is thus strongly analogous to Kant's view of autonomy in that the latter involves not merely thinking on one's own without external constraints but also thinking rationally.

The implied subjectivism in the states' rights view contradicts its own affirmation of popular sovereignty. For example, "either ratification of the Constitution does or does not make a claim to moral validity: if ratification does, it presupposes the prior presence and authorization of 'we the people' (the national view) as the final ruling power; if ratification makes no such claim, the states' rights view reduces to subjectivism" (*MN*, 217). On the national view that Gamwell defends, it is morality that underlies and permits popular sovereignty. In the last chapter of the present book, I will defend the method of reflective equilibrium and the modest moral foundations operative in this method. If moral relativism, subjectivism, and the states' rights view are all self-refuting, it is because they conflict with the transcendental nature of the moral law as it is articulated in terms of reflective equilibrium. If no political decision can be rationally defensible, such that relations among citizens are based on nothing more than strategic deliberation (as in the states' rights view), then the political community is a civil war waiting to happen. On this basis the best that we can hope for is a mere *modus vivendi*, to use the Rawlsian designation.

Gamwell, however, hopes for much more, especially that the promise of the *concepts* of justice, liberty, and equality found in the Declaration of Independence will be more than mere promissory notes and that we will find more particularized *conceptions* and institutional structures conducive to the asymptotic realization of these concepts. Further, it does not escape Gamwell's notice that, although the concept of God is not mentioned in the Constitution, it is in fact invoked explicitly in the Declaration of Independence, with the earlier document providing the moral background for the Constitution (*MN*, 218–19, 247).

It is understandable that there might be grey areas between formative and substantive principles. For example, some people might want an economic right to a living wage enshrined in the Constitution. In fact, some have such strong convictions on this matter that they might risk revolution if their convictions were not realized in practice. Gamwell joins the majority view among scholars of the US Constitution that, given the distinction between formal and material claims about justice (which to a significant extent maps the distinction between formative and substantive principles of justice), economic conditions fall on the material side of the divide. But even if the majority view is incorrect, revolution is difficult, but not impossible, to justify. The political instability and violence involved in revolution can be justified only if such a pursuit is the only way to bring about a more democratic Constitution (*MRF*, 176–77).

The communicative respect that is constitutive of formative principles of justice nonetheless presupposes that there are substantive norms of some sort. Only the compound character of justice—formative and substantive—can do the theoretical work necessary in the effort to bring about a just society. Because severe ignorance or poverty counts against the claim that a particular society is just, substantive matters are an essential part of the story. Gamwell puts the issue in the strongest possible terms as follows: "Formative justice *implies and is implied by* a substantive principle or set of principles" (*EG*, 168, also 164–71). The question of *which* substantive principles are implied will be addressed in due course.

CHAPTER NINE

Religious Freedom

There is no other political prescription that is more widely accepted as an expression of modern (in contrast to premodern) politics than the first amendment to the US Constitution: "Congress shall make no law respecting an establishment of religion, or prohibiting the free exercise thereof." In this chapter I will examine Gamwell's nuanced views on religious freedom, largely saving for the following chapter a critique of those views. Although transcendental argument does not make its presence felt here to the same degree felt elsewhere in Gamwell's thought, it is by no means entirely absent in debates regarding religious freedom. A persistent division is evident between contemporary "separationists" (who emphasize the first clause in the first amendment, the [dis]establishment clause) and the "religionists" (who emphasize the second clause, the free exercise clause). For most religionists, religious conviction is essential to civic virtue. Whereas religionists often claim that separationists not only disestablish religion but in addition deny its free exercise, separationists often claim that religionists not only affirm free exercise but in addition establish religious conviction. Gamwell does not directly enter into the debate, but rather, as is typical, wants to call attention to more general or philosophical (indeed metaphysical) aspects of the debate. In fact, he thinks that the contemporary impasse regarding the debate is largely due to philosophical confusion (*MRF*, 3–4).

It is widely assumed that religious beliefs cannot be the subject of public debate or rational assessment, either because they are primal and hence are antecedent to rational discourse or are above and beyond reason. That is, the problem of religious freedom involves not only issues in political philosophy but also in philosophy of religion. The theory of religion as nonrational (or subrational or suprarational) has as many defenders inside of religion as in agnostic or atheist circles. Although it is widely believed that, given pervasive religious pluralism in the modern world, toleration is a good thing, there are nonetheless questions regarding what toleration exactly means and what the reasonable grounds are to support the concept of toleration. For example, one meaning of "toleration" is compatible with an established religion so long as nonestablished religions are permitted. Gamwell assumes, rightly, that this meaning of the term is not a coherent solution to the modern problem of religious freedom in a pervasively pluralistic society. Religious freedom is not so much an answer to a question as it is a question to be pursued. Gamwell's response to this question is to say that religious freedom is ultimately constituted by free and full discourse in a democracy about religious topics. Democratic civility is not only consistent with religious adherence; it actually implies religious freedom (*MRF*, 5–11).

If any understanding of comprehensive purpose is a possible religion, then freedom of religion involves both a private and a public liberty. Regarding the former, participants in discourse have a right to freedom of conscience. And regarding the latter, one can say that democratic discourse is not only *free* but also *full* in the sense that no moral claim is immune from public dissent and argumentative assessment. Nonetheless, those who hold on religious grounds that comprehensive purpose can be known only through special revelation (i.e., without the use of reason or with diminished use of reason) are legitimate participants in public discourse. That is, rational assessment of religious belief is extended even to those who think that religion is "beyond reason" because they are still offering a response to a rational question regarding comprehensive purpose (*DP*, 234–40).

Gamwell argues against the separation of justice from the good (or comprehensive purpose). He thinks that the widespread belief in such a separation derives from a confusion between logical contradictories and contraries:

> If religious establishment and the separation of justice from the good were contradictories, then one could not consistently deny one without affirming the other. But these two alternatives are logical contraries, so that one can consistently deny both. The disestablishment of all religions does not imply that justice is independent of any one because there is another alternative. This third option is the compound character of justice, which means that formative principles of a democratic constitution are

differentiated from the substantive principle or principles that, through the democratic discourse, ought to control the decisions of the political association. On the conception of justice as compound, the constitution may not explicitly affirm or deny any [substantive] theory of justice because the political association is properly constituted as a full and free discourse among all such theories. As a political principle, religious freedom stipulates nothing more or less than this political discourse, so that other constitutional provisions properly legislate only formative conditions of it. (*DP*, 249–50)

Religions are politically important because each one includes, or at least implies, a conviction about the ultimate terms of political assessment as well as the terms of one's comprehensive orientation in life. In fact, one may designate religious freedom as *the* inclusive constitutional right of each citizen. The fact that political liberalism started as a theoretical solution to the wars of religion in the early modern period is not accidental. What is noteworthy about Gamwell's approach to religious freedom is the degree to which he is committed to argumentative redemption for religious beliefs with the Constitution providing institutional support for the formative principle of communicative respect. Making a political claim, including a political claim regarding religion, is like making a promise. It is a pledge that one's claim can be rationally assessed. In a way, the fact that some thinkers find Gamwell's commitment to rational assessment surprising is itself surprising in that the alternative to his view flirts with authoritarianism:

The supposed need for an authoritarian appeal can itself be defended only by an authoritarian appeal. As a consequence, disagreement about whether ultimate principles answer a rational question has the following form: Those for whom the question is not rational cannot *argue* for their denial and thus can only assert it. But those for whom the question is rational can argue for their affirmation, namely, by arguing for the truth of some fundamental conviction and, thereby, arguing against authoritarians. (*EG*, 162)

Religious beliefs are differing attempts to represent explicitly what is implicit in everyone: a perspective on ultimate reality, the practical or substantive terms of which can be the objects of political assessment (*EG*, 159–63).

Religion as well as politics are forms or patterns of culture, but Gamwell sees religion as the primary form of culture because it deals explicitly with the comprehensive question or questions regarding ultimacy. Because human beings have the capacity for self-understanding, they are distinctively constituted to deal with these questions; hence there is no option to ignore altogether religion if one is to remain authentic. Because the particular implies the general, any particular self-understanding implies a response to the most general questions. No doubt we may be mistaken in what we say about comprehensive purpose, given human fallibility, but we can nonetheless see that a *comprehensive* purpose is the common presupposition of more particular purposes. Any particular moral claim is a specification of the comprehensive purpose to certain circumstances (*MRF*, 13–20).

Although there is a moral as well as metaphysical aspect of religion, it is the moral aspect that is inclusive. That is, religion is something more than its metaphysical claim, a claim that is very abstract. The character of human authenticity as such (i.e., the comprehensive moral purpose) presupposes the relation to the character of reality as such, but not vice versa. Further, if religion is defined in terms of explicit treatment of the comprehensive question, then all of the great traditions that arose in what Karl Jaspers called the axial age are religions: the Abrahamic faiths, but also Hinduism, Buddhism, Confucianism, et cetera; thus religions do not have to include a defense of a "transcendent reality." The distinguishing feature of religious *activity* is to cultivate the virtuous lives of religious adherents in the pursuit of comprehensive self-understanding. Critical analysis of these traditions is a secondary form of reflection built on the primary mode of internecine interrogation within these different traditions. Religious freedom, for example, requires this sort of "secondary" self-critical activity (*MRF*, 20–29; *WTP*, 202).

Gamwell is to be thanked for pointing out that a broad understanding of religion is required in order to respond adequately to the modern political problematic characterized by pervasive pluralism: "Religion is the primary form of culture in terms of which the comprehensive question is explicitly asked and answered and, further, so answered that human authenticity is derived from the character of reality as such" (*MRF*, 30). Every response to the comprehensive question has a metaphysical aspect in addition to all of the other functions religions perform: aesthetic, sociological, et cetera. If religion is the specific form of association that asks and responds to the comprehensive question, politics is the specific form of association that asks and responds to the question of the state. Religious freedom, it should be noted, is a religious as well as political question. The former attends to human activity as such and the latter attends to human activity vis-à-vis a state (*MRF*, 30–37).

Religious freedom is a political expression of the comprehensive question. But a modern democratic political community must be constituted by the question itself or by responses to this question, rather than in terms of *the* answer to it, as would be the case if there were an established religion. (One wishes that Gamwell referred to "responses" to the comprehensive question rather than "answers," the latter term obscuring his best points on the topic of religious freedom.) Nor would it be just to have an established religion that nonetheless permitted or tolerated other religions, as in Great Britain, in that the established religion would have an officially recognized answer to the comprehensive question that would at least implicitly denigrate other religions. There are similar problems with a system of multiple establishments, as existed in colonial America. The fact that an established religion receives "merely verbal" support from citizens is a non sequitur in that, if a political community is constituted by the comprehensive question itself, then trivializing this ultimate question is almost as bothersome as offering an *answer* (rather than response) to it. It is high time, Gamwell seems to say, for democratic societies *and religions* to grow up and face the comprehensive question in terms of rational assessment, rather than in terms of dogmatic assertion or trivializing neglect (*MRF*, 38–41).

I would now like to initiate a comparison of Gamwell's view of religious freedom with three influential contrasting views: the *privatist* view of Rawls, the *partisan* view of John Courtney Murray, and the *pluralist* view of Kent Greenawalt. I will deal with the privatist view in this and the following chapter, and I will get to the partisan and pluralist views later in the present chapter.

First, the privatist view is one wherein (allegedly) none of the religious convictions of citizens are important in politics. This view is widely shared in liberal democracies, as are the reasons in its defense. For example, it is often held that civil peace requires the privatization of religion; hence defenders of this view can be called either "separationists" (such that there is a strict separation of church and state) or "privatists." Apel sees this view as part of a "complementarity system" wherein the private or "subrational" religious views of citizens are combined (but not mixed) with the public views expressed in political thought. Others see the privatist view as an understandable consequence of the "rationalization" of society detailed by Max Weber. Gamwell thinks that the complementarity system is often unfortunately connected to the thesis that the comprehensive question is not a rational one. But even in a more subtle version of the privatist stance, where it is not assumed that religion is sub- or suprarational, some thinkers simply refuse to allow religious convictions to enter the public square (*MRF*, 47–49).

The issue is a big one when it is realized that religious freedom is *the* conception that Rawls's famous work *Political Liberalism* is meant to defend. Whereas Rawls's even more famous early work *A Theory of Justice* was actually built on what Rawls later called a comprehensive doctrine, the later Rawls realized, according to Gamwell, that it was unrealistic to expect all citizens who are free and reasonable/rational to agree on the same comprehensive doctrine. In *Political Liberalism* Rawls distinguishes between a *comprehensive doctrine* and a *political conception of justice*. Rawls also distinguishes between fully comprehensive and partially comprehensive doctrines, with the former exhibiting a family resemblance to Gamwell's comprehensive purpose in that a fully comprehensive doctrine in Rawls concerns all of the virtues and values that deal with the largest questions in life. But the later Rawls, on Gamwell's interpretation, simply refuses the comprehensive order of reflection, both full and partial. A political conception for the later Rawls is not derived from *any* comprehensive doctrine; hence it is in Rawls's terminology "freestanding."

In this regard, Rawls further distinguishes between *comprehensive* liberalisms that have a conception of justice that receives foundational (if not metaphysical) backing (as in the liberalisms of Kant, Mill, and the Rawls of *A Theory of Justice*) and *political* liberalism, where the concept of justice is freestanding (as in the Rawls of *Political Liberalism*). Even without foundations, however, Rawls's view in *Political Liberalism* is not totally adrift in that abstract reasoning and concrete judgments or intuitions can settle into a sort of *reflective equilibrium*, to use Rawls's designation, as we will see in the final chapter. For example, the rejection of slavery is a "settled" judgment even without strong foundations in the sense that contemporary defenses of slavery are in disequilibrium with all of the other beliefs with which reasonable people agree (*MRF*, 50–53).

Rawls identifies two moral powers: the capacity to be *reasonable* and the capacity to be *rational*. The former consists in the capacity for a sense of justice and a willingness to abide by fair terms of agreement, whereas rationality consists in the ability to follow and assess arguments and to deliberate carefully about the good life. A helpful motto is that it takes a reasonable person to enter the Rawlsian original position and a rational person to deliberate there. Or again, reasonableness concerns *the just or the right*, whereas rationality concerns *the good*. The hypothetical device of the *original position* seeks to identify a reasonable point of view the search for which is facilitated by the well-known *veil of ignorance* where the particular features of one's identity are hidden from one so as to help eliminate bias and the temptation to tailor the principles of justice to one's own benefit. Another way to put the Rawlsian view is to say that the two moral powers are a sense of justice and a sense of the good. All citizens require the same primary goods—both material goods like food and shelter and formal goods like freedom of speech and religion—and hence a just society is one that provides these for all citizens (*MRF*, 54–55).

One remarkable feature of Rawls's thought is that he claims that *all* reasonable-rational agents of construction in the original position would, when deliberating about justice behind a veil of ignorance, reach the same conclusions regarding the abstract contours of a just society, which would be characterized by two (actually three in that the second principle of justice can be divided in half) major principles, as can be expressed in the following popular terms: the *equality principle* ensures that all basic goods—again, both material and formal—should be distributed equally; the *opportunity principle* requires that when distributing a larger slice of the pie to some once basic goods are distributed to all the opportunity for the unequal share be open to all; and the *difference principle* requires that when distributing a larger slice of the pie for some once basic goods are distributed to all the larger share for some be to everyone's advantage, especially the least advantaged. Further, one sees here an analogy between the equality principle in Rawls and the egalitarian character of Gamwell's formative rights in contrast to the partially inegalitarian character of the Rawlsian opportunity and difference principles, which Gamwell sees as more substantive (*DP* 304–11).

In the determination of these principles of justice, the right (or just) is prior to the good, or put differently, the reasonable is prior to the rational. These principles are determined (problematically so, according to Gamwell) independently of any concept of *the* good, except for the basic goods mentioned above. The problem, as Gamwell sees things, is that Rawls's view is vulnerable to the transcendental argument that, in order to develop a political concept of justice without presupposing a particular metaphysical doctrine, one is nonetheless offering support to a metaphysical thesis: *no* metaphysical doctrine is required for this purpose. Or again, the distinction between the reasonable and the rationally true *must itself* be true. Gamwell once again refers us to a type of philosophizing that asks about the a priori or necessary conditions of human activity (*MRF*, 56–59).

Gamwell admits that Rawls's political liberalism must be worked out in two stages. In the first stage, principles of justice are determined as a freestanding view, and in the second stage it is determined how these principles can preserve stability in a society where citizens affirm many different comprehensive doctrines, sometimes uncompromisingly so. Although the problem of stability was not solved in *A Theory of Justice* (due to the unlikelihood of everyone adhering to the same comprehensive doctrine), in *Political Liberalism* stability is achieved through *overlapping consensus* among reasonable-rational citizens, whatever their comprehensive doctrines, who nonetheless agree on the aforementioned three principles of justice. That is, there is consensus among adherents to reasonable comprehensive doctrines on the concept of justice, if not on the concept of the good life. Of course, Rawls admits that some comprehensive doctrines are unreasonable or irrational, as when religious fanatics in the early modern period were willing to persecute members of rival comprehensive doctrines. The goal is to allow citizens to pursue their conceptions of the good so long as they are not unreasonable (i.e., so long as they do not violate what would be agreed to in the original position behind a veil of ignorance) (*MRF*, 60–64).

We will see that Rawls's view might not be as privatist as Gamwell alleges. At present, however, I would like to highlight Gamwell's concern that Rawls's alleged overlapping consensus might actually be something much weaker in terms of a *modus vivendi* or a mere convergence of interests or temporary truce that could break apart at any time. A true overlapping consensus, he thinks, requires an agreement regarding moral principle, rather than a happenstance balance of relative forces. An overlapping consensus is more stable than a *modus vivendi* because as long as the political conception is affirmed on *moral* grounds (rather than, say, on grounds of self-interest) each party will continue to support it. Gamwell thinks that this implies that a concept of justice must be part of some comprehensive doctrine or other (*MRF*, 65–70).

Actually, Gamwell's critique goes much deeper. He alleges that no religious adherent would ever accept Rawls's privatist account. As we will see, I am a religious adherent who *does* accept Rawls's account, but I am not convinced that it is as privatist as Gamwell suggests. But I am not suggesting that Gamwell has not read Rawls carefully. He has. For example, he notes that for Rawls the concept of justice is a module that can be (must be!) inserted into a wider view, indeed into a comprehensive doctrine. However, Gamwell wants more. He wants a view wherein it is *only* on the basis of a comprehensive view that a concept of justice can be adequately defended.

I will try in the following chapter to reach rapprochement with Gamwell on this significant point. On Gamwell's interpretation, Rawls's view is nonfoundational *simpliciter*, whereas on my interpretation Rawls's view can be classified as one having modest foundations, as we will see. Although Rawls is comfortable with the distinctions between a concept of justice and a comprehensive doctrine, on the one hand, and between reasonableness and rationality, on the other, Gamwell thinks that there has to be a backing *for these distinctions themselves.* Such a backing involves an argument that necessarily, he thinks, relies on a comprehensive view (*MRF*, 70–75).

Liberal theorists are virtually united in tracing the problem to be solved back to the early modern period, when it became clear that religious diversity had to be tolerated if the twin dangers of anarchy and tyranny were to be avoided. That is, liberal political theory is a conceptual response to the challenge posed by religious diversity. In fact, political liberals in general tend to see their views as the only ones where religious plurality can be civilized. Gamwell is deeply indebted to several thinkers in this tradition, but he does not think that, in order to benefit from the great successes of liberal theorists, one needs to separate justice from the comprehensive good. This is because he thinks that the formative principle of democracy itself implies a comprehensive purpose (*DP*, 238–40).

Gamwell sees Rawls as offering the most sophisticated version of separatist or privatist theory, especially in *Political Liberalism.* This is because Rawls is at least aware of the problem that theory of justice cannot survive for long if it is not embedded in *some* comprehensive purpose, just as, say, a fish cannot live for long without water in which to swim (my image, not Gamwell's). Holding that justice is separate from a comprehensive good *itself* implies that the concept of justice is comprehensive. The "distinction" between justice and the good in Rawls amounts to a "separation" between the two. Another terminological device favored by Gamwell is that "freestanding" refers to standing apart from any universal moral good. He also notices, but does not emphasize, that Rawls's justification for his view is *pro tanto*. In due course I will argue that one pays a heavy price for this lack of emphasis on *pro tanto* justification. But Gamwell is buoyed by the admission in Rawls that his theory of justice exemplifies but does not define political liberalism. That is, there is a family of liberal doctrines and there is an internecine debate, entered by Gamwell, regarding which member of the family is best. He is not buoyed, however, by Rawls's concession in "the proviso" that some parts of some religious comprehensive doctrines can be admitted into the public square. I will argue that, like the concept of *pro tanto* justification, there is more in Rawls that should be to Gamwell's liking than Gamwell is willing to admit (*DP*, 266–71).

Some scholars might fear that Gamwell's opposition to the freestanding character of justice in Rawls's view might lead to religious establishment on Gamwell's part. But Gamwell insists in a crucial passage (*DP*, 272) that this is not the case. The reason why Gamwell's view does not lead to religious establishment is based on the aforementioned compound character of justice. The comprehensive purpose on which the concept of justice is based is strictly formative. It can lead to any number of substantive principles as these are found in different religious and political proposals. Only *some* universal principles can be redeemed in democratic discourse, not the panoply of contested political assertions. The theses that democracy implies a comprehensive purpose and that justice has a compound character go together hand in glove. Of course, there is still a distance between Gamwell's view and that of Rawlsian liberals. This is in evidence when Gamwell attributes to the Rawlsians the stance that there is *no* universalist concept of justice, a claim that, true to form, Gamwell says contains a statement regarding what is universally the case: that *all* concepts of justice are historically specific. If one says that *all* principles of justice are historically specific, then one has asserted a universal principle of justice in spite of oneself (*DP*, 272–74).

The indictment against Gamwell's view is likely to be that it is inconsistent with democratic neutrality on the part of the government and might even lead to religious establishment. We have seen that Gamwell's response to this criticism is to champion the compound character of justice. An abstract commitment to discourse concerning the ultimate terms of political assessment (analogous, as we have seen, to Robert's Rules of Order for meetings at a local level) is different from the realm of contested political claims. A general commitment to assess contested claims by argument is hardly a move in the direction of religious establishment. Nor is treating all others as potential participants in moral discourse a problem (*EG*, 147–53; *MN*, 241; *WTP*, 3). The goal of Gamwell's response is to challenge the at least implicit denial that religious beliefs or religious associations are important for politics. Indeed, the privatization of such beliefs is now taken for granted, rather than being the conclusion to cogent argumentation, he thinks. This is odd when it is considered that the very soundness of moral claims presupposes the existence of God (*DG*, xi–xii).

Second, whereas, on Gamwell's interpretation, Rawls thinks that *no* religious convictions are important in politics (hence the label *privatist view*), there is also the *partisan view* of Murray, where the political process *depends* on some religious views. State neutrality, on this view, does not extend to the distinction between theistic religion and secularism. The former is preferred because, as the founders of the United States believed, theistic religion is necessary for civic virtue. Theistic religion is here seen as providing the motivation for pursuit of the common good. It is also seen by Murray and other "religionists" as required in order to answer the important question: Why be moral? (*MRF*, 77–81).

A somewhat less partisan, and perhaps more appealing, way of expressing Murray's defense of the role of the Judeo-Christian tradition in politics is to say that a pluralist civil order is possible only if diversity shares a commitment to political civility, which is a rational, deliberative quality (from the Latin *deliberare*, a scale metaphor requiring a weighing of reasons in the determination of which of two competing views is better). Whatever resemblance this view has to Rawls's stance is mitigated, however, by Murray's insistence on the traditional distinction between natural law and eternal law, the latter of which is not answerable to rational analysis. This also puts Murray at odds with Gamwell, who does not agree with Murray's insistence that political reason has no authority with respect to ultimate questions (*MRF*, 81–82).

More precisely, the natural law, which is rational, is nonetheless included in the eternal law, on Murray's Thomistic stance. As a result, the comprehensive order of reflection includes rationality, but it is not exhausted by rationality. This is a stance that is not as friendly to secularism as the Rawlsian stance, which is simultaneously post-religious *and* post-secular. That is, the Rawlsian view is opposed to both confessional states, on the one hand, and to officially secular states, on the other. The latter includes both the frightening implications of communist states and the soft authoritarian secularism found in the *laicite* doctrine in France. Both Rawls and Gamwell can find common ground with Murray in his fear that in the contemporary world reasoned argument would be replaced with successive soliloquies. But even if there were a robust culture of rational discourse among citizens, Murray would still be open to the possibility of an established religion, indeed to the desirability of an established religion, *if* we were not in a condition of pervasive pluralism. The policies of no establishment and freedom of religion, as defended by Murray, are meant to foster public peace and to avoid violent societal discord. This is related to Murray's stance that indifference to theistic religion (in relation to the secular) threatens public civility (*MRF*, 83–86).

Gamwell notices how odd it is to endorse religious freedom, as Murray does, while simultaneously affirming theistic religion as a constitutional essential. He is also bothered by Murray's idea that there can be no strictly rational response to the question "Why be moral?" What is most troubling about the partisan view, however, as Gamwell sees things, is that it, like the privatist view, denies that the comprehensive question can be responded to adequately by rational means. In Murray's partisan view, this involves supporting comprehensive convictions by appeal to supernatural grounds. Or more precisely, there is conflicting evidence from Murray in that at times he emphasizes, along with the natural law tradition, that reason is sufficient to articulate and defend the common good, but at other times he emphasizes the necessity to bring in superrational support. In this regard it should be noted, however, that the principle justifying religious freedom is not a particular theistic conviction, but the natural law (rational) principle regarding the need for civic peace and the avoidance of violence. In the final analysis, Gamwell detects a contradiction in Murray between the content of the common good, which is rational, and the motive to pursue it, which depends on superrational conviction. It is this latter element that problematically leads Murray to endorse (at least in theory if not in practice) an established religion. That is, Murray's affirmation of God's sovereignty over all nations is at odds with his affirmation of human freedom (*MRF*, 87–95, 172; *DP*, 237).

Third, in addition to the privatist (separationist) and partisan (religionist) views of religious freedom, Gamwell also distinguishes his stance from the *pluralist* view, as exemplified by Greenawalt. Whereas the religionist thinks that the separationist never really acknowledges the existence of *religious* freedom, the separationist thinks that the religionist never really acknowledges the existence of religious *freedom*. The pluralist tries to overcome this impasse. Unfortunately, according to Gamwell, this third alternative also fails to acknowledge the possibility of rational religion. Although Greenawalt tries to refute the claim that liberal citizens should exclude their theistic convictions from deliberations that lead to political choices, he does not agree with Murray's claim that citizens should be adherents to some theistic religion. That is, Greenawalt takes "religion" broadly to refer to both theistic and secular responses to the comprehensive question. But both sorts of response are outside the realm of publicly accessible reasons. Greenawalt's key idea is that when rational theories regarding justice cannot resolve critical questions of fact or disputes regarding political issues, people can appropriately rely on religious (or secular) convictions so as to respond to these questions (*MRF*, 97–103).

But reliance on religious convictions is warranted *only* when publicly accessible reasons are inconclusive, according to Greenawalt. Thus, he does not completely exclude the political relevance of religion. He thinks that there are many public issues where reasons are inconclusive; hence on these issues (as in the abortion debate and the debate regarding nonhuman animal rights) nonpublic grounds for decision are fitting. By mediating between the privatist and partisan views, Greenawalt thinks he has a firm basis for both *religious* freedom (in his qualified defense of religious convictions) and religious *freedom* (*MRF*, 104–7).

Gamwell cannot find good reasons in Greenawalt why reliance on religious convictions should be limited to situations where reasoning is inconclusive. Although Greenawalt admits that religion *may* be nonrational, Gamwell wonders whether Greenawalt is really committed to its being nonrational necessarily. Gamwell asks the following: "If our polity provides any space for reliance on overriding convictions that cannot be publicly assessed, why should its religious citizens maintain reliance on publicly assessable reasons when the two conflict? The guest for whom Greenawalt prepares a room in the mansion of liberal democracy seems willing to move in only if she or he can rule the house" (*MRF*, 111). In this regard, Gamwell sees affinity between Greenawalt and Rawls. What justifies the liberal commitment to the idea that religious convictions *ever* have a public importance? Gamwell sees a contradiction in Greenawalt that, because of his similarity to Rawls, affects the latter thinker as well: "Either (1) religious convictions are important to politics even if in principle they cannot be rationally assessed, in which case there is no reason why religious citizens should affirm an overriding commitment to publicly accessible or secular reasons, or (2) citizens as such should affirm some commitment to reason, in which case there are no grounds on which this commitment could be limited" (*MRF*, 113). This dilemma can be restated with respect to the very meaning of "religious freedom": "This term is either (1) a legitimation of a plurality of religions, as it must be, in which case there are no grounds on which to believe that the political community can be unified, or (2) a political principle, as it must also be, in which case there are no grounds on which to admit a nonrational basis for decision" (*MRF*, 113). The contradictions that Gamwell sees in Greenawalt (and Rawls) are parts of his familiar use of transcendental argumentation in that the claim that nonrational convictions can be legitimate in politics is itself a *comprehensive* nonrational claim (*MRF*, 108–15). In the following chapter I will criticize Gamwell's view of religious freedom primarily from a Rawlsian point of view.

Gamwell finds an unwitting ally in the thought of Ronald Dworkin in the effort to make political thought responsible to universal moral principles. This is somewhat ironic in that Dworkin defends religion without God.

(Dworkin does not so much argue against theistic metaphysics as he assumes that Hume and Kant have refuted it once and for all. Further, he assumes that any religious ethics will get impaled on the horns of the Euthyphro dilemma.) For Dworkin, the principle of religious freedom should be expanded to include a general right to ethical freedom. What makes Dworkin's view appealing to Gamwell is that it offers, once again unwittingly, the necessary character of moral truth. Also appealing in Dworkin's thought is a distinction between morality (standards regarding how we ought to treat each other) and ethics (how we ourselves ought to live). Here we have a vague reminder of Gamwell's distinction between formative and substantive principles. The aforementioned necessary character of moral truth is built on the idea that every assertion about how one decides among available alternatives is itself a putative moral principle in that all decisions one makes should be consistent with it. Further, moral thinking is inescapable because the reality of moral truth is a transcendental feature of decision-making. Here "transcendental" refers to a necessary feature of subjectivity as such; every denial of a transcendental feature is pragmatically self-refuting in that every act of denial implies what is denied (*MN*, 141–52, 236).

I say that Dworkin is an unwitting ally of Gamwell because Dworkin defends the claim that all moral beliefs are held contingently and are parts of something like reflective equilibrium, which will be discussed in the final chapter of the present book. Although on the surface Dworkin holds that no interpretive thinking requires a transcendental principle, the presence of moral truth as a necessary feature of subjectivity as such becomes apparent when we think about its denial. Subjective decisions regarding moral matters seek reflective equilibrium by pursuing, at least implicitly, and in very general terms, what practical thought *ought to be*. A denial of a moral truth *itself* is an example of such. The exercise of freedom involves at least implicitly a decision in favor of some supreme principle in terms of which specific alternatives are evaluated (*MN*, 153–57, 174).

Another difference between Gamwell and Dworkin is that the former insists on a moral teleology involving a telos defined by reality as such, a view that was the norm in ancient and medieval thought. By contrast, Dworkin neither asserts nor denies the (or a) good life for which all persons ought to strive. But he does hold that morality defines the lanes, as it were, that separate swimmers; morality is prior to ethics. That is, Dworkin tells us what we cannot do but has comparatively little to say about the comprehensive good. One wonders, however, how this view can hold. Is it not the case that to falsify with assurance presupposes *some* understanding of the stable background of truth against which the claim that something is false must be seen? Gamwell is forthright in claiming that religious discourse (which includes discourse about the comprehensive good) is a contribution to the political process. In sharper terms, (Dworkin-like) nonteleology as a theory about the ultimate terms of evaluation cannot be rationally defended because, by defining moral principles as constraints, one has *already* evaluated such principles morally, an account that is self-refuting. Nonteleological principles imply what they deny. The way of reason implies moral teleology such that if religious (and Dworkin's ethical) freedom makes sense, then a telos is implied as defined by the ultimate nature of things (*MN*, 158–67).

CHAPTER TEN

A Rawlsian Response

John Rawls is widely acknowledged to be the most influential political philosopher of the twentieth century. But the implications of his views for both religious belief and religious believers are hotly contested. Some think that he is largely on the right track, indeed that he solves many of the traditional (and bloody) problems regarding the relationship between politics and religion (see, e.g., Freeman 2007a, 2007b; Pogge 2007). Others are critical of his approach (see, e.g., Weithman 2002; Wolterstorff 2008; Eberle 2002). Perhaps the most insightful of these critics of Rawls, who argues from the perspective of a metaphysical view or a comprehensive religious doctrine, is Gamwell. It will be the purpose of the present chapter to both order Gamwell's criticisms of Rawls, which are spread across several books that span several decades, and to offer a Rawlsian response to Gamwell's criticisms.

Some terminological issues should be treated at the outset. By "comprehensive doctrine" Rawls means an overall view of what is valuable in life and that covers all recognized values and virtues in a rather precisely articulated system. One reason he uses this label rather than "religion" is to make it clear that, in addition to religious comprehensive doctrines, there are also nonreligious, or at least nontheistic, comprehensive doctrines affirmed by many reasonable citizens in contemporary democratic societies.

Rawls's "comprehensive doctrine" has at least a family resemblance to Gamwell's "comprehensive question" or the "comprehensive order of reflection," where human beings question and reflect on what the meaning to human life is in the context of the wider cosmos. Rawls's "comprehensive doctrine" is also similar to what Gamwell calls a "metaphysical view," but this latter designation also has more precise meanings in Gamwell, as we have seen. To be specific, metaphysics in the strict sense is the critical study of what must be the case regarding *everything* that exists. Gamwell's metaphysics in the restricted (he calls it "broad") sense is also transcendental in the sense that it studies what is the case in every *experience* of the real.

Thus, it makes sense from a Rawlsian point of view to say that Gamwell's metaphysics is but one among many comprehensive doctrines in a contemporary liberal democracy. Gamwell does not accept this characterization of his position, but not because of any religious intolerance or claim to religious exceptionalism on his part. This is why his thought is so very interesting and poses a challenge to Rawlsian theory.

That is, Gamwell defends a view of metaphysics that purports to stand above the conflicting comprehensive doctrines in contemporary democratic societies; hence he implies an exemption from the restrictions Rawls places on comprehensive doctrines. In effect, there are two different senses of "metaphysics" that have to be distinguished in addition to the aforementioned distinction between metaphysics in the strict sense and metaphysics in the restricted sense. Metaphysics-1 refers to any general worldview that orders values and virtues and is roughly synonymous with Rawls's "comprehensive doctrine," whereas metaphysics-2 refers to the study of the *really* abstract and ubiquitous features of *all* reality or *all* subjectivity (i.e., metaphysics-2 has both a strict and a restricted sense). Or again, metaphysics-2 refers to the discipline that discovers and articulates the general ideas that are indispensable to the analysis of *everything* that happens. Gamwell uses "metaphysics" in both senses, although his primary interest is metaphysics-2, the type of metaphysics that is the subject of the above-mentioned exemption. While metaphysics-1 roughly corresponds to Rawls's "comprehensive doctrine," it is only metaphysics-2 that is *truly* comprehensive, as Gamwell insightfully sees things. That is, the aforementioned distinction between strict and restricted metaphysics is *within* what I am now calling metaphysics-2.

We have seen that readers of Gamwell's books have to come to terms with two main areas: first, his view, derived from Hartshorne, that if a metaphysical-2 claim in the strict sense is true, it is true about everything; and second, his view that there is a tight connection between metaphysics-2 and political philosophy. In this chapter I will pull these two areas apart. Enthusiastic (Hartshornian) support for Gamwell as a metaphysician does not necessarily mean the same for Gamwell's thesis that a response to "the comprehensive question" is integral to any effort to theoretically understand what a just society would be like. My questions regarding Gamwell as a democratic political philosopher are nonetheless compatible with the belief that he is the most insightful thinker to date of those who think that it is fitting that one unqualifiedly bring one's comprehensive doctrine to bear on political questions, even in a condition of pervasive pluralism. That is, the real comprehensiveness of what Gamwell calls "the comprehensive question" both counts in favor of his metaphysics-2 and creates some questions for his political philosophy.

My procedure will be to lay out eight criticisms that I detect in Gamwell's profound reading of Rawls (five of which are explicitly directed at Rawls and three of which point the way toward Gamwell's own view), then to offer a spirited Rawlsian response to these eight criticisms so as to highlight the fruitful, complementary relationship between Rawls's and Gamwell's respective philosophies.

Rawls is well known for his distinction between the concept of justice (or the right), on the one hand, and the concept of the good, on the other. These two must be separated, he thinks, because of the plurality of opposed concepts of the good that reasonable people defend, sometimes uncompromisingly so. But such opposition, he thinks, need not be a political problem if we can nonetheless agree on democratic principles and procedures that will enable us to live in peace and prosperity and in a fair manner. That is, Rawls thinks that although we cannot agree (or at least that we do not in fact agree) regarding the comprehensive *good*—some are Catholics, some are Jews, some are Buddhists, some are agnostics, et cetera—we can (and often do, in democratic societies) agree regarding the procedures that should be followed in a *just* society.

For at least five nuanced reasons Gamwell is not convinced. First, Rawls's separation of justice from the comprehensive good *violates* those who defend such a comprehensive doctrine, at least if it is truly comprehensive or metaphysical (metaphysics-2). Relatively early in his career Gamwell indicated that he saw certain versions of liberalism as "seriously flawed." This criticism of liberalism was due to his desire to return to "the religious character of the comprehensive religious variable." By this variable he meant that in terms of which all possible existents are understood and evaluated. On this view, the public world only becomes a meaningful concept when diverse and fragmentary human communications are part of a divine, comprehensive unity-in-diversity. That is, a maximal public ideal finds its justification in God (*BP*, ix, 151).

Later Gamwell indicated, and no doubt he always realized, that liberalism in general arose as a specific kind of political theory that was meant to deal with the insistence and persistence of religious diversity, both between religious communities and within them. The religious wars of the early modern period were, as Gamwell notes, ruinous. So in addition to the need for *comprehensiveness* there is also the fact of *diversity*, the latter of which must in some fashion be tolerated if politics is to avoid both anarchy and coerced uniformity. The distinctive task of liberal theory has been to define the terms on which religious plurality can be civilized (*DP*, 238). To put the point in interrogative fashion, how can toleration be given reasonable grounds? (*MRF*, 9).

The Rawlsian, politically liberal response to this question, Gamwell thinks, violates popular sovereignty by offering a *freestanding* view that is independent of, or separated from, ideas of the comprehensive good. The violation presumably occurs with respect to those like Gamwell (and me) who defend comprehensive doctrines that really are comprehensive (i.e., that constitute a metaphysics-2 view), in contrast to those who hold "comprehensive" doctrines that are only nominally so. Although the Rawlsian freestanding view is very abstract, it nonetheless fails to be "self-democratizing" in light of the above alleged violation (*PCV*, 41). Here Gamwell enlists Habermas's support in his criticism of Rawls: practical discourse is compromised if the state insists that only its narrowly construed liberal conception of justice can be tolerated (*DP*, 248).

Granted, "liberalism" can mean many different things to many different thinkers. On one use of the term, any form of democracy where there is government by the people is liberal; on another use, the term refers to the view that politics is instrumental to diverse ends; on still another, it refers to maximal want-satisfaction, as detailed above in the first chapter. When Gamwell criticizes political liberalism, what he has in mind is the idea that there should be a separation of principles of justice from the comprehensive good, a separation that is unfair to those who defend truly comprehensive doctrines because the very idea of the *separation* of justice from the good militates against comprehensiveness; the concept of a freestanding concept of the just does the same.

Second, Rawls's *refusal* to consider comprehensive doctrines in politics amounts to a *denial* that any such doctrine could be true. Gamwell's critique is rooted in a concern voiced by Whitehead in the 1930s: that democracy without metaphysics loses its intellectual justification (Whitehead 1967a, 36). We will see that the issue here is whether "without metaphysics" necessarily means "antimetaphysics" and whether "without comprehensive religious backing" means "antireligious." Gamwell thinks that the Rawlsian view *is* antimetaphysical and antireligious; indeed, it is a type of secularism (*EG*, essay 2, part 1).

In this regard Rawls is, as Gamwell sees things, in the lineage of Kantian thinkers who assert that rights are independent of any inclusive telos; thus democratic rights are solely the creatures of historical context. As Gamwell sees things, however, the moral status of human beings cannot even be articulated, much less defended, in a nonteleological way. Thus, the Kantian-Rawlsian project is self-destructive because religious comprehensive doctrines give to their adherents the very terms for political evaluation. By seeking neither to assert nor to deny any particular comprehensive doctrine, Rawls ends up simply refusing (or more forcefully, denying) the comprehensive order of reflection. For Gamwell, there is no relevant distinction between refusing to consider comprehensive doctrines and denying their legitimacy.

Although I think that there *is* an important distinction here, it should not escape our notice that in the effort to conflate refusal and denial Gamwell sheds light on the complex development of Rawls's thought. Gamwell insightfully wonders about the transition from Rawls's early essay "Two Concepts of Rules" (1955) to *A Theory of Justice* (1971), to *Political Liberalism* (1993). In the early essay Rawls defends the idea that the justification of a practice, in contrast to the justification of a particular action falling under it, appeals to utilitarian principles (see Rawls 1999). Yet by the time of *A Theory of Justice* nonteleological principles are highlighted. Why? Gamwell floats the hypothesis that Rawls was spellbound by the Kantian conviction that political theory must be independent of a metaphysical telos. Although he left the impression that he was a comprehensive liberal in *A Theory of Justice* (with *comprehensive* liberalism, in contrast to *political* liberalism, consisting in an overall view that competes with other comprehensive doctrines for our allegiance), the fact that he was uneasy about this impression, along with the fact that he altered his view in *Political Liberalism*, highlights this Kantian conviction, which is the ultimate object of Gamwell's criticisms (*DP*, 185–87, 304–5).

Third, Rawlsian separation of the just from the good means that individuals' conceptions of the good are *privatized* and hence *relativized*. The separation that leads to privatization is a problem, according to Gamwell, because religious conviction involves a self-understanding that should be exemplified without duplicity in *all* human activity, including political activity. (This is why Gamwell opts for metaphysics-2 and for a comprehensive doctrine that is truly so.) Indeed, we have seen that Gamwell labels Rawls's stance, by contrast, as "the privatist view."

Because Rawls denies the comprehensive order of reflection, he implicitly asserts that political activity is always, even in the condemnation of slavery, relative to given historical and cultural conditions. In anticipation of the fifth criticism below, Gamwell thinks that relativism itself is ironically a comprehensive doctrine to the extent that it asserts a moral comparison of human activities: *all* these activities are historically and culturally specific. We will see that Gamwell thinks that all such responses to the comprehensive question are self-refuting.

To sum up the criticisms thus far, privatist, putative refusal to consider the comprehensive order of reflection *is* a denial, Gamwell thinks, and such a denial oddly leads to comprehensive, oppressive relativism: "To assert that one's choice of a purpose is never bound by a norm is also to assert a norm . . . namely, that human authenticity as such is always and in all respects particular or relative to the activity in question" (*MRF*, 141, also 139–43).

Fourth, as a result of the privatization and relativization of the good, the most that one can hope for on a Rawlsian basis is a *modus vivendi* (or a Hobbesian truce that is temporary because there is no genuine meeting of minds). That is, overlapping consensus (where those with differing comprehensive doctrines nonetheless *agree* on the concept of justice) is not possible. To be precise, Gamwell admits that Rawls's view is compatible with some "comprehensive" doctrines, but only those that are not truly comprehensive. That is, his political liberalism is incompatible with comprehensive doctrines that have a universalist conception of justice. Democracy implies a truly comprehensive purpose, on Gamwell's interpretation; hence the title of one of his books alludes to democracy *on purpose*. The strongest terms he uses are the following ones: a "nonteleological theory of justice" is as self-refuting as a "nontheoretical theory of justice" (*DP*, 277–79). Without a telos justice is purely (Gamwell might say "merely") procedural; hence the best we could hope for under a nonteleological theory of justice would be a *modus vivendi*, contra Rawls's obvious intent to be arguing for something more than a *modus vivendi* in terms of an overlapping consensus (*PCV*, 42).

Without metaphysical backing, justice as fairness has to remain a type of *modus vivendi*, Gamwell thinks, and cannot rise to the level of overlapping consensus. If we get along with each other on a Rawlsian basis, it has to be due to a contingent and fortunate convergence of interests rather than to an adherence to commonly held and necessarily true principles (*MRF*, 66–67). As a result, Gamwell thinks that no defender of a really comprehensive doctrine could ever accept an explicitly freestanding and implicitly *modus vivendi* conception of justice. On Gamwell's view, it is the comprehensive doctrine that justifies the political principles rather than the other way around. In fact, it is *only* a true comprehensive doctrine that could justify political principles. Gamwell puts the point directly and controversially as follows: "There is simply no such thing as a reasonable religious conviction or reasonable answer to the comprehensive question" (*MRF*, 72, also 70). Here he is assuming the Rawlsian distinction between the reasonable and the rational. The former refers to a willingness to abide by fair terms of agreement and the latter refers to the ability to follow arguments and to adjust means to ends. As before, it takes a *reasonable* person to willingly enter the Rawlsian original position (the place where the hypothetical decision-making procedure takes place in the effort to find the abstract principles that would obtain in a just society) and a *rational* person to deliberate there.

But even with this distinction in mind it is easy to misunderstand Gamwell's point. The quotation in the previous paragraph could easily be taken to mean that Gamwell is opposed to toleration of religious beliefs (or nonbeliefs) different from his own. Nothing could be further from the truth. I think that what Gamwell means is that when doing metaphysics-2 one is dealing with those *most abstract* features of all reality and of our experiences of it, such that when doing metaphysics-2 there is simply no need to reasonably adjudicate disputes regarding more concrete and more contentious aspects of comprehensive doctrines found at the level of metaphysics-1.

It is true that there are also differences of opinion regarding metaphysics-2 claims (e.g., regarding whether becoming should take precedence over being), but Gamwell thinks that *these* differences are not the sort that people literally fight over or that destroy the basis for a just society. These differences of opinion concern questions as to whether "something exists" or "God exists" are necessarily true. I agree with Gamwell's affirmative responses to both of these questions, although we will see that I am a bit skittish as to whether the latter question is as politically innocuous as Gamwell thinks.

Fifth, nonetheless, despite what has been said in the above four criticisms, Rawls's view of justice does, in spite of itself, involve a *comprehensive doctrine*; in fact, it amounts to an *established religion*. Because of the counterintuitiveness of this criticism, it will be worthwhile to try to understand Gamwell's point. The major problem, and an unnoticed one, with Rawls's theory, he thinks, is that any proposed separation of justice and the good implies a concept of justice that involves *its own* concept of the good; hence any such proposed separation involves a performative self-contradiction (*PCV*, 119; also see Griffin 2001 regarding performative self-contradiction). That is, the separation of justice from concepts of the comprehensive good nonetheless itself involves the creation of another such concept, Gamwell thinks; hence such a separation cannot unify politically a diversity of such concepts (*EG*, essay 5).

Gamwell once again thinks that the very statement that *no* universal concept is valid is itself a statement of what is universally the case (*DP*, 272–74). The attempt to avoid metaphysics is futile, Gamwell thinks, because the denial of all universalist concepts is contradicted by the confident assertion of a supposedly nonuniversalist one. Here Gamwell pushes Rorty and Rawls together in a joint denial of the claim that comprehensive doctrines that are truly comprehensive are reasonable. The problem with this view, on Gamwell's grounds, is that democratic discourse itself requires a substantive principle that is universal—in Rawlsian language, it requires a comprehensive doctrine (*DP*, 275–76; *MRF*, 136).

All of Rawls's talk of separation is merely on the surface in that Gamwell thinks that by refusing or denying the comprehensive question, Rawls ironically ends up with a metaphysical position: that *no* metaphysics is ever required for the purposes of politics (*MRF*, 47–58). "Irony" may be too weak a word here because Gamwell thinks that the Rawlsian project is plagued with "internal incoherence" (*MRF*, 68, 136–37). Gamwell detects in Rawls an awareness of the criticism being leveled against him (especially in Rawls 1996, 29). The Rawlsian distinction between the *reasonable* and the rationally discoverable *true* must itself be true for Rawlsian political philosophy to make sense. That is, Rawls cannot consistently deny metaphysical commitments. And, as before, metaphysics-2 is conceived by Gamwell not as the articulation of just any general view but, in Hartshornian fashion, as the articulation of the a priori or necessary conditions of reality and human (and other) activity. On this basis he is willing to grant to Rawls that no *particular* metaphysical view has to be affirmed if some of the traditional metaphysical views are kept in mind (e.g., Cartesian vs. Leibnizian), but regarding the most comprehensive aspects of comprehensive views Rawls cannot remain neutral (*MRF*, 58–59).

Of course, some religious adherents are reasonable and some are not, despite the language above regarding the claim that there is no such thing as a reasonable answer to the comprehensive question. The former, on Gamwell's account, are those who believe that comprehensive convictions can be publicly assessed and the latter are those who are not prepared to defend their comprehensive doctrines in a public forum. On this account it is Rawls himself who is unreasonable in that he is not willing to admit that justice as fairness *is* (at least implicitly) a comprehensive doctrine; hence *a fortiori* he is not willing to defend it in public as such. "The turn in Rawls's thought from *A Theory of Justice* to *Political Liberalism* has failed to achieve its principal purpose, namely, to propose a political theory that is not itself part of a comprehensive doctrine" (*MRF*, 74). Part of this failure lies in the tendency of the privatist view to assert that *none* of the religious convictions in the community are important in politics (*MRF*, 119).

These five criticisms are aimed directly at Rawls's view and they prepare the way for three more that illuminate Gamwell's own positive alternative to Rawlsian separation, or better, "separation." Sixth, every moral claim at least implicitly *includes its metaethical grounding.* This claim is crucial for Gamwell's view and applies to all moral claims, including not only those in one's personal morality but also those in political philosophy. He calls this stance, as we have seen, the "compound character of justice" in that the democratic principles enshrined in the Constitution, say, are more abstract than particular political judgments, but even these democratic principles must rest on something more basic. In Gamwell's terms, justice is both formative and substantive and neither of these components can be eliminated (*DP*, 232). To put Gamwell's point in Rawlsian language, a concept of justice cannot be freestanding because it must involve a concept of the comprehensive good.

Seventh, Gamwell goes even further. *Only* a true comprehensive doctrine can redeem political prescriptions. Not only does Gamwell claim that the separation of justice and the good in effect slips in through the back door an implicit concept of the good; it also slips in what amounts to an established religion: the religion of separation. Gamwell does not discuss in detail, although he does notice, that the Rawlsian view is *pro tanto* (to be discussed later) and that, because Rawls's political liberalism is not meant to be universalist, it is a poor candidate for status as a comprehensive doctrine. Only a view that is universalist, in the sense that adherents to the view think that it *alone* can redeem political prescriptions, can be really comprehensive. That is, on Gamwell's view an authentic comprehensive doctrine is incompatible with the Rawlsian *translation proviso,* wherein one's own comprehensive doctrine can be brought into the public sphere only if its terms can be translated in such a way that any reasonable-rational citizen could understand and possibly accept such terms (*DP*, 266–71).

Gamwell insists that opposition to Rawlsian separation does not itself imply religious establishment, but rather only implies that *some* universal principle or principles could be redeemed in political discourse. Such redemption *might*, if it were successful, *somewhat* reduce the need for the Rawlsian method of *reflective equilibrium* among various factors that would have to be balanced within public reason. This method works on the assumption that there are no convenient algorithms available for determining what a just society would be like. Rather, one must work hard, on the basis of this method, to think through how all of the relevant factors are to be brought into harmony with each other. That is, if one factor is overemphasized, we are put into an uncomfortable disequilibrium. Or again, on Gamwell's interpretation of Rawls, in *partial* contrast to Rawlsian reflective equilibrium, a zero-sum game is involved in political philosophy: if political liberalism is defensible then every universalist theory or truly comprehensive doctrine is invalid.

And eighth, religious convictions can be *rationally defended* and hence are amenable to public debate. One of the most distinctive of Gamwell's challenging theses is the claim that religious convictions are rationally defensible. In this regard he is commendably militating against the commonly held view that religious convictions are based on personal preferences and are thus not legitimate parts of our common moral (including political) enterprise. But religious convictions, he argues, have no wider comprehensive scope than Rawls's principles of justice. That is, Rawls's refusal to consider (or denial of) comprehensive claims is universal, and if there is a true concept of human authenticity, as Gamwell thinks there is, it would likewise be true under all conditions (*MRF*, 135–45).

Gamwell grants that the critique of traditional metaphysics that began with Kant led many thinkers to discredit normative ethics as well. He thinks that Rawls is one of the heroes in the effort to reclaim a central place for normative ethics and politics in philosophy. But Gamwell thinks that Rawls's achievement is attenuated because of his refusal to consider, or denial of, rationally intelligible metaphysical claims regarding the comprehensive good (*EG*, preface).

The truncated Rawlsian approach has nonetheless had a profound effect on Gamwell's theory of distributive justice, which is formulated in Hartshornian process terms: maximize the general conditions of creativity to which all have equal access. All three principles in Rawls—the principle of *equal basic liberties*, the principle of fair *equality of opportunity* with respect to any inequalities in the distribution of goods, and the *difference principle* wherein any inequalities or differences in the distribution of goods will work to everyone's advantage (especially the least advantaged)—inform positively Gamwell's view, especially the idea at the core of the difference principle that talents won in the natural and social lotteries are justified only if they advantage the least advantaged. Although there are also obvious dissimilarities between Rawls's view and Gamwell's theory regarding the general conditions of emancipation, the significant overlap regarding their theories of distributive justice deserves emphasis. That is, on Gamwell's view there is much that is accomplished on the attenuated basis of Rawlsian political philosophy (*DG*, 201–2; *PCV*, 91–92; *DP*, 294, 310).

Nor is Gamwell necessarily opposed to the overall method at work in Rawls that was briefly discussed above: reflective equilibrium. Particular convictions that we have no reason to question (commitment to democracy, opposition to racism, etc.) are easier to bring into equilibrium than those convictions that are easily criticized. But this method, once again, could be seen as attenuated because, although it works well as moral philosophy, it does not work as moral Philosophy (Gamwell's capitalization) in terms of "a foundation or grounding for the moral theory reached in reflective equilibrium" (*DG*, 116). Because there is no transcendental grounding offered for reflective equilibrium, its results could be seen to be tinged with arbitrariness, hence the charge of relativism articulated above (*DG*, 123–24). This eighth criticism therefore deals not so much with the lack of rationality in Rawls as the lack of Rationality. I will return in detail to reflective equilibrium in the final chapter of the book.

I would now like to offer responses—several in the form of friendly amendments—to Gamwell's eight criticisms. Regarding the first criticism, that political liberalism violates those who defend truly comprehensive doctrines, the following can be said in reply. Gamwell is well aware of the problem created by the pluralism of comprehensive doctrines that citizens affirm, very often uncompromisingly. To put the question in his terms: How can religious plurality be civilized? But his response to this question is somewhat different from the response that is given by political liberals like me.

Gamwell thinks that religious toleration can be given reasonable grounds by requiring religious believers (at least some of them, if I understand correctly) to give a public defense of the comprehensive doctrine that they affirm. If such a defense is truly *public* it will require civil discourse, which in turn requires toleration. The politically liberal response to the question at issue, by way of partial contrast, is to take the truth or falsity of comprehensive doctrines off the table *in politics* for at least two reasons. Either defenders of comprehensive doctrines themselves might not be willing to give a rational articulation of their view (after all, fideism, or the idea that religious belief is based on faith rather than reason, has had the upper hand in both philosophy of religion and religious circles at least since the time of Kant), or, if they are willing to offer a rational, publicly articulated version of their view, it might be hopelessly at odds with conflicting articulations.

It should be noted that Gamwell is not only encouraging religious believers to develop rationally (i.e., publicly) defensible versions of their beliefs, but he is also basing the continued existence of civil society on the ability of religious believers to develop such publicly defensible versions of their beliefs. One wonders what would happen if most religious believers remained steadfast in their fideism and did not see the need for, or even the appropriateness of, rationalized religion. I would like to make it clear that I personally see a strong role for reason in religion, but I am also painfully aware of the fact that there is no swarming multitude in addition to Gamwell that agrees with me in this regard.

There is a certain irony in the fact that, despite the fortunate circumstance that Gamwell and I share roughly the same (Hartshornian) metaphysical-2 view, he thinks any defenders of a truly comprehensive view are treated unfairly in political liberalism. I would not think that I would be treated unfairly if my comprehensive doctrine did not provide *the* metaethical support for liberal toleration. As Hartshorne himself put the point, liberals are thinkers who know that they are not God (Hartshorne 1984a, 9). It should also be remembered that Whitehead, like Hartshorne, was a liberal in politics (see Morris 1991), such that his view could be interpreted as saying, as Rawls's view could be interpreted as saying, that liberal political beliefs require the backing provided by *some* comprehensive doctrine, but which one?

It makes sense to distinguish between toleration of reasonable comprehensive doctrines and toleration of different conceptions of justice. Gamwell's appropiation of Habermas seems to indicate that he thinks that Rawls is intolerant in the latter case. Another way to look at the matter, however, is to suggest that Rawls is very tolerant of different conceptions of justice *within the politically liberal family*, which includes a large number of well-known political philosophers. Nonliberal conceptions of justice (e.g., as defended by Straussians, Marxists, etc.) are not so much the victims of intoleration as they are ignored (although Rawls discusses Marx's own views in detail; see Rawls 2007, 319–72).

I think that we should commend Rawls in this regard. The argument for such relative neglect, which might understandably strike some as flippant, relates to reflective equilibrium. That is, if we adopted the Straussian or Marxist stances, which in their different ways actually denigrate justice as either a convenient foil for the unwise or as a bourgeois fetish, respectively, we would put into disequilibrium most of the important beliefs held by reflective citizens in contemporary democracies. Among these beliefs are that in politics citizens should be viewed as ends-in-themselves who are free and equal, reasonable and rational. If these beliefs were false, then admittedly nonliberal conceptions of justice would look more attractive. But as it stands, with these beliefs assumed as relatively stable, one would pay far too great a price by adopting a nonliberal conception of justice.

Regarding the second criticism, that Rawls's refusal to consider comprehensive doctrines in politics amounts to a denial of them, several different responses are in order. Gamwell moves too quickly, I think, from politically liberal principles that do not rely on metaphysical support to the idea that such principles are antimetaphysical. Likewise, he moves too quickly from the idea that politically liberal principles can be articulated without comprehensive religious backing to the idea that such principles are antireligious. These "offside" infractions by Gamwell (if the North American football metaphor be permitted) are prompted by his assumption that Rawlsian political philosophy is a variety of secularism.

This assumption deserves scrutiny. Granted, modern liberal thinkers like Kant, Mill, and Dewey seemed to think that as citizens became more enlightened, and hence less attracted to traditional religious understandings of politics, a secular utopia could be approximated. But the later Rawls clearly tries to distance himself from these varieties of *comprehensive* liberalism, which were meant as replacements for what was thought to be the outmoded wisdom of the Judeo-Christian ages. Rawls thinks of comprehensive liberalism as just one more comprehensive doctrine that must be brought within the sweep of *politically* liberal institutions. Indeed, Rawls thinks that comprehensive liberalism can lead, and historically has led, to messianic and imperialistic forays that were actually at odds with liberal political principles. That is, it might be more accurate to view Rawlsian political philosophy as post-secular rather than as secular. The very fact that Rawls uses the label "comprehensive doctrine" rather than "religion" indicates, as we have seen, that he thinks that *both* religious believers and nonbelievers have to submit to reasonable criteria developed in fair decision-making procedures, such as those found in the Rawlsian original positions at both the domestic and international levels (see Malone-France 2012).

Or again, Gamwell thinks that political liberalism, in addition to being anti-metaphysical and anti-religious, is also anti-teleological. There is a grain of truth in his position here, but I think that a more accurate way to put the point would be to say that no single telos can be isolated that captures the various (and at times conflicting) ends that reasonable citizens affirm in contemporary democracies: the greater glory of God, pleasure, sexual liberation, artistic excellence, wealth, et cetera. In fact, it is not too much of a stretch to say that, rather than being anti-teleological, political liberalism is hyper-teleological in that it permits as many ends as are compatible with justice.

Although it is correct, as Gamwell notices, that Rawls rejects what Gamwell calls the "comprehensive order of reflection" *in politics*, the point of such rejection is to make the conceptual world safe for the comprehensive order of reflection in other areas: the academy, churches, the arts, responsible journalism, et cetera. If the comprehensive order of reflection yielded only one concept of *the* good (as Aristotle and Thomas Aquinas, for example, thought), then political matters would be much simpler than they are in the polyglot conceptual world that we inhabit at present and for the foreseeable future.

The third criticism, that Rawlsian separation of the just from the good both privatizes and relativizes the good, is problematic for several reasons. The contrasting term to "public" in Rawls is "nonpublic" rather than "private." This last term is etymologically related to the negativity associated with privation or lack or deficiency. There is nothing in political liberalism, however, that associates religious belief with privation. People just happen to believe and there is nothing lacking in them in this regard. Further, religious believers tend to worship together in community and to identify themselves with their religious communities; hence "nonpublic," although not the ideal term, is nonetheless better than "private" when describing religious believers' conceptions of the good.

Further, it is not the case that religious believers are required to sequester their conceptions of the good. In political liberalism they are permitted to do intellectual work with them, even in the public square, *as long as* the terms of the translation proviso are met (see, e.g., Rawls 1996, li). As I see things, these terms are not onerous or unfair to defenders of either religious or nonreligious comprehensive doctrines. Once one acknowledges that reasonable citizens affirm many different conceptions of the good, one comes to realize that it would be a sign of disrespect to enact laws (especially those that use the coercive apparatus of the state to restrict the freedom of citizens) that are based on the terms of a single comprehensive doctrine that many citizens could not accept.

For example, Martin Luther King (or those he influenced) easily could have met the terms of the translation proviso by providing for his agnostic listeners, in addition to his appeal to religious grounds, a nonreligious explanation of why he advocated a discrimination-free society on the basis of race. Or again, Rawls himself, who was a defender of abortion rights for women, nonetheless commended Joseph Bernardin, the Catholic cardinal of Chicago, for trying to defend opposition to abortion in terms that were compatible with *public* reason. On Rawlsian grounds Bernardin may have been wrong, but by fulfilling the terms of the translation proviso he was at least being respectful of fellow citizens (see Rawls 1996, lvi). There is no good reason to abandon the translation proviso so as to allow the use of one comprehensive doctrine to trump the concepts of the good found in others. I will return to Gamwell's view of abortion later.

It is true that *some* religious beliefs (e.g., belief in the trinity or in the dual nature of Christ) might not be amenable to the rational articulation that is the hallmark of public reason, but it is precisely these beliefs that are least political in that we can easily imagine a just polis where there is reasonable disagreement on these matters. Whereas some religious beliefs are overdetermined in the sense that they could be justified either in line with public reason or on religious grounds (e.g., that murder is wrong), and hence are easily amenable to the terms of the translation proviso, other religious beliefs seem to be justifiable only on nonpublic grounds. These latter beliefs are not appropriate bases for public policy in a democracy, as I see things.

The stable beliefs that are the subjects of widespread agreement in contemporary democracies (e.g., that slavery is wrong, that women deserve political equality with men, et cetera) are shared by all reasonable parties, whatever their comprehensive doctrine. This is fortunate because abandonment of these beliefs would most egregiously put our moral lives into disequilibrium. In other words, it is rational to think that we pay too great a price for abandoning these beliefs; hence it is not accurate to say that political liberalism merely *privatizes* such belief.

The fixed points within political liberalism (e.g., that citizens should be seen as politically free and equal, reasonable and rational), the abandonment of which produces a dangerous disequilibrium with respect to morality, in general, and political philosophy, in particular, are, of course, open for discussion. But this is a far cry from suggesting that the results of such a discussion among reasonable and rational parties would lead to the abandonment of human authenticity, as Gamwell suggests. These beliefs are stable precisely because reasonable citizens who lead authentic lives affirm them (albeit in many different ways).

My response to the fourth criticism, that the most one can hope for in political liberalism is a *modus vivendi* rather than an overlapping consensus, follows from what has been said above. In logic it is clear that one can reach the same conclusion (X) starting from several different sets of premises (a, b, c), either directly

$$\begin{array}{ccc} a & b & c \\ & X & \end{array}$$

or indirectly

$$\begin{array}{ccc} a & b & c \\ d & e & f \\ & X & \end{array}$$

If something analogous can be said in political philosophy, then overlapping consensus (perhaps even Gamwell's "comprehensive purpose") is possible in that X can be agreed to by all reasonable parties.

I understand what Gamwell has in mind when he says that political liberalism can achieve only a convenient *modus vivendi* because it is nonteleological. We cannot decide *in politics* among a's, b's, or c's ends. Likewise, it is nontheoretical *in the sense that* we cannot decide in political philosophy about whether a, b, or c is true. If these are mutually exclusive options, however, we *can* know that they cannot all be true and that some of them (but which ones?) are false.

What Gamwell wants in politics are both commonly held principles (which is what overlapping consensus is all about) and necessarily true principles. Regarding the latter, political liberalism *in a way* admittedly falls short. Although necessarily true principles are not denied in political liberalism, as Gamwell alleges, they *are* left to metaphysicians like Gamwell and me to deal with. Decisions regarding necessarily true principles (and I think that Gamwell and I would largely decide in similar ways) should occur at scholarly conferences and in academic journals, in religious councils and in theological discourse, rather than in the halls of congress or in courthouses.

Gamwell is correct to be suspicious regarding a *modus vivendi*, however. The question is whether political liberalism can achieve something greater in terms of overlapping consensus. The problem with a *modus vivendi* is that it lacks stability and can fall apart at any time. The reason for this is that there is no meeting of minds or like-mindedness in a *modus vivendi*, only a truce that could easily be violated when the forces arrayed on the other side are diminished. It should be noted that over time a *modus vivendi* can develop into an overlapping consensus as mutual trust develops. It should also be noted as a concession to Gamwell that an overlapping consensus can over time degenerate into a *modus vivendi* as trust wanes and as political opponents in a friendly *agon* gradually come to be viewed as hated enemies (see Dombrowski 2009).

The fifth criticism is that Rawls develops a comprehensive doctrine and an established religion in spite of himself. The first point that should be made in this regard is that if Rawls's view is in fact a comprehensive doctrine, as Gamwell alleges, it is not very comprehensive. There is no statement for or against the existence of God in Rawls, no stance regarding the afterlife, no theodicy. There is not even a theory of human nature other than an articulation of the parameters within which a *political* person as free and equal, reasonable and rational, can maneuver. There is no stated view regarding the mind-body problem (the greatest philosophical problem since the seventeenth century) and no resolution to the problem of human identity over time other than how this problem relates to *political* agency. Rawls has no stated metaphysical view regarding the status of universals, the problem of the one and the many, or the relationship between being and becoming. There is not even a general theory of axiology that deals with moral as well as aesthetic value. And, perhaps most significantly, there is no developed theory regarding *why* human beings are ends-in-themselves, dignified subjects worthy of respect, as would be the case if he had a truly comprehensive doctrine.

To say that Rawls also implies an established religion (of separation) is to elicit a response to the effect that it would be a very odd established religion because Jews, Christians, Moslems, atheists and agnostics, et cetera, would not only be tolerated but they would also be afforded political equality with all other citizens. As we have seen, the separation of the just from the good is not absolute or "religious" in Rawls due to the translation proviso. Between pure exclusivists, like Rorty, who would utterly prohibit religion in politics, and pure inclusivists, like Nicholas Wolterstorff, who would seemingly permit religious believers to bring *any* of their religious beliefs into the public square so long as they did not contain threats of violence, lies Rawls and his partial inclusivism. It is true, however, that Rawls is closer to Rorty on this continuum than he is to Wolterstorff in that if the terms of the translation proviso are not met Rawls thinks that the exclusion of one's particular concept of the good from politics is a good thing. However, some religious convictions *are* very important in politics, that is, those that are reasonable and translatable. An example would be the religious conviction that human beings are made in the image of God, which can be translated (not without remainder, to be sure, but translated well enough to do significant intellectual work, in Wittgensteinian fashion) into the language of rights and respect (see Schilbrack 2013). It should also be noted that Gamwell is not entirely at Wolterstorff's end of the spectrum due to his insistence that religious believers defend their beliefs rationally. That is, both Rawls and Gamwell avoid the two extremes and hence have more in common with each other than Gamwell realizes.

Gamwell is at his best when he points out performative self-contradictions, but it is hard for me to see how Rawls falls victim. Rawls admits that a *thin* theory of the good is required in theory of justice, which is a theory of the good that involves basic things that would be required in *any* thicker and wider theory of the good that is reasonable. When Rawls separates justice from the good it is this thicker and wider concept of the good that is separated, not the thin theory. Perhaps it would have been less confusing if Rawls had called the thin theory of the good a theory of (Martha Nussbaum–like) capabilities or (Aristotelian) requirements so as to avoid the appearance of contradiction.

It is futile, Gamwell thinks, to try to avoid metaphysics. In a peculiar way a Rawlsian could agree with this claim in that, because political philosophy is only a part of an overall moral philosophy, *some* conception of the good is required in order to deal with all of the questions that are not spelled out in theory of justice. As the cliché has it, politics is not the whole of life, even if it affects everything else. Another way to put the point is to say that it is misleading to suggest that no concept of the comprehensive good is required in political liberalism; rather, several different metaphysical views and their concomitant comprehensive goods are compatible with justice. Hence there is no incoherence in eschewing any particular metaphysical view *in politics* while permitting one, encouraging one, perhaps even requiring one elsewhere!

Rawls assumes, and so should we, that each citizen affirms both a view of justice *and* a comprehensive doctrine. In some cases, the political conception is simply the consequence of, or is at least continuous with, the citizen's comprehensive doctrine; or it might be an acceptable approximation of such a doctrine. The political conception might need to be *presented* as freestanding and yet be part of, or derivable from, a comprehensive doctrine. But all citizens at least implicitly affirm a comprehensive doctrine of some sort to which the political conception they accept is in *some* way related. Thus, citizens' views have two parts: one deals with the publicly recognized political conception of justice and the other is a full or partial comprehensive doctrine to which the political conception is in some manner related. A political conception of justice is no more indifferent to truth (in a comprehensive doctrine) than the principle of toleration is indifferent to truth (in religion). The difference between a political conception of justice and a comprehensive doctrine is a matter of scope, with the latter being wider than the former in that it deals with what is of ultimate value and with questions of virtue and character. For a conception to be even partially comprehensive, it must extend beyond the limited scope of the political (see Rawls 1996, xxi, 12, 38, 140, 150, 175).

Very early in *A Theory of Justice* Rawls makes it clear that justice is the first virtue of social institutions, just as truth is the first virtue of systems of thought (Rawls 1971, 3). There is no principled opposition in political liberalism to truth. So Gamwell in a way is insightfully correct to say that the Rawlsian distinction between the reasonable and the rationally discoverable true itself must be true. But this very abstract truth is clearly not the whole truth or the less abstract truth found in a comprehensive doctrine or in metaphysics-1. That is, political liberalism is not challenged in any significant way when it is claimed that it cannot remain neutral regarding all of the abstract aspects of truly comprehensive doctrines.

It should now be clear how I would respond to the sixth criticism, that Rawls does not submit to the idea that any moral claim at least implicitly includes its metaethical grounding. This is another way of objecting to Rawls's idea that theory of justice should be freestanding. My response relies on a distinction between two different senses of "freestanding." The first connotes the idea that a theory of justice should be freestanding in the sense that it does not rely on *any particular* metaethical view, whereas the second stands for the idea that a theory of justice should not rely on *any* metaethical stance. The second sense is, as Gamwell rightly thinks, problematic for several reasons. But it is the first sense that a political liberal should defend and it is not clear what is wrong with freestandingness in this sense.

The seventh criticism (that political liberalism lacks a true comprehensive doctrine, that only such a comprehensive doctrine can redeem political prescriptions, and that such a true comprehensive doctrine does not amount to an established religion) should be addressed in terms of Rawls's admission that his view of political philosophy is *pro tanto*, as was mentioned above in the introduction. Literally these Latin words mean to pay in part, as when in a legal context someone in debt escapes penalty by paying part of the debt on the pledge to pay the remainder at a later time. *Pro tanto* pledges are quite different from bankruptcies, where one is under no obligation to repay the remaining debt. Given this distinction, one can interpret Rawls to be saying that one pays one's "debt" in moral philosophy in two stages (or better, in two different ways, in that I am speaking of logical stages here and not temporal ones). "First" one needs to get clear on the abstract principles of justice that would guide a democratic society in a condition of reasonable pluralism; "then" one needs to deal with all of the other questions in moral philosophy that are not primarily questions regarding justice.

Because the second payment involves one of the two moral powers that are individually necessary and jointly sufficient in the moral life—a sense of the right or the just *and* a sense of the good—no bankruptcy proceedings are appropriate here. Whereas Gamwell speaks as if Rawlsian political philosophy is a type of bankruptcy proceeding (in that the sense of the good is not exercised in the effort to understand the comprehensive order, indeed it is *denied*), it would perhaps be more accurate to say that it is *postponed*. Or better, because one's concept of the good may antedate one's concept of justice, it might be even more accurate to say that it is not so much postponed as it is *relegated* to a different part of moral theory and the moral life.

Not to engage in this sort of *pro tanto* postponement or relegation is to run the risk that one *would* end up with an explicit or implicit established religion (or anti-religion, depending on the comprehensive doctrine in question). To say of one's favored universalist concept of good that it *alone* can redeem political prescriptions is to flirt with the possibility that overlapping consensus would disintegrate into a *modus vivendi* or worse.

Of course, there is something messy about *pro tanto* reasoning, in particular, and about reflective equilibrium, in general. But this is because reflective equilibrium is a type of dialectic; and this generic philosophical method (*the* method of philosophy, according to Scanlon 2003, 149) always involves some unfinished business and some questions only partially answered. The hope for a philosophic method that moves beyond dialectic has a long history, dating back to the attempt at the topmost rung in Plato's divided line to achieve a level of reality beyond being (*hyperousia*). But there is an equally long history, also dating back to Plato, of returning to dialectic once the effort to move beyond it is over.

Gamwell's own effort to develop a universalistic concept of good, such that only in its terms could political prescriptions be redeemed, itself is open to dialectical criticism and to further clarification (as Gamwell himself would no doubt admit). We have seen that, in defense of Gamwell, his metaphyics of politics operates at the most abstract level and at a more concrete level is very much compatible with Rawls's own views. The Hartshornian way to make the point is to say that if we are lucky enough to reach necessary truth, this fact itself will be contingent. We have no viable alternative to the back-and-forth movement involved in the process of reflective equilibrium: intuition, rational argument, counterargument, response to counterargument, new intuition, et cetera. The regional resolution of the problem of justice that this processual method has produced is the sediment associated with political liberalism. No doubt improved versions of liberalism may be in the offing, but the disequilibrium that would be brought about by radical shifts to the right or left (as in adopting the Straussian or Marxist views mentioned above) continues to be unpersuasive. There is nothing arbitrary in accepting the provisional results of dialectical argument in political philosophy. The disastrous results of disequilibrium make this readily apparent.

However, in a way I am in agreement with Gamwell's eighth criticism, that religious convictions at the most abstract level (e.g., regarding the existence of God or regarding the features properly connected to the concept of that than which no greater can be conceived) are rationally defensible. My agreement here with Gamwell, however, is as a metaphysician, not as a political philosopher dealing with some of the more concrete issues in politics. It should be clear that we are in a minority regarding the defensibility of the ontological argument; and our common belief that creation *ex nihilo* is unintelligible is also controversial even in (especially in) religious circles, as is the belief that opposition to truth inevitably leads one into performative self-contradiction. That is, in political theory, in contrast to metaphysics, we will have to rest content with philosophy rather than Philosophy, with rationality rather than Rationality, unless we are dealing with politics at the most abstract level.

I would like to make it clear that I share Gamwell's concern that religious conviction ought to be exemplified without duplicity (*MRF*, 49). But I do not see duplicity at work in trying to understand philosophically and to implement practically the biblical advice "Let both grow together until the harvest" (Matthew 13:24–30). Taken literally, "both" refers to wheat and weeds, but here I am taking it to refer to true and false comprehensive doctrines. I have previously admitted that some comprehensive doctrines must be false. This is a logical point in that when comprehensive doctrines contradict each other one realizes that they cannot both be true.

My point here is not merely logical, however. I agree wholeheartedly with Gamwell's belief that there are convincing reasons for thinking that neoclassical or process theism *is* true. I do not so much hide this belief in public, and hence behave duplicitously, as I refrain from calling attention to it unless it seems both effective to do so in politics (largely it is not) *and* respectful to do so (sometimes it is, per the translation proviso, sometimes it is not).

I also share Gamwell's fear of postmodern refusal or denial of metaphysics and metanarratives (which often conceal an implicit metaphysics and metanarrative). But I have tried to show how the freestanding character of political liberalism enables one to be nonmetaphysical in one sense and as committed to metaphysics as one would like to be in another *as long as* one is reasonable. The problem here is, in Whiteheadian fashion, misplaced concreteness. The locus for integration of political principles and metaphysical ones is not at the societal level as long as many reasonable citizens either eschew metaphysics or defend different metaphysical views from one's own. Rather, the locus for such integration is at the individual or associational level.

As I see things, until all rational beings agree at the level of comprehensive doctrine (the "harvest"), we have a duty to be reasonable. As the biblical image makes clear, one danger is that by prematurely pulling the weeds the wheat itself might be ruined. Finally, it seems to me that it would be a mistake to view this stance as religion lite (I have no reason to believe that Gamwell thinks this); instead it should be viewed as religion come of age, given the long history of religious intoleration that both Gamwell and I deplore.

CHAPTER ELEVEN

American Intellectual History

We have seen that there are significant differences among theories that strictly privatize religion, those that allow religious convictions into the public square so long as something like the translation proviso is met, and those that more widely permit (with or without qualification) religious convictions into political discourse. In the present chapter I will explore the question as to how, given the wide pluralism of both religious convictions and views regarding religious freedom, there can be a common allegiance to a democratic form of government. This question will be explored in terms of Gamwell's appropriation of several thinkers in the American intellectual tradition, including Thomas Jefferson and Abraham Lincoln (as interpreted by John Burt), along with the historian David Strauss (not to be confused with the conservative political philosopher Leo Strauss), who introduces dynamism into scholarship regarding the US Constitution and who provides a bridge between Jefferson and Lincoln. Jefferson, despite his well-known weaknesses regarding slavery, appreciated this question and, as a result, had an abiding commitment to reasoned inquiry. In fact, Gamwell thinks of Jefferson, again despite his weaknesses in other areas, as the primary voice in favor of religious freedom among the Founders of the United States. James Madison's 1787 role in the passage of the first amendment to the US Constitution is pivotal, but Jefferson's authorship of the 1777 Bill for Establishing Religious Freedom in the state of Virginia has been seen as "the most decisive element in the epochal shift in the Western world's approach to relations between civil and religious spheres of life" (Marty 1988, 1). On Jefferson's view, religious freedom functions as a prior constraint on government power (*WTP*, 1–4).

Jefferson's precursor to Rawlsian overlapping consensus was the search for the "moral precepts" common to all religions, including Judaism, Christianity, Islam, Hinduism, et cetera (but not secularism, which was not much of an option in the eighteenth century). These moral precepts were seen to be different from "the dogmas of religion" that divided various sects. Benjamin Franklin called the common principles "the essentials" of every religion. The hope was that there would be no significant conflict between religious freedom and commitment to democratic government due to these common or essential moral principles. That is, in American intellectual history there always has been a religionist account of the ethics of democratic citizenship. Indeed, Jefferson thought that democracy *depends* on religious essentials. Gamwell defends Jefferson here, even if he wishes to differentiate his defense from the aforementioned views held by Murray and Greenawalt. The important thing is that we *all* stay "locked together in argument." In this regard, Gamwell commends Jefferson for being reticent throughout his career to talk about his own religious beliefs, but for being more than willing to talk about commitment to rational argument (*WTP*, 5–11).

Gamwell doubts if Jefferson would have fully agreed with Rawlsian (alleged) separationism, even when mitigated by the translation proviso that religious convictions can enter the public square when they are framed in rational terms amenable to public debate in a condition of pervasive pluralism. This is because Jefferson would have seen a tight connection between rationality itself and theism, between morality itself and theism. In different terms, Jefferson believed in Truth with a capital "T," which is what gave him confidence that the clash of ideas in a democracy over time would lead to the elimination of error. Errors cease to be dangerous when they can be corrected over time by rational criticism engaged against the background of an omniscient knower. Gamwell is to be admired for his critical appropriation of Jefferson's view wherein democracy does not require agreement on constitutive elements in any religious view. Nor does it rely on an established religion. It *does* rely, however, on the conviction that the comprehensive question can be dealt with rationally. Gamwell thinks that he has Jefferson on his side in thinking that "comprehensive assessment" and "religious freedom" are rough synonyms. The *ultimate* terms of political evaluation are essential parts of the story that must be told in political philosophy, even if such terms do not tell the whole story in its concrete richness (*WTP*, 12–18).

This foray into Jefferson's thought is instructive today due to the way that Jefferson indicates the grains of truth in both the separationist *and* religionist perspectives on religious freedom. as Gamwell argues: "His . . . most apparent proposals seem to advance, on the one hand, a religionist view, on which certain supposed essentials of all religions in the conventional sense will be commonly affirmed, and on the other, a separationist view, on which common consent is possible because republican morality is independent of whether any conventional religion is true" (*WTP*, 19). Jefferson's allegiance to reason should be our own, as Gamwell argues, because *any* democratic political claim at all is, at least implicitly, a commitment to adjudicate contested claims by way of reason. As before, in making any democratic political claim one is issuing a pledge or a promise that, if the claim is contested, one must give reasons in support of the claim. The practice of political discourse, of testing contested claims by way of rational argument, is a metaethical feature of democratic government. This practice is self-imposed by virtuous citizens in a democracy (*WTP*, 20–21).

It must be admitted that sometimes promises cannot be kept due to future contingencies that were not foreseen at the time the promise was made. But the practice of promise-making retains *prima facie* its strength. Likewise, the pledge to supply reasons for one's political claims indicates a commitment to democratic practice even when unforeseen events make it difficult to follow through on one's pledge. Gamwell is understandably saddened to notice the threats to this Jeffersonian legacy in both politics *and* academe. Indeed, Gamwell thinks that there is at present unfortunately a virtually unanimous refusal of the positive aspect of Jefferson's legacy that contested claims regarding comprehensive questions be adjudicated by reason! The assertion that religious claims cannot be supported by reason *itself* is a statement that cannot be supported by reason. If democracy *depends* on the commitment to resolve disagreements by argument, then we abandon this commitment at our democratic peril. This peril will likely surface as political paralysis or instability, conditions that invite exercises in power that are not characterized by epistemic constraint. It must also be admitted that there is something idealistic about the Jeffersonian view, but Gamwell thinks that it nonetheless receives warrant from a theistic realism that sees both self-regarding *and* social impulses in human nature (*WTP*, 22–27).

Jefferson's commitment to rational assessment of religious claims is precisely what makes him, according to Gamwell, the principal mind responsible for American commitment to religious freedom. This commitment is based on a widely held experience of divine reality, as well as on the pervasive experience of morality and truth. These common experiences were infamously violated by Jefferson himself regarding the institution of slavery, an institution that over time has ironically not withstood the test of Jeffersonian rationality. The way of reason is, in the final analysis, authorized by the reality of God. Error is obviously a problem, but the best way to deal with it is to make it possible for reason to combat it, with God as omniscient providing a standard for what reasonable beings, when they are thinking reasonably, would over the long haul assert (*WTP*, 28–29; *MN*, 240, 242).

As a process thinker, it is not surprising that Gamwell is congenial to the scholarship of David Strauss, who defends a view of the US Constitution as open to change as a living document, in contrast to so-called originalism. By "originalism" is meant the view that the meaning of the Constitution is that intended by those who drafted or ratified the written text. Strauss and Gamwell think that this theory is inadequate, especially when it is realized that it would permit government discrimination against women and people of color, given the original understanding of the document in 1787. Originalism is also problematic because it requires that interpreters be sophisticated intellectual historians, which few judges are. Further, it is in some cases impossible to know what the original understandings or intentions were. Originalism requires that we translate prescriptions from centuries ago to a contemporary idiom, which may be extremely difficult, given the fact that we now live in a largely urban, high-tech society that would have been foreign to the eighteenth-century drafters and ratifiers of the Constitution. Indeed, in what Strauss calls the Jefferson problem, one generation is to a later one as one independent nation is to another (*WTP*, 31–33).

The grain of truth in originalism, despite its debilitating problems, is that one would want to prevent arbitrary interpretations of the Constitution. The processual views of Strauss and Gamwell rely heavily on common law, which, like culture, develops over time. But it is not arbitrary in that common law gains authority over time as it becomes generally accepted. It is originalism, by contrast, that is shot through with indeterminacy. Common law militates against such indeterminacy and arbitrariness because it relies on a patient and cautious sort of empiricism that allows laws to change over time, albeit slowly. The function of the Constitution does not depend on veneration of our ancestors. Rather, it is valuable because it provides a common ground to settle disputes and it narrows the range of disagreement, in part by eliminating the need to keep reopening issues all the time. It should also be noted that there is a difference between the *hermeneutical* question regarding how to interpret the Constitution and the *normative* question regarding what makes the Constitution, however we interpret it, authoritative. Because constitutional law is not my area of expertise, I have no desire to speak with confidence in this area. But I would like to locate Gamwell's views on the matter within his metaphysics. The Constitution, the Declaration of Independence, and the Federalist Papers are all clear that the abiding character of American government centers on the idea that the United States is a republican form of government, that is, a form of government that derives its powers directly or indirectly from the people. Although one should not expect metaphysics or transcendental argumentation to specify the details of the Constitution, one can expect the metaethical duty to maximize creativity for all over the long term to be exemplified in *some* type of popular sovereignty (*WTP*, 34–44).

Of course, there are an enormous number of issues that need to be decided at more and more concrete levels, including the question as to whether republican government should be in terms of direct democracy or in terms of indirect representation. The semantic issues here are thorny, say if "democracy" is reserved for direct participation in government and is opposed to indirect representation. The key point here in relation to the topic of the present book is that the legitimation of the government derives from popular sovereignty and that the ultimate terms of political justification rest on a metaphysics of maximal creativity (*WTP*, 45–49).

Whereas the Declaration of Independence makes reference to God, the Constitution does not do so. Gamwell thinks this is a good thing because a constitutional provision affirming theism would be inconsistent with popular sovereignty. We are once again reminded of the fact that Gamwell's theism is affirmed at a very abstract level so as to provide an adequate response to the comprehensive question. It is *not* affirmed so as to exclude other theists or religious skeptics from fair treatment in a republic. But leaving God out of the Constitution does not deny democracy's theistic grounding. Regarding the Declaration of Independence's theism, it is crucial to notice that popular sovereignty in the eighteenth century was not necessarily violated by God-talk in public documents. This is in contrast to the increasingly agnostic world of the twenty-first century. It might be argued that the drafters and ratifiers of the Constitution showed a prescience not found in the Declaration of Independence. It might also be argued, by partial contrast, that theism is implicit in the Constitution in that this document is based on the promissory note delivered in the Declaration of Independence, where theism is explicit. Once again, the interpretive difficulties here are enormous. But this does not mean that one cannot criticize religious skepticism as a half-hearted response to the comprehensive question. Further, the Declaration of Independence explicitly depends more on natural law (which, in turn, depends on theism) than does the Constitution, although the latter may be implicitly reliant on the natural law tradition (*WTP*, 50–52).

Gamwell's desire is to advance the constitutional tradition. In 1787, as is well known, women, blacks, indigenous people, and even poor white males were denied the right to vote. The concessions to slavery at the Constitutional Convention were, on some interpretations, a compromise for the sake of the Union, a compromise that was accepted with the expectation, or at least the hope, that slavery would eventually be abolished. The "abiding character" of the Constitution is worked out processually or advanced *over time*. Popular sovereignty implies politics by way of reason. It implies that the government cannot invalidate by mere stipulation. The importance of reason in Gamwell is most prominent when he suggests that citizens must answer questions like: Is democracy the best form of government? If so, why? These questions lead Gamwell to suspect that the Constitution implies a universal moral principle or an encompassing moral purpose, even if only the Declaration of Independence affirms explicitly such a principle or purpose. Here Gamwell seems to depart from Strauss, who shies away from metaphysical speculations, despite his processual leanings (*WTP*, 53–60).

Lincoln, it should be emphasized, never had a political feeling that did not spring from the sentiments in the Declaration of Independence. Human equality, inalienable rights, and consent of the governed were the bases for all of his political views. The affinity between Lincoln and Gamwell comes into focus when it is realized that Lincoln read the Constitution *through* the Declaration of Independence. In fact, the Declaration of Independence *authorizes* the Constitution. Here Gamwell cites H. L. A. Hart's distinction between a *concept* and a *conception*, a distinction that is analogous to Gamwell's own distinction between formative and constitutive or substantive ideas, respectively. For Hart, a concept is a deep value that conceptions are meant to serve. It can be claimed that the Declaration of Independence states the concept of American liberty, which is more concretely realized in the conceptions of the Constitution. This distinction, as I see things, plays into the hands of Gamwell's levels of abstraction, culminating at the most abstract level in the comprehensive question. It must be admitted that Lincoln, but to a lesser extent than Jefferson, did not always act from pristine motives, but we must take seriously the fact that he continually recurred to a *moral* argument against slavery that soared above party politics and personal ambition. It is also in Lincoln's favor that he was aware of, and felt guilty about, his shortcomings, as argued by John Burt, who in turn is influenced by Rawls. For example, Rawlsian overlapping consensus allows that public values can be shared by several people for different reasons, as we have seen. It should not bother us, therefore, that people were opposed to slavery for quite different reasons and that Lincoln himself opposed slavery for different reasons at different stages of his career. Some of our reasons rely on the better angels of our nature, to use Lincoln's own phrase, some do not (*WTP*, 61–69).

Clearly Lincoln was no (later) Rawlsian in the sense that he, unlike Rawls, believed that human equality was built into the moral (natural) law, which plays only a peripheral (but not nonexistent) role in Rawls's philosophy, as we will see. Justice as authorized by the moral law affirms the substantive moral equality of all citizens, which finds its proper location in politics with consent of the governed. Lincoln's commitment to the Declaration of Independence only makes sense in terms of his religious beliefs in that the moral law, as he saw things, was providential. If humanity was created in the image of God, justice had to be extended to *all* humans. Unfortunately, Lincoln seems to have been a classical theistic fatalist under the influence of Calvinism. On the basis of this view, it seems that God willed the Civil War. Nonetheless, his belief in divine control did not evoke passivity. This may very well have been inconsistent on Lincoln's part, but thankfully so in that he came to see himself as God's unworthy vehicle for saving the Union and for abolishing slavery. Gamwell is helpful in pointing us toward Whitehead's view that each of us is distinctive because each individual makes with each relatively minor choice an all-embracing decision about what gives meaning to everything that we do. We have previously seen that Gamwell refers to this as an original decision, in contrast to the better-known original sin. This decision is incurably solitary and incurably religious. Lincoln seemed to have believed that only God can give life ultimate worth. Further, he thought that the Union should be saved only if it was worth saving (*WTP*, 70–85).

In part because of Lincoln's command of the English language, Lincoln became America's preeminent public theologian; hence his views are worthy of our consideration in the present book. In addition to his commitment to the Declaration's ideals of human equality, inalienable rights, and popular sovereignty, he added the memorable sentiment of "with malice toward none, with charity for all" to our common vocabulary, as exemplified most notably in the life of Martin Luther King Jr. Lincoln is also helpful in supporting one of Gamwell's own abiding achievements: the understanding that purportedly relativizes all human knowledge and morality cannot itself consistently be relativized. The moral law, Lincoln knew, required the abolition of slavery in order to reclaim the Declaration of Independence's authority. Lincoln's theology, of course, is criticizable from a process perspective, especially regarding the idea of an omnipotent God who controls history and who knows the outcome to future "contingencies" before they occur. But these ideas can be rejected while still affirming with Lincoln the processual idea that democratic justice is rooted in divine purpose. If there is no ultimate worth to our lives, Whitehead may very well be correct that they are passing whiffs of insignificance, as I have previously emphasized (Whitehead 1941, 698). The permanence of worth requires a permanent personal reality to which all that we decide makes a difference. On a relativistic basis, there is always the possibility that in some circumstances (e.g., when practiced by indigenous peoples) slavery would be morally permissible. With Lincoln, however, we should defend the claim that slavery is wrong *simpliciter* (*WTP*, 86–90; also see Dombrowski 2024).

We have seen that, for Gamwell, religious freedom has no coherent meaning if religion is theorized as nonrational. In order to shed further light on Gamwell's view, we should consider the thought of Sidney Mead, a noted historian of religion in the United States. Mead, along with Gamwell, thinks that the religious freedom developed at the founding of the United States was one of the most profound revolutions in the history of the church. The recognition of Christianity as the official view of the state lasted in the West from the time of Constantine in the fourth century until at least the eighteenth century. The solidarity of the people in *one* church was long assumed to be necessary for social order. Colonial religious establishments gave way to the presence of religious freedom as a matter of religious *principle*, rather than seeing religious toleration as a merely pragmatic concession to religious pluralism. The practical difficulties involved in a national established church led to theoretical support for religious freedom. Multiple establishments in the individual states were rejected for good *reasons*, even if these reasons were initially appreciated, according to Mead, by only a few thinkers like Jefferson, Madison, and Franklin. The Enlightenment clearly played a large role in the development of these thinkers' views. But these Enlightenment rationalists were not intent on establishing an officially secular state. Rather, the aforementioned essentials in all religions were rational. That is, religious neutrality by the government should not be identified, as it often is, with secularization. It should instead be identified with de-sectarianization (*MRF*, 119–26).

These religious essentials (the importance of a life of virtue, doing good to others, etc.), which bear a resemblance to what was traditionally called the natural law, in effect constitute the democratic ideal *as a religion*, an ideal that was often inculcated into school children as something sacro-sanct. The religion of the republic is the common commitment to seek via democratic discussion both justice *and* the ultimate meaning of the universe (the latter of which is now widely denied). Such discussion requires freedom of speech, including religious speech, such that all opinions could have a hearing (subject to restraints on extreme cases like incitement to immanent violence). Truth, even objective truth, *emerges* processually through exchange of ideas. If the theory of religion as nonrational is correct, then there is not much point to discussing (much less debating) religion at all (*MRF*, 127–34; *DP*, 236).

Gamwell interprets the first amendment to the Constitution as suggesting that, as the only viable alternative to religious establishment (whether religious in the conventional sense or secularistic), there should be creative public discussion about what matters to people. As Gamwell puts the point, "Religious freedom is nothing other than a political expression of the comprehensive question" (*MRF*, 157). That is, "religious freedom constitutes the body politic by the question itself" (*MRF*, 158).

Everyone agrees that at least *some* comprehensive convictions are immune to public assessment, but some scholars go so far as to claim that religious activities cannot be substantially burdened by law unless a compelling state interest cannot be served in a less restrictive way. This leads one to wonder about the extent of religious exemption to drug laws in the case of peyote use in Native American religions, to health laws in the case of conservative religious opposition to contraception and abortion, and to conscription laws in the case of religious pacifism. Gamwell cannot, of course, resolve these thorny issues *as a metaphysician*, but he uses these examples to illustrate the distinction between the content of a comprehensive conviction and the particular cultural formation of signs and symbols with which a given group cultivates this conviction. Another important distinction is between a given comprehensive confession's prescription of a certain activity for its adherents and a given comprehensive confession's prescription for the general public. The latter is not even a plausible candidate for exemption; the former is a possible candidate for exemption from a generally applicable law. In the (in)famous Hobby Lobby case, Gamwell objects to the exemption from the Affordable Care Act because the plaintiff did not appeal to religious prescriptions applicable only to adherents; rather, the plaintiff tried to prescribe for all citizens by declaring the act a bad law. Further, because a democratic constitution is properly formative rather than constitutive, its goal is to establish full and free discourse. Hence, any exemptions to the law should be provided by statute and should not be seen as constitutional essentials (*MN*, 169–73, 178–91).

We have seen that Gamwell affirms free political discussion and debate among responses to the comprehensive question. Although he knows he is risking hyperbole, Gamwell floats the hypothesis that religious freedom *is* the Constitution in the sense that other constitutional prescriptions are stipulations necessary for religious freedom. Or again, religious freedom can be seen as the *only* constitutional principle in the sense that the state is not permitted to answer definitively the comprehensive question; hence the key task of the Constitution is to facilitate responses to this question on the part of citizens and associations. Of course, no full and free debate can be anarchistic; hence there has been a need throughout American intellectual history for the *regulation* of speech, if not its *restriction*. The regulating itself can also be a topic of debate in that there are alternative ways to establish fair procedures, both in the state and in academe. Debates regarding regulation of speech, however, should not get in the way of free speech itself because, as Lincoln held, religious freedom is the democratic way. This view is nonetheless compatible with the claim that the *specifics* regarding how debate is to be organized can be historically variable, at times resembling a Socratic dialogue in the *agora*, at other times like a medieval university disputation, and at still other times like a New England town meeting. (Gamwell is influenced here by Popper.) Perhaps fair online conversations/debates will be in play in the future. The distinction between formal and material conditions of justice seems to remain invariant, however (*MRF*, 161–76).

No doubt it will be objected to Gamwell's philosophy that it is impractical if it requires of all citizens that they become sophisticated philosophers. But Gamwell is not claiming that discourse about the comprehensive question is the only aspect of full and free political discourse, even if it is a necessary (albeit largely neglected) aspect of it. *Someone* should attend to the comprehensive question, especially when it is realized that implicit and inchoate responses to the question abound. Analogously, we cannot expect all citizens to deal with economic problems that only those with doctorates in economics could understand, but it is essential that *someone* deals with these questions. Democracy as such, however, *is* demanding, even for ordinary citizens, in the sense that each has a duty to understand as much as is realistically possible about the issues at hand. In this regard there is the common complaint that in large measure what passes as public debate in contemporary American democracy is sophistic rhetoric, systematically distorted communication, or even outright mendacity (*MRF*, 180–83).

As was argued in the previous chapter, it is sometimes hard to see the gap that Gamwell sees between his own stance and Rawls's views. For example, for the sake of argument one can grant Gamwell's position that it is legitimate for the state in some circumstances to say that it is fighting a just war, but it would not be legitimate for the state to claim that the war was required by divine command. Rawls agrees. Not only just war, but also opposition to racial discrimination, the duty to pay taxes, and rules regarding the market are noncomprehensive prescriptions. Here Gamwell is tempted, however, to agree with Robert Bellah that there is something called "civil religion," which contains certain affirmations regarding human authenticity that are different from those in any particular disestablished religion. Here Gamwell and Bellah and Rawls sound like the founders regarding "the essentials" of religion, which are the bases of civic virtue. (There is a stronger version of civil religion in Bellah that seems to be rejected by Gamwell because it *does* attribute an answer to the comprehensive question by the state.) The development of civic virtue is especially needed when the belief becomes widespread that politics is essentially or primarily a conflict of power, when mere assertion replaces argument. When such a belief becomes widespread, the aforementioned distorted communication and mendacity become more popular and are accepted with a shrug of the shoulders. That is, civility is the key virtue of democratic citizens who are committed to the common good. Gamwell sums up his view succinctly in the following terms (*MRF*, 185–204):

> The democratic resolution is, we may conclude, both separationist and religionist in the following senses: All religions are separated from the state in the sense that the state may not explicitly endorse any answer to the comprehensive question. At the same time, religion is essential to the body politic in the sense that political decisions should imply the valid comprehensive conviction. Politics is consistent in principle with a plurality of legitimate religions because they are united through democratic discourse. (*MRF*, 205)

Obviously, a major feature of American intellectual history is the prominence of human rights, which is not at all at odds with Gamwell's teleological approach, despite what some critics might allege. Maximal flourishing in the future for the greatest number actually *requires* a strong role for deontological constraints. Gamwell's main criticism of the Kantian deontological tradition in ethics, once again, concerns the partialist fallacy wherein it might be assumed that the important *part* played by rights or deontological constraints is the whole story. But the idea that the human rights of the innocent can be easily cancelled is strongly counterintuitive, according to Gamwell, and puts most of our prior commitments in ethics into disequilibrium. Our prime duty is indeed to maximize the good, but this duty, it will be remembered, is an imperfect one (in the Kantian sense) that both allows for elbow room on the part of the moral agent and offers protection of basic rights, especially those of the innocent: "Pursuit of the maximal good permits actions in violation of certain guiding rules only in rare circumstances." Or again, "act in accord with the guiding rules . . . except in rare circumstances" (*EG* 118). In the relevant sense, "rare" refers to circumstances in which the greater good is clearly served by acting against the rules, as in some well-known *in extremis* cases (see Walzer 1977, 157–58). In effect, Gamwell asks us to think in a more nuanced way than the manner in which ethics has been taught in recent decades, where teleologists ground morality in some good to be maximized *simpliciter* and deontologists assert adherence to principles whatever the consequences (*EG*, 115–19).

The pursuit of maximal creativity in the future is a common enterprise that implies *and is implied by* a social practice of respect for all subjects. As before, the principle of communicative respect is transcendental in that it is necessary for the moral enterprise itself. If one *claims* to be released from the duty to communicative respect, one simultaneously affirms it as universally applicable. Belief in the comprehensive good and belief in communicative respect mutually reinforce each other. Some human rights are nonmetaphysical and depend on the understanding of certain social practices, but the principle of communicative respect itself is transcendental in the sense that it is implied in the very effort to understand and enhance the common world of relations among subjects maximizing the creative possibilities of all. It is hard to make sense of our moral hopes and strivings without an original belief in our relation to the good, which we have seen Gamwell refer to as an original decision, in contrast to original sin. Religion can be seen as a cultural formation wherein adherents explicitly affirm such a decision. A true religion, on this account "is one that decisively represents in this way our original belief in our existence as a coenactment of the divine and thus a communion with God, who empowers us to decide for maximal creativity in the future as such and, thereby, to maximize our worth to the all-inclusive and ever-enriching unity of all things" (*EG*, 126, also 120–25). By contrast, the consensus for the past few centuries has been that democratic principles are properly separated from *any* understanding of existence or reality as such. This consensus is at odds with "the original decision." Although Rawls is the primary example of this consensus who is engaged by Gamwell, Jeffrey Stout is another American thinker who energizes Gamwell's view, both positively and negatively. Stout tries to defend democracy without metaphysics. But Stout is opposed both to Rawlsian contractarianism and to "the new traditionalism" of thinkers like Alasdair MacIntyre, John Milbank, and Stanley Hauerwas. These latter thinkers encourage in different ways withdrawal from liberal political participation. Gamwell shows himself to be thoroughly ensconced within the American political tradition by energetically discouraging such a withdrawal. A distinction in Stout that Gamwell finds productive is that between secular*ism* and secularized discourse in politics. The latter does not necessarily indicate a commitment to secularism as a comprehensive doctrine. It only indicates an abandonment of the assumption that one can take for granted that one's interlocutors in political discourse understand religion the way you do. They may very well have no understanding of religion at all or have only a very rudimentary understanding of it. In fact, the secularized norms of discourse allow discussion of secular*ism*. In regard to this distinction between secular*ism* and secularized discourse in politics, we should notice how similar Gamwell *and* Stout are to Rawls, their pro-testations to the contrary notwithstanding. What Gamwell especially likes in Stout is emphasis of the idea that, in contrast to the new traditionalists, with their authoritative texts and/or authoritative interpretations of texts, democracy itself has its *own* tradition that deserves our attention. It also has its own well-known characteristic virtues (*EG*, 127–34).

The stumbling block between Gamwell and Stout is precisely the lat-ter's opposition to metaphysics, a discipline that Stout sees as fruitless. The present book is intended to show what some of the fruits of metaphysical discourse might be. For example, in an attempt to defend himself against the charge of relativism, Stout distinguishes between justification and truth, with metaphysicians committed to defending truth and pragmatists like Stout resting content with justified belief. But Gamwell wonders about the status of this very distinction. Is *it* true? Stout implies that it is, thereby contradicting himself. Stout has no objection to some uses of "truth" in everyday discourse, where the term often functions in a cautionary way to avoid disaster, but he is skeptical of the term when used as part of a cor-respondence theory with no explanatory value. In a way, Stout is trying to operate on a strictly negative view of truth (i.e., truth as *not* correspondence), but one wonders along with Gamwell what this amounts to. It should be noted that, if there *could* be a successful metaphysical argument, then there *must* be metaphysical backing to political thought at the most abstract. level. This is because metaphysical principles cannot be absent unless they are necessarily absent, contra the assumption of Stout in his contingency-driven version of nonmetaphysical pragmatism, as such is presented within secularized democratic debate (*EG*, 135–43).

Stout's view can be criticized in the following way: to assert the absence of metaphysical conditions anywhere is *itself* to imply a metaphysical claim, the metaphysical assertion that *no* metaphysical assertions are true. It is Gamwell's belief that every attempt to defend democratic norms without metaphysics (like Stout's attempt) refutes itself by implying metaphysical conditions of politics. Making explicit what is implicit in any practical inference is incomplete without a statement of its necessary conditions. Getting clear on this point is needed if Stout's and Gamwell's common project of refuting the new traditionalists is to succeed. The problem with the new traditionalists is that they do not think that understandings of reality or of politics are possible by way of reasoned adjudication: "If differing beliefs about the most basic principles of political belief are beyond the reach of argumentative assessment, a political community inclusive of this plurality can avoid sheer coercion by the stronger only so long as adherents of each find some other form of decision making strategically acceptable" (*EG*, 161, also 144–46, 192). However, there is nothing hyperbolic in Gamwell's affirmation of the reach of rational argumentation.

CHAPTER TWELVE

Community

Because Gamwell wishes to defend a version of political liberalism (specifically *reformed* liberalism based on a *public view* of religious freedom), it will be worthwhile to respond to two influential criticisms of political liberalism: C. B. Macpherson's view that liberalism is a ruse for possessive individualism and Michael Sandel's view that liberalism involves a retreat from community (and morality). This defense of Gamwell will emphasize the importance of community (and cognate concepts) in his thought as well as the degree to which Gamwell's view is more similar to Rawls's view than Gamwell is often willing to admit; hence careful attention will again be paid to Rawls in this chapter. That is, Rawls and Gamwell can serve to mutually illuminate and support each other.

Perhaps the safest characterization of Gamwell's and Rawls's view of community (or social union) is that their stance is a moderate one between two extremes. At one extreme is a weak sense of community found in Hobbesian stances wherein there is a *modus vivendi* established between contesting parties that do not share a sense of justice. This is merely an expedient truce that is meant to halt hostilities among the contesting parties; hence it is an inadequate basis for stability over time in that if one of the contesting parties got the upper hand, the truce could be broken and the party with the greatest threat advantage could, in effect, ram its views down the throats of everyone else. At the other extreme are Aristotelian stances that prescribe a unity constituted by widespread acceptance of a particular conception of the good life or of what Rawls calls a comprehensive doctrine. These views can be called weak and strong communitarianism, respectively.

The moderate stance found in Gamwell and Rawls is that of a *political* community wherein there is widespread acceptance by the population of a certain conception of *justice* (contra Hobbesian views), but where there is not widespread acceptance of any particular view of the *good* or of any particular comprehensive doctrine (contra Aristotelian views). This political community in Rawls's *Political Liberalism* comes about through an overlapping consensus regarding justice among people who affirm (very often uncompromisingly) different conceptions of the good. This means that Rawlsian political community may very well be affirmed by people for somewhat different reasons. But Rawlsian community, like Gamwell's, is indeed affirmed for moral reasons, in contrast to the reasons of expediency that characterize Hobbesian views.

One consequence of this view is that Aristotelian or strong communitarianism (often in popular discourse referred to simply as communitarianism), which has a state-endorsed conception of the good life, should be abandoned in a condition of pervasive pluralism regarding the comprehensive doctrines that citizens affirm. Comprehensive doctrines apply to many topics other than political justice. Rawls is happy to affirm a consensus regarding the latter only, given the wide array of comprehensive doctrines: utilitarianism, various types of perfectionism, various (and sometimes contentious) religious conceptions of the good, Marxism, hedonism, et cetera. The hope is that we could attain a political community that could accommodate diversity by removing many difficult philosophical/religious issues from the political agenda, in Rawls's case, or that we would open the comprehensive question to public debate while simultaneously prohibiting the state from establishing any particular response to this question as *the* official one, in Gamwell's case.

The task of political philosophy in such a community is to analyze and give a coherent linguistic formulation to popular culture in constitutional democracy. In periods of turmoil political philosophy may be highlighted more than when there is a stable concept of justice at work in political institutions and in popular culture, when the work of politicians, journalists, and others comes to the fore. One is reminded of Thomas Kuhn's famous distinction between revolutionary and normal science, respectively. The important thing is that toleration on the ground be widespread and a matter of intuitive conviction on the part of citizens, given the fact of pervasive pluralism. That is, one need not have an *established* answer to the comprehensive question in order to have political community and agreement about justice, as Gamwell would agree.

The thesis of the present chapter is that the aforementioned moderate Gamwellian and Rawlsian view of community is worthy of explication and defense. This explication and defense will occur over several stages in that I will first deal with the topic of individuation through community, then move to the complementarity among citizens that characterizes a just society. The communal virtues will be considered along with the importance of the Rawlsian difference principle, with which Gamwell agrees, for the concept of community. We will see that justice as fairness is by no means opposed to the importance of community. The chapter ends with a consideration of the relationship between communal love/benevolence and Gamwellian and Rawlsian justice.

There is a communitarian strand to Gamwell's and Rawls's theory of justice due to the fact that the very constitution of the individuals requires cooperation and a sense of mutuality and reciprocity. Members of the community as a result must share in the distribution of benefits as stipulated in Rawls's famous two (actually three) principles of justice. Far from endorsing the "unencumbered self" so often ascribed to his theory (especially by Sandel), Rawls, as well as Gamwell in *BP*, emphasizes the individual's membership in a family and various associations that form the individual's character, for good or for ill. It comes as a surprise to some readers that Rawls thinks of the *social* basis of self-respect as the most important primary good (Rawls 1971, 440). A person's endeavors need to be at least implicitly appreciated by others in a shared community of interests in order to confirm such self-respect. Self-respect involves not merely (and not primarily) one's own norms, but also (and primarily) the norms that are anchored in familial or communal bodies.

It is a mistake to depict the famous liberalism-communitarianism debate as a conflict between an individual's judgment and society. This is because the ends an individual chooses are already intertwined with others' approval. Perhaps an Emersonian self would be willing to stand up for its moral independence regardless of what a community of shared interests might think, but this is not the Gamwellian or Rawlsian view. It is true that Gamwell and Rawls defend vigorously *political* autonomy, but not a *comprehensive* autonomy that is destructive of associative ties. A community of shared interests provides standards of worthiness that are crucial to the primary good of self-respect. It is membership in a community of shared interests that fosters self-esteem, not the other way around. That is, the issue of whether the self is prior to its ends or vice versa involves a blurred distinction. A developed sense of justice requires the presence of (familial and associative) others (Rawls 1971, 462–79). In this regard we should not exaggerate the alleged difference between supposed liberal ("Western") individualism and the communitarian self that is found in various nonliberal cultures.

Before individuals choose the sort of persons they want to be, they have already been shaped by communal values. In this regard even the Rawls of *A Theory of Justice* had anticipated Sandel's critique. We are historical individuals who are parts of some social tradition such that only in social union is an individual complete (Rawls 1971, 525). Community is not a mere attribute of an individual but is partially constitutive of the process of individuation. If the *social* basis of self-respect is secured, it is more likely that citizens will engage in genuine Gamwellian mutuality and be willing to reciprocate with others in a system of mutual benefit. In turn, this willingness makes it more likely that society can be organized in such a way that the demands of the two (really three) Rawlsian principles of justice will actually be met, principles with which Gamwell largely agrees (*DP*, chs. 5–6).

Given what has been said thus far, a sketch of Gamwellian and Rawlsian responses to strong communitarian critiques can be seen. Sandel seems to miss altogether moderate communitarianism largely because it is not the strong sort that Sandel himself defends. That is, Sandel assumes a definition of "community" that is too restrictive. MacIntyre worries that without strong communitarianism justice cannot be sustained, in which case there is not much hope for contemporary democracies, given the fact that there are competing concepts of the good and comprehensive doctrines that citizens affirm. But democracies *do* thrive in the contemporary world, even when threatened by autocrats. This continued success of liberal democracy should call into question the assumption that strong communitarianism is a necessary condition for democracy to flourish. And Charles Taylor contends, in partial agreement with Gamwell, that liberalism itself *is* a conception of the good, thus implying that Rawlsian justice itself *is* a comprehensive doctrine. But the qualities stipulated of the parties in the Rawlsian original position are not intended as clues regarding a comprehensive view of human nature any more than the need for political autonomy is an implicit way of sneaking in comprehensive autonomy. Rawls is doing something very specific in his political philosophy and is not trying to replace the wider aims of comprehensive doctrines, which are tolerated, and even encouraged or required, in a condition of reasonable pluralism, as we have seen.

Thus far I have tried to call attention to two points (in reverse order): (1) A citizen's sense of justice and conception of the good presuppose habituation into some communal values at the familial and associational levels. And (2), due to the pervasive pluralism of conceptions of the good and comprehensive doctrines in contemporary societies, strong communitarianism can hold sway at the societal level only through the illegitimate use of force. Nonetheless there can be a *political* community based on a common view of justice, rather than a common view of the good, even if Gamwell is to be commended for defending at a very abstract level the view that *the* good is presupposed by any comparative moral judgment (*DP*, ch. 3). Moderate communitarian justice can more accurately be described as a (just) social union of (particular communal) social union*s* (Rawls 1971, 527, 529; 1996, 201, 304, 323).

Any social union, including that found in the original position, involves complementarity, which Rawls analogizes to the musical players in a symphony orchestra (Rawls 1971, 524; 1996, 321). Each player could have learned to play well every instrument in the orchestra, but each becomes proficient on a single instrument due to the difficulty involved in learning them all. The word "symphony" itself literally means to sound together, to harmonize together, despite individual differences among the players. The orchestra metaphor evokes the democratic harmonic resolution of any tension between individual and society. Behind the veil of ignorance, as it were, each participant could theoretically play any instrument, but in reality each has to rely on the other players to complement individual insufficiencies. When the veil—on this metaphor, a curtain—lifts, we can play together in an aesthetically pleasing way, a view that is congenial to Gamwell (see *BP*, 108–14).

As is well known, over time Rawls became somewhat dissatisfied with the shape his theory of justice had originally taken. The principles of justice in *A Theory of Justice* were seen as parts of an overarching moral theory. A society based on them would be stable because all reasonable and rational people would agree with them. Rawls came to see that a better concept of stability was needed, which led in *Political Liberalism* to the idea of overlapping consensus. We have seen that this idea operates even in a condition of pluralism with respect to comprehensive doctrines, yet nonetheless provides a greater sense of community than the weak Hobbesian sort found in a *modus vivendi*. Overlapping consensus is admittedly not deep, but this is a commendable feature in that overlapping consensus *is*, as a result of its not being deep but wide, conducive to widespread agreement regarding justice in a democratic society. Gamwell's view, I contend, can be made compatible with that of the later Rawls *so long as* the deep comprehensive question is asked and responded to at some point (*MRF*, ch. 3).

Establishing terms for social cooperation for mutual benefit remains Gamwell's and Rawls's primary concern, but the principles of justice are now seen more accurately in *Political Liberalism* as political, rather than as comprehensive. These principles function as modules that can be inserted into various comprehensive doctrines with their deeper communal ties. This is a point that serves to reconcile Gamwell and Rawls. Even if citizens disagree strenuously regarding some particular issue or piece of legislation, they may nonetheless be members committed to political community in that the community in question centers on the basic framework of a just society and on institutional essentials, rather than on various concrete particulars. Stability for the right reasons requires that commitment to this framework not be a mere *modus vivendi*, but a matter of *principled* conviction so as to secure political community and the complementarity involved in such community.

In addition to the criticism of liberal political philosophers not being sufficiently committed to community, it is also common to hear that they do not pay sufficient attention to the virtues. However, it is important to note the distinction between two sorts of virtue: political virtues and those linked to the relatively nonpolitical lives of citizens with their separate comprehensive doctrines. Liberal political philosophers are especially interested in the *political* virtues: toleration of reasonable differences, civility, a sense of fairness, and reasonableness itself. Further, Gamwell (especially in *BP*) and Rawls note the importance of the virtues connected with the socialization process of citizens in families and associations (including neighborhoods and sports teams and churches). That is, socialization into a virtuous life of some sort may be needed in order to eventually have mature citizens capable of the political virtues. But a just society cannot expect all citizens to develop those virtues that are idiosyncratic to some comprehensive doctrines but not others, as in theological virtues found in some religions but not others and certainly not in the lives of religious skeptics. Faith is a prime example here. In different terms, the common good of common goods that characterizes a just society *requires* the political virtues that are essential parts of the societal common good, in general, but only *permits* those found in the more specific common goods at the associational level of differing comprehensive doctrines.

In a limited sense, liberal neutrality extends to both communities and virtues, although a just state is not neutral regarding the need for political virtues nor regarding the need to develop cooperative virtues within familial and associational life, a development that, like capital, can accumulate over time (Rawls 1996, 157). One thinks here of the way that both churches and youth sport teams inculcate the virtues of respect for others, sportspersonship, and team cooperation. It would be a gross error to think that Gamwell or Rawls privatize virtue in that "the personal" is by no means synonymous with "the private." Indeed, well-ordered societies *depend on* the existence of citizens who have developed the communal virtues, both the cooperative virtues developed within the context of one's familial/associational life and the political virtues per se (*BP*, 114–22).

Liberal political community consists in a social union of social unions. This idea, when tethered to the famous difference principle, defended as well by Gamwell, as we have seen, gives rise to questions regarding how this view will bring about and/or sustain community when principles of justice are, in turn, tethered to some economic system or other (see *DP*, 304–20). A social union of social unions is meant to deflect the charge that political liberals cannot account for the value of community, but Rawls is acutely aware of the fact that our communal or social nature can be easily trivialized (Rawls 1971, 456–59). After all, not even egoists can learn to speak or even to develop their own egoistic concerns outside of specific communities. Genuine human sociability requires the difference principle rather than the "privatized" society that finds its natural habitat in theories that are overly enthusiastic about competitive markets (see *BP*, ch. 1). Gamwell and Rawls argue for a complementary good for all. Rawls offers various mechanisms, seemingly agreeable as well to Gamwell, meant to hold in check instrumental market relations that get in the way of political community, especially the difference principle and the public funding of elections so as to combat the curse of money (Rawls 1971, 226, 275, 302; 1996, lviii–lvix, 235, 328, 357–60; *PCV*, 88–99; *BTP*, ch. 3, 8).

However, the nature of a just society requires further specification regarding what sort of economic system could bring this about. Here I would like to emphasize the fact that, although Gamwell and Rawls provide only limited support for meritocratic notions, they do not offer a blanket repudiation of them. In fact, the general ideas of merit and desert are so central to our judgments and practices that their complete elimination would put everything else we believe in ethics into disequilibrium. The question is not "Do people sometimes deserve differential treatment based on differences in character or performance?" (they do), but rather "Do people deserve unequal and unjust income or power based solely or primarily on these?" (they do not). That is, informal practices of praise and blame can easily be brought into equilibrium with liberal political community. Citizens in a just society are motivated to participate in political and economic systems that are consistently aimed at providing *everyone* with the means to exercise and develop their capacities of self-determination and Gamwellian creativity. We want to make sure, however, that goods that might be idealized at the high end do not generate conditions in which many people cannot secure more modest goods that are essential for such flourishing (see Dombrowski 2011, ch. 4; *PCV*, 150–61).

The purpose of the present chapter is to explore the concept of community or, to use a roughly synonymous designation, the common good. It will no doubt be objected that political liberalism is basically a political philosophy meant to justify toleration, but toleration is not enough. Critics might wonder where the liberal notion of community or the common good is to be found. These critics might not be willing to buy into political liberalism without a clear indication of how this view is conducive to community or the common good. David Hollenbach provides a prominent example of this sort of skepticism. To achieve a polis, it will be alleged, and here Gamwell would agree with Hollenbach, one needs to do more than show toleration and a live-and-let-live attitude that avoids introducing concepts of the full human good into political discourse. The liberal method of avoidance is part of a commendable hope to neutralize potential conflicts, but, according to Hollenbach, what we need is the realization that a human being is, as Aristotle suggested, a political animal (*zoon politikon*), although Hollenbach does not seem to notice that Rawls and Gamwell also in a way agree with this claim (Hollenbach 1998, 8).

Hollenbach assumes that political liberalism violates the communitarian nature of religious and other groups by placing us in an "individualistic isolation" that "is finally a prison." The question seems to be, from the perspective of political liberalism, whether the call received by, say, religious communities (which in itself is perfectly compatible with liberal justice) means that the whole body politic is being called. Another question is whether the reasonableness required to participate in the original position, and the resulting principles of justice that are agreeable to Gamwell, can plausibly be described as leading to "individualistic isolation." Nonetheless common ground between Hollenbach and political liberalism, including both

Gamwell and Rawls, can be established when Hollenbach rightly emphasizes that justice is the premier social virtue.

We have seen that two sorts of community or common good or solidarity should be distinguished: (1) the common good as established through some singular comprehensive religious (or philosophical) doctrine; and (2) the common good as established through a pervasive willingness to abide by fair terms of agreement among people with different comprehensive religious (or philosophical) doctrines. The latter is a type of community or solidarity—indeed a type of love or a type of metacommunity—largely ignored by Hollenbach.

Hollenbach, like Gamwell, sees a shift in Rawls from the Kantian character of *A Theory of Justice* to the pragmatist character of *Political Liberalism*, where, he alleges, the original position has been largely replaced by the historical presuppositions of Western constitutional democracy. Hollenbach is on thin ice here for two reasons. First, Rawls explicitly retains the original position in *Political Liberalism*; and second, the presuppositions of Western constitutional democracy were not absent in *A Theory of Justice* (see, e.g., Rawls 1996, 50, 54, 116, 304–10; 1971, 195, 222, 226, 243, 295, 354–57, 360, 363, 382–86, 492). There is some legitimacy in Hollenbach's (and Gamwell's) point here, however, when it is noticed that the theory of justice in *Political Liberalism* is not intended as an argumentative coup de grace directed at those who do not already share the propositions of Western constitutional democracy (see Hollenbach 1994, 133–34; *MRF*, ch. 3).

Rawls is not claiming, as Hollenbach alleges, that presuppositions about the common or ultimate good are "private," because the ideals of churches and other communal associations are certainly "public" at least within the church or association, and perhaps are public in a more general sense if they overlap with the comprehensive doctrines of others. Virtue and justice, as Hollenbach correctly notes, become matters of cooperation among people with conflicting views of community; and human rights are the necessary conditions for such cooperation, as Gamwell agrees (*MRF*, ch. 8).

Hollenbach's fear is that political liberalism would not provide such a space, nor would it help to resolve disputes regarding the common good if political liberalism really does involve a commitment to the method of avoidance. In fairness to Gamwell and Rawls, it should be emphasized that they are not prohibiting critical engagement with others who have different views of community or the common good from one's own. Indeed, they (especially Gamwell!) encourage such engagement. What we should not do *in politics*, however, is establish any *particular* communal religious (or philosophical) comprehensive doctrine, not even one that is reasonable. *This is what is meant by "avoidance."* It may well be the case that Rorty's (in contrast to Gamwell's and Rawls's) version of liberalism fosters indifference to the truth of all moral and religious claims; hence Hollenbach should rightly fear Rorty's view because in the long run it may very well threaten the dignity of persons. That is, because of Rorty's rejection of the correspondence theory of truth, he also rejects the truth of all moral and religious claims, whereas Gamwell and Rawls are open to the truth of such claims. Further, according to Gamwell, because such claims are often mutually exclusive, we can know that some of them *must be* false (*DG*, 94–114).

Political liberalism not only permits different views of community or the common good, it *encourages* them, but only when they are expressed appropriately, reasonably. The forms of permissible public reason are always several, especially regarding controversial issues. And they are very often in flux as new variations are proposed and some older views are no longer represented. Communitarian beliefs that are parts of some comprehensive doctrine are welcome in the political arena *as long as* they are reasonable in liberal terms. This suggests that some comprehensive communal views—whether religious or nonreligious—are not reasonable, but hegemonic, dogmatic, and unfair. Rawls's idea of the traditional view of the common good seems to be derived primarily from Thomas Aquinas himself and from the more recent Thomistic perspectives offered by Jacques Maritain and John Finnis. That is, the political liberal's view of the common good is not an ersatz addition to modern or postmodern individualism, but is rooted in ideas that can be traced back to the premodern period (see Dombrowski 2022). However, Gamwell and Rawls are well aware of the changes that have occurred in the natural law tradition that have informed much that has been said about strong communitarianism. Likewise, they are open to changes that may have to occur in the future regarding political liberalism, although it is extremely unlikely that pluralism of communities or comprehensive doctrines will go away any time in the near future (*MN*, 123–29).

The relationship between Gamwell and Rawls, on the one hand, and Aristotle and Aquinas, on the other, is complicated. Aristotle's influential eudaemonistic perfectionism is connected to his commitment to community or the common good (*DG*, 19–29). This commitment is compatible with political liberalism as long as it is expressed in terms of *political* values, rather than in terms of a particular community or a particular comprehensive doctrine. In the latter case it is subject to the restrictions on comprehensive doctrines, in general, that are required in a condition of reasonable pluralism.

Nevertheless, Rawls acknowledges that Aristotle's treatment of happiness as an inclusive end for a human life (rather than as a dominant end) is the most influential in the history of philosophy and even influences Rawls's own treatment of a rational plan of life (Rawls 1971, 481). Aristotle's perfectionism led him to affirm only one reasonable and rational good; institutions were justifiable to the extent that they promoted this good, on Rawls's interpretation of Aristotle (Rawls 1996, 134).

Gamwell's and Rawls's views of community are also related to Thomas Aquinas's view in a complicated way. Justice is a complex of three ideas—liberty, equality, and reward for services contributing to the common good (once primary goods are fulfilled regardless of contribution)—and these ideas are compatible with Thomas Aquinas's political philosophy. But Thomas Aquinas failed to draw out the implicit egalitarianism of these three ideas. What is needed is not merely the announcement of these ideas, but also their interpretation and application. In a similar way, Rawls's view is compatible with Thomas Aquinas's stance regarding the dignity of the human person when it is expressed as a political conception of the person, rather than in terms of a particular comprehensive doctrine. Regarding the latter, Thomists tend to say that all human beings desire, even if unknown to themselves, the vision of God, just as Platonists tend to say that all human beings desire a vision of the good. Political liberalism sets aside comprehensive accounts of human nature such as these, although it should be noted that it permits them as long as they are reasonable. Indeed, Gamwell and Rawls encourage them at the associational and personal levels (*EG*, 171–77).

Gamwell's and Rawls's view is especially at odds with Thomas Aquinas's (and the Protestant reformers') stance that there is only one reasonable and rational established good such that political institutions are justifiable to the extent that they promote this good. On this basis, intoleration of those who impede this good is justifiable. This sort of intoleration, which is based on (very often dogmatic) confidence in one's own comprehensive doctrine, is different from (very often reluctant) intoleration based on a concern for justice in a liberal society (Rawls 1971, 189–90; 1996, 34). Likewise, in Rawls's later works comprehensive liberalism, in contrast to political liberalism, is a type of utopian communitarianism in the pejorative sense and is no better than the comprehensive religious views of Thomas Aquinas or Martin Luther; but Rawls anticipated this point even in *A Theory of Justice* in his rejection of the communitarianism found in the "omnicompetent laicist state" (Rawls 1971,186). Rawls nonetheless agrees with Thomas Aquinas on the common good when simpler cases are involved, concerning which reasonable people do not disagree (e.g., that cruelty is wrong). Here he is also in agreement with philosophers who have been positively influenced by Thomas Aquinas like Philippa Foot (Rawls 1971, 350–51). That is, the importance of natural duty in Rawls (Rawls 1971, 293–301) indicates an overlap with Thomas Aquinas's view of natural duty, although in Rawls's case natural duty is affirmed without a metaphysical account of its underlying basis, as would be desired by Gamwell (see *EG*, 101–7).

It should now be clear that political liberalism includes a view of community or the common good in several senses, including a basic concern for reasonable regulations to maintain interest in public order, health, and safety. And the difference principle demands that those who are more advantaged than others cannot say that they should be permitted to acquire benefits that do not contribute to the welfare of others; their natural or social advantages should be seen in political liberalism as part of a common inheritance in that they are not deserved. So also, and this point is almost always neglected in criticisms of justice as fairness, we are not to illegitimately gain from the cooperative labors of others by avoiding doing our fair share. Laziness is as morally bothersome, it seems, as unreasonably gaining by virtue of traits we do not deserve. Egoism comes in many forms. Luckily in a fair decision-making procedure no one would agree to egoism (Rawls 1971, 97, 104, 112, 119, 240). Here Gamwell is in complete agreement with Rawls (*PCV*, 88–99, especially 92).

In Gamwell and Rawls it makes sense to require sacrifices from citizens in times of social emergency when all must pitch in for the communal good. But this is a tricky point because what may be required *in extremis* is not necessarily a helpful guide regarding normal circumstances. For example, if one entered a burning building and only had time to save one of two people inside, one's own child and one's neighbor, one would surely be justified in saving one's child. But this does not mean that in other circumstances it would be legitimate to harvest organs from the neighbor so as to save the life of one's child with a deadly disease. So also, the fact that we can require sacrifices of citizens in emergencies for the sake of the common good does not necessarily mean that in other circumstances we can adopt in political philosophy a comprehensive utilitarian view wherein some citizens' life prospects are routinely sacrificed for the sake of the life prospects of others (Rawls 1971, 178; *DP*, 132, 140, 305).

This criticism of utilitarianism, that when it is made into a political philosophy it often requires sacrifices on the part of individuals for the sake of the communal good that are disrespectful of those individuals, is not an attack on the very notion of Gamwellian teleology or of the communal good. The public good or the communal good is equivalent to that enshrined in the medieval maxim that what touches all concerns all. This maxim should be taken seriously and declared as the public intention as long as the government does not aim at the common good in an exploitative way. Political liberalism certainly permits utilitarianism as a reasonable comprehensive philosophical doctrine, but it is not to be equated with a defensible *political* philosophy (see Rawls 1971, 222–25, 233). Further, we have seen previously that Gamwell's very abstract teleological view is not to be confused with utilitarianism (*EG*, 191).

Since bitter dissensions exist in politics (think of paramilitary groups or sharp religious antagonisms), sometimes liberty has to be restricted if it conflicts with the common good *in the sense that* such liberty violates the fair terms of agreement that would arise as a result of an impartial decision-making procedure. But intolerant sects are not a permanent aspect of political life; just institutions can, over time, eliminate or at least mitigate their intolerance. In what comes closest to Rawls's definition of the communal good, which is very much compatible with Gamwell's view, he says, "The common good I think of as certain general conditions that are in an appropriate sense equally to everyone's advantage" (Rawls 1971, 246, also 130, 242–43, 245, 258–59). Although Rawls is skeptical as to whether a definition can settle any fundamental question, from this definition of the common good we can see that for Rawls the common good is largely connected to the original position and to the principles that would be agreed to there and to the contents of overlapping consensus. He leaves open the choice between a private property economy and a soft socialist one, but either way a just society would have to be one that fostered the equality, opportunity, and difference principles and hence legitimate community or the common good. Once again, here Gamwell is very much in agreement with Rawls (*DP*, ch. 6).

Political liberalism has a central place for the value of community, but it is best not to rely on either an undefined loose concept of community or an aggressive view of community as an organic whole with a life of its own distinct from, and superior to, that of its members. Community or the common good is best served when everyone is treated fairly, when basic goods are distributed equally, and when unequal shares of other goods are open to all and to everyone's advantage, especially the least advantaged. These are both formal and material conditions for the just Gamwellian society, contra the claim that the liberal's view of community or the common good is purely formal (*DP*, ch. 4, 6).

In the effort to support the common good certain "externalities" will be produced that counteract the very communal good that is the goal, as in negative environmental impact produced by public utilities or private enterprise. One essential task of government is to institute the necessary corrections (Rawls 1971, 264–68; *DP*, 284, 286, 305, 313). The idea that political rule is established solely or primarily on human propensity to self-interest is not, as Gamwell sees things, a defensible view (see *BP*). Once again, either a private property or a socialist society (or, what might be best, some hybrid economic system) could do well or poorly in preventing injustices and damage to the environment. The key is to have the economic system that is in place adhere to the principles of justice that are found in the original position (Rawls 1971, 271).

Concerning certain public goods, the market has historically failed altogether, and regarding the freedom of citizens to have a choice of careers (and of comprehensive doctrines) collectivist varieties of socialism, with their forced and central direction of labor and ideology, have a rather dismal track record. In fact, command societies in general seem to be inconsistent with the liberties that citizens can legitimately expect. In this regard a system of markets that decentralizes the exercise of economic power is to be commended, a decentralization that may very well require strong antitrust intervention on the part of the state. In any event, as Gamwell argues, there are limits to what any philosophical view of justice can accomplish when trying to detail the economic and political machinery in advance. It is nonetheless crucial to indicate how a liberal regime, whether under a soft socialist or a capitalist market-oriented or a mixed economy, fosters community or the communal good, contra Hollenbach (see Rawls 1971, 272, 274, 280), and maximizes Gamwellian creativity (*DP*, 122–31, also ch. 4).

Acceptance of the principles of justice forges the bonds of civic friendship that are conducive to community or the common good in a constitutional democracy. These bonds are important when it is realized that no one person can do everything she is capable of doing. Everyone must select a course of life with the confidence that others will do the remaining tasks necessary for life lived at a high level. It is through the social union based on the needs and potentialities of others that each person can benefit from the assets of all collectively. In this regard we are once again led to imagine a community of humankind spread over time on the analogy of orchestra musicians, each one of whom could have trained to play any instrument in the orchestra, but by a kind of implicit agreement perfected skills on one instrument to help realize the powers of all in their joint performance.

It is only in such a tacit Gamwellian social union that any individual is complete (see Rawls 1971, 517, 523–25; 1996, 204, 321; *DP*, 185–209).

The development of science, art, religion, and culture itself can be thought of in analogous terms to the above orchestra example. There is a shared final end emphasized by Gamwell that is nonetheless arrived at through free activity of individuals. These are not examples of perfectionism in the strong sense, however, in that the assessment of excellences in each of these examples takes place within a democratic context. There are many types of social union. A well-ordered and just society is in effect a social union of social unions in which the regulative principle is that each citizen wants others to act from principles that would be agreed to in an initial condition of equality. But the larger social plan that contains many smaller plans or social unions does *not* establish a dominant end in politics, as in the greatest excellence of culture or a religious superunity. It is rather a social union (or common good or community) of social unions (or common goods or communities) in which each can participate as a free and equal member (Rawls 1971, 526–29, 569; *WTP*, 96–99).

A conception of the good is ultimately connected to some (relatively) comprehensive religious or philosophical doctrine, as Gamwell urges. Each conception of the good, it should be noted, is not fixed, but develops as the persons holding it mature over the course of life. A shared political life does not necessarily require a shared comprehensive doctrine, nor does it require a Kantian comprehensive autonomy, but only a commitment to *political* autonomy in a context where pluralism is a given, and where reasonable people seek common ground. Such a search is what justice as fairness is all about. The procedures developed very often appear to be neutral, and are intended as such, but there are also substantive claims at work in liberal proceduralism (as in the desirability of political equality, autonomy, and reasonableness) that nonetheless fall short of what Rawls calls comprehensive liberalism, the latter a view that contradicts the beliefs of many citizens, especially many religious communitarians (Rawls 1996, 19–20, 98, 192). But such a search is also compatible with, or even requires, that attention be paid to what Gamwell sees as the *really* comprehensive question (*MRF*, 135–45).

It should now be clear that even the idea of political community should be rejected *if* this idea means a unity based on one *particular* comprehensive doctrine. Political community should be embraced, however, if it is based on an overlapping consensus of different comprehensive doctrines. The mutual dependence involved in overlapping consensus is in no way mysterious.

In fact, it is found whenever there is cooperation among people with different particular comprehensive doctrines. The glue that holds together a liberal society is not *a* conception of the good (which is not to deny that such exists at an abstract level, as Gamwell rightly insists), but rather a shared public concept of justice and overlapping, ongoing conceptions of goodness. As before, Hart's distinction between a very abstract *concept* and more particular *conceptions* is crucial in the effort to understand Rawls and especially Gamwell. Gamwell's view of justice as compound is also relevant here. By accommodating a plurality of conceptions of the good, liberal society seen as a social union of social unions can coordinate the various activities made possible by human diversity into a just society (Rawls 1996, 201, 304, 323; *DP*, ch. 5).

Another comment is needed on Hollenbach's desire to return to the stronger community inspired by Aristotle. It should not escape our notice that in preindustrial societies individuals were indeed incorporated into groups in a stronger sense than the inclusion found in political liberalism, but the preindustrial incorporation was brought about in ways that Gamwell and Rawls would not find livable or justifiable today. For example, Aristotle's polis had few free citizens in that most were slaves or aliens. In addition, most were illiterate, which no doubt was conducive to the stronger sense of community there than in a liberal state, as Walter Ong has emphasized, in that literacy has a tendency to foster free thinking (see Ong 1998, 43–44).

A distinction between primary and nonprimary goods is required for understanding Gamwell's and Rawls's view. Any person with self-respect would, from the perspective of the original position, desire that the former be present no matter what else is wanted. Further, there is general agreement among philosophers of various persuasions, especially Gamwell, that goodness be seen, as above, as rationality. Hence, it makes sense to suspect that a good person, rather than a good assassin or a good farmer, is one who has to a higher degree than the average person the properties that, from the perspective of the original position, it is rational to want in a person. These properties would include, I assume, being a self-respecting member in good standing of some particular community and engaging in cooperative efforts with members of other communities. Evil people, by way of contrast, violate the rights of others in ways that parties in the original position would deem unjustifiable. Beyond primary goods (freedom of thought, movement, and choice of occupation; income and wealth; etc.) and those principles mentioned above that would be chosen in the original position, however, we should remain cautious (Rawls 1971, 433–40, 456; also 1996, 308; *PCV*, 83, 102, 122–23).

This caution is due to several factors, including the possibility that citizens will change their minds about which conception of the good they will adhere to, as Gamwell and Rawls realize. One's moral power to form and rationally pursue a conception of the good is such that this conception is, for various reasons, subject to revision. Therefore, we should not stipulate in detail what the good will be for each person based on the community to which they belong. It is true that if we suddenly lost the convictions that dominate our community, we would become disoriented. Usually when changes occur to our view of the good they are gradual, but sometimes they occur suddenly such that in a very real sense we are not the same person as before. Rawls himself cites the example of Saul of Tarsus on the road to Damascus, who became St. Paul (Rawls 1996, 30–31).

For the purposes of public life, Saul of Tarsus and St. Paul are the same person, and it is important from a political point of view that people be allowed to convert from one community to another without being persecuted. Otherwise, people are, to varying degrees, treated like slaves who are, in effect, socially dead because they are not sources of claims. By way of contrast, citizens who at any given time have a determinate conception of the good are politically autonomous. They are free within the limits of political justice to pursue any permissible conception of the good. Each of these permissible conceptions will, presumably, require primary goods that are the necessary conditions for pursuing higher-order interests, whether in public or nonpublic life, as Gamwell and Rawls rightly see things (Rawls 1996, 32–33, 74, 76, 79; also see *DP*, 20–22, regarding the process view of individuals over time).

Because we are reasonable, we can understand various communities and their conceptions of the good, and we may be drawn to at least one (or some) of them. Any attractive political (rather than comprehensive) conception of the good will conform to the goodness as rationality thesis and to the idea of there being primary goods. Members of a democratic society have, at least in an intuitive way, a rational plan of life. To claim this much is not to specify any particular political view or any particular community's view of the good. Such specification ought not to be made by the government, either. It should no more maximize the fulfillment of wants or strong perfectionistic values than it should act to advance one community over another. Obviously, the government should prohibit the enactment of some conceptions of the good found in some communities, those that violate basic rights and liberties. But if these are not violated, we are free to affirm our own conception of the good, which need not be, and probably is not, idiosyncratic in that it is likely a communal value of some sort, as Gamwell and Rawls argue (Rawls 1996, 85, 176–79, 187, 313; *BP*, 94, 102–8, 136).

What is most likely is that we will affirm a conception of the good rooted in some community in which we have been raised, educated, or both. When we reach the age of reason we find some view at the center of our loyalties. Some take this view on faith or are satisfied with it precisely because it is the traditional view; still others use a subtle blend of faith and reason. The fact that many have communal views of the good based largely on faith is no problem for political liberalism as long as these faith-informed views are within the bounds of justice. To have a defensible *theory* of justice, however, or a theory regarding the place of the good in political justice, requires rational argumentation, as Gamwell more than anyone rightly emphasizes, and the participants in the original position must be willing to be moved by reasons of justice as such (Rawls 1996, 314, 316; *MRF*, 145–53, also the appendix).

Of course, it is not only intellectuals who have determinate conceptions of the good, which is appropriate because if citizens had no conceptions of the good/common good that they tried to enact, a just society would have no point. Some have the impression that Rawls needs to make this claim in order to respond to strong communitarian critics of liberalism, but he makes no such concession in that the point is crucial to theory of justice and to political liberalism themselves regardless of the strong communitarian stance (Rawls 1996, xix, 318, 334). Justice as fairness assumes that citizens have *some* determinate conception of the good and *some* communal ties that prompt them to perform supererogatory acts beyond the confines of justice. No obstacles are put in the path of those who desire to explicate and act on Gamwellian higher-order moral sentiments that serve to bind a community of persons together *as long as* such higher-order sentiments are not imposed on others through the political process (Rawls 1971, x, 192).

I would like to conclude this chapter by considering the relationship between love/benevolence and community, a relationship that is much more complicated than liberalism's strong communitarian critics realize. A consideration of this relationship will also serve to bring together the various threads of my treatment of political liberalism and community, in general. It will also help us to better understand Gamwell's thought regarding the biblical Great Commandment regarding love of God and neighbor, which is a major theme in Gamwell's *PCV*.

First, Rawls defines love and benevolence in very similar ways as the desire to advance another person's good as that person's rational self-assessment would require or as beneficial action that is performed for another person's good (Rawls 1971, 190, 438, 487). Second, some might wonder why we do not build up a political philosophy on the communal basis of such loving warmth, in contrast to the allegedly cold procedure found in original position and Gamwellian rationalism. And third, Rawls responds to this criticism by pointing out that there is a difficulty that arises when it is noticed that love of several persons will likely lead to conflict if these distinct persons desire goods that are at odds with each other (and assuredly will lead to conflict if the love in question is love of "mankind" in general). In this situation benevolence is at sea and requires principles of justice so as to adjudicate the disputes that occur in a condition of conflicting loves.

Love and benevolence are second-order notions in that they are concerned with one's own desires or actions in relation to the desires or actions of others whom we want to advance. In this regard Rawls notices the analogy between the oft-noted hazards of love and the hazards of justice. In each case our own happiness is threatened when others are harmed. Because of the problem of conflicting loves, there is a need for *some* sort of impartial decision-making procedure. But what sort? It might be asked. Rawls is intent to show the inferiority of the Humean/utilitarian theory of the impartial spectator to the deliberations that occur in the original position, where principles of justice are determined by the litigants themselves. We have also seen that Gamwell is skeptical of this utilitarian ethical tradition. In a rebuke of those who see all objective procedures as cold and ahistorical and acommunal, Rawls says that "the fault of the utilitarian doctrine is that it mistakes impersonality for impartiality" (Rawls 1971, 190, also 573). That is, it is real persons with real historical and communal backgrounds who are the participants in the original position.

The fact that the sense of justice and love are continuous (Rawls 1971, 476; *PCV*, ch. 4) is confirmed by three "moments," especially in the integral connection between love and community in these moments. As before, however, when many objects of love are opposed, principles of justice are needed to offer guidance.

The first moment occurs in the lives of children who come to love their parents because their parents love them. The pervasiveness of this quite natural (although admittedly not universal) occurrence is a precondition for a just society (Rawls 1971, 463–66). It is a precondition for a just society because such mutual love is the basis for all-important reciprocity. When we are loved, our sense of self-esteem is enhanced, which in turn secures the social basis for self-respect that is one of the most important primary goods. Community would soon dissolve if love were answered with hate. Indeed, evolutionary history would have weeded out any "communities" wherein hate would be a normal response to love (Rawls 1971, 494–95). In short, being a member of loving familial and associative communities is a natural circumstance of society, a circumstance that is presupposed by any Gamwellian society that approximates justice (Rawls 1971, 438; *PCV*, 82–88; also see *BP*).

A second moment occurs in the relationship between love and the original position, while the third occurs "after" the original position when love plays various different roles in the comprehensive doctrines that citizens affirm and in the various communities within which citizens live and flourish. Despite the analogy between love and a sense of justice, love very often involves a greater intensity of desire than a sense of justice and hence often prompts supererogatory actions beyond those that are required as a matter of basic justice (Rawls 1971, 190, 478–79, 484). Building on what I have said above regarding the plurality of concepts of good that citizens affirm, the loves that are parts of some reasonable comprehensive doctrines, but not others that are not reasonable, are to be permitted, even encouraged (*PCV*, 88–99).

The close relationship between love and just communities is evidenced by the fact that it is found not only in communal life that antedates and postdates the original position (moments one and three, respectively), but also in the complicated relationship between love and the original position itself. It must be admitted that there is nothing to be gained by attributing love or benevolence to parties in the original position in that such attribution would be seen as "cooking the books" in favor of the principles of justice. But the fact that the parties in the original position are, strictly speaking, not so much individuals as "continuing strands" of families and communities, and of the loves found in families and communities, is noteworthy (Rawls 1971, 190–91; *DP*, 290–311).

In a key, yet largely neglected, passage Rawls says the following:

Now the combination of mutual disinterest and the veil of ignorance achieves the same purpose as benevolence. For this combination of conditions forces each person in the original position to take the good of others into account. In justice as fairness, then, the effects of good will are brought about by several conditions working jointly. The feeling that this conception of justice is egoistic is an illusion fostered by looking at but one of the elements of the original position. (Rawls 1971, 148)

I am claiming that Gamwell's and Rawls's view is that *a just society is composed at the most general level of a loving political community of more particular loving communities.* The combination of mutual disinterest *and* the veil of ignorance (rather than the former alone) quite remarkably achieves the same results as would be achieved if the society in question were established by a committee of saints, by a committee of loving or benevolent agents! This is because in the original position the deliberating parties are forced to take the good of others into account (which, it will be remembered, is the distinguishing feature of love and benevolence). The fact that Rawls is able to achieve the goal of defensible principles of justice on such a parsimonious basis remains the greatest accomplishment in political philosophy of the past 150 years. It is for this reason that it counts in Gamwell's favor that his views regarding justice are close to those of Rawls, even if Gamwell goes beyond Rawls by placing these principles within a metaphysics of maximal creativity (*DP*, ch. 6).

Our duty to maximize mutuality in the long run can be recast in terms of a duty to love. Political realism, that is, is not an end but a counsel for the course toward it. This duty to love (both God and our fellow creatures) implies a democratic commitment to justice. The fact that democratic procedures do not reach an explicit verdict regarding which of contending religious convictions are true does not mean that the justice of any particular political decision can be intelligibly stripped from its ultimate ground of worth (*PCV*, 79–99, 106–17).

CHAPTER THIRTEEN

Applied Ethics

Both Gamwell and Rawls are often accused of being overly abstract. Even if this accusation is misguided, as I think it is, there is no doubt that these thinkers require some sort of framework to simplify the application of their abstract principles, especially in a condition where citizens' judgments are likely to differ at the most concrete level of issues in applied ethics. The political process can be seen as a device whereby social decisions are made in conformity with philosophical principles at a higher level of abstraction. Further, the greater the disagreements at street level, the greater the need for abstract thought at a height that enables us to comprehend heated disputes on the ground. Gamwell and Rawls are more than willing to engage in the requisite abstract thinking. Because there is no predetermined correct way to solve thorny problems in applied ethics, only imperfect procedural justice is possible, in contrast to perfect procedural justice, where *the* right decision can be known independently of the procedure, as in the procedure to have the person who cuts the cake choose last among three people who desire to eat cake. An accurate scale provides the independent standard that enables us to determine fair slicing.

We have seen at least two distinctions in Gamwell that are helpful in the effort to bridge any gap that might exist between abstract and concrete: relatively abstract *formative* principles and more concrete *substantive* principles, on the one hand, and Hart's distinction between relatively abstract *concepts* and more particular *conceptions*, on the other. To these very helpful distinctions we can add the equally helpful Rawlsian four-stage sequence (see Rawls 1971, sec. 31). Regarding the latter, which seems to be acceptable to Gamwell and in any event helps to elucidate Gamwell's thought, after the parties in the *original position* have adopted the principles of justice, there is a need to think carefully about what the best constitution would be, as constrained by these principles of justice. At this *theoretical constitutional convention*, the veil of ignorance is partially lifted in that the intellectual framers now know the relevant general facts about their own society, a knowledge that was not found in the original position. At the conclusion of this second stage, we can be sure that a just society would be some sort of constitutional democracy. The third stage is *legislative*, on the assumption that no scheme of procedural justice can ensure unjust legislation will not be enacted. Just legislation is more likely when the abstract principles of justice, along with the elements of a just constitution, guide deliberations among elected legislators. Ideal legislators remain ignorant of their own particulars in the effort to avoid bias. It should be noted that the need for equal liberties and for equality of opportunity offer more guidance than is possible regarding the details of the difference principle due to the greater indeterminacy regarding which economic arrangements would be most conducive to justice. The last stage is the *application of rules* to particular cases by judges and government officials, and the following of these rules by citizens generally.

This four-stage sequence adds some flesh to Gamwell's distinctions between formative and substantive principles and between concepts and conceptions. In each case, the indeterminacy of theory is not itself a defect, but is rather an understandable feature of abstract theory: its need for particular, contingent exemplification. In the present chapter I plan to explore Gamwell's thought at the most concrete exemplification of his wide-ranging theory, that admittedly goes deeper than Rawls in the effort to articulate the metaphysical basis of comprehensive doctrines. That is, Rawls's theoretical ambitions are not as extensive as Gamwell's, either at the most abstract end, obviously, or even at the most concrete end, counterintuitively, in that Rawls was, with only a few exceptions, generally reluctant to join the fray at the level of applied ethics. I will deal with four topics in Gamwell's applied ethics: abortion, animal rights (and environmental ethics), affirmative action, and distributive justice.

Gamwell thinks that abortion continues to be a vexing issue that precludes any hope of a definitive resolution. But one helpful distinction that is often forgotten is that between politics and morality in that the state should not be expected to determine in detail what the latter requires. For example, promises should be kept, but no one thinks it a good idea that the state should define in detail the exceptions to promise-making. *If* abortion violates the state's prohibition of murder, then it has a constitutional duty to prohibit abortion, but the hypothetical character of this judgment makes prohibition of abortion very difficult to defend. Writing before the *Dobbs* decision in the U S Supreme Court in 2022, Gamwell emphasizes the fact that the *Roe* decision in 1973 ruled that an emerging human prior to birth is not a person in the constitutional or moral sense. Thus, abortion prior to viability (around the end of the second trimester or the beginning of the third trimester) was seen as constitutionally permissible. Gamwell agrees morally. In addition to the debated constitutional and moral status of the fetus is the unquestioned constitutional and moral status of the pregnant woman who has a right both to control her own body and to make decisions on the basis of her own conscience. Statutory prohibition of abortion would, Gamwell argues, illegitimately infringe on these rights (*PCV*, 130–34; *BTP*, ch. 5).

Gamwell, like Rawls (Rawls 1996, 243–46), thinks that the permissibility of abortion in the first two trimesters can be defended even if the personhood status of the fetus cannot be definitively resolved. The fact that the personhood status of the fetus cannot be *convincingly* redeemed in public discourse, as can the personhood status of the pregnant woman as well as that of a newborn child, is telling. Legal protection for the *potential* of the fetus conflicts with the *actual* rights of the pregnant woman to control her own body and to make decisions according to her conscience. That is, democratic commitment to public discourse is sufficient to command agreement with the moral permissibility of abortion, given the fact that the personhood status of the early fetus is typically established on nonpublic grounds. Gamwell admits that the state is not barred from considering lives that do not have constitutional rights, but presumably such lives would at least have to exhibit the capacity to suffer. What harm could be done to a pre-sentient being? In this regard we should, along with Hartshorne, defend Gamwell's processual view of the fetus in that, although individual nerve cells appear relatively early in pregnancy, a central nervous *system* (and hence sentiency per se) does not appear until the end of the second trimester or the beginning of the third trimester, which is also (and understandably) when viability occurs (*PCV*, 135–41; also Morowitz and Trefil 1992).

Gamwell's views regarding abortion are consistent with, and insightfully exemplify, the way of reason that he defends in every aspect of his philosophy, even when others despair of reason due to problems like abortion. Further, his stance regarding the moral status of the (late) fetus has more in common with religious tradition than many realize, given the facts that abortion is never treated explicitly in the bible and that delayed hominization of the fetus was the dominant view in the history of Western Christianity until at least the seventeenth century (see Dombrowski 2000). As far back as Aristotle it was common to view fetal development as dynamic in the emergence of a morally considerable human. Gamwell's aforementioned commitment to be creative and to foster creativity in others cannot ignore the vast differences between a pre-sentient fetus (in the sense of sentiency per se in contrast to microscopic sentiency) and a pregnant woman who is not only sentient but rational. *Her* rights and creative plans for the future are vastly superior to those (assuming for the sake of argument that these exist at all) of the pre-sentient fetus (*PCV*, 142; *MRF*, 105).

It is relatively noncontroversial to say that the criterion for moral agency (i.e., the ability to *act* morally or immorally, to make moral decisions, and to be held responsible for one's actions) is rationality and related qualities. In Gamwellian terms, a necessary condition for being a moral agent is the capacity to have a comprehensive purpose in light of which moral judgments can be made. As Whitehead puts a similar point, morality of outlook involves generality of outlook (Whitehead 1978, 15). On the neoclassical view, however, one's identity as a moral agent is not substantial. Rather, a moral agent's identity is abstract and is actualized by momentary states. The requisite generality of outlook and capacity for comprehensive purpose is not found in fetuses at any stage or in nonhuman animals like dogs. That is, they are not moral agents in that immoral activity occurs only in a being who decides for the false even while knowing what is true. Immorality typically involves self-deception (*MN*, 130–33).

Of course, it might be objected at this point that on these grounds very young children are not moral agents either, but only potential moral agents. This objection is correct (*MN*, 234, 244). Gamwell makes sense when he endorses Whitehead's classificatory scheme where four grades of events in the universe are distinguished. The lowest two—in so-called "inorganic" nature and in the vegetative world—exhibit possibilities for creativity that are severely limited. In nonhuman animals with central nervous systems, however, there is far greater unity-in-variety and possibilities for creative action, even if these beings still fall short of moral agency status. It is in self-conscious experiences typically found in adult human beings that creativity and moral responsibility are immensely extended (*BP*, 139).

But the criterion for moral patiency status is much more controversial. A moral patient is a being who can *receive* harm from others and hence have its rights violated. Regarding the abortion issue, Gamwell, Hartshorne, and

Rawls are all reticent to attribute moral patiency status to fetuses who are nonsentient or pre-sentient in the early stages of pregnancy (in the sense of sentiency *per se* as found in beings with central nervous systems, in partial contrast to the proto-sentiency found in single-celled organisms, plants without central nervous systems, etc.). This reticence has implications for how Gamwell views nonhuman animals. Although the cognitive differences between most human beings and sentient nonhuman animals is a matter of degree, the extent of the degree makes all the difference. To be specific, human beings typically cross the Rubicon of moral agency status due to their superior cognitive capacities vis-à-vis nonhuman animals, but "higher" nonhuman animals cross the Rubicon of moral patiency status due to their sentiency (see Whitehead 1968, 36–38; 1978, 113). Gamwell does not say much about issues in environmental ethics, except that the destruction of *some* subhuman value is morally justified, but *only if* it is required to maximize the happiness of all. This is a far cry from condoning *every* invasion of nature that is executed in the name of human purpose. Indeed, as Gamwell insightfully points out, maximal human happiness itself depends to a great extent on appreciation and respect for nature, especially for sentient animals. Extreme and enduring inequality of potential is the essential condition that enables us to determine where the above-mentioned Rubicons are located. The key factor is that the proper guide for moral deliberation is maximizing happiness or creativity as such, thus linking Gamwell's approach to applied ethics with his most abstract work in metaphysics (*BP*, 140–41).

The substantive principle of justice that Gamwell is advancing is that we should maximize the general conditions of emancipation. Rational beings (of whatever species, but typically human) require more by way of emancipatory conditions than those beings who are not rational but sentient. In turn, sentient beings (of whatever species) require more by way of emancipatory conditions than those beings that are not sentient (assuming, for the sake of argument, that these latter beings can in fact be emancipated). Gamwell does not wish to be more precise than this on the Aristotelian assumption that we should expect only as much precision as the subject matter will bear, in this case the subject matter being the metaphysical foundations for applied ethics and the importance of the distinction between formative and substantive principles. Borderline cases are to be expected (see Dombrowski 1997). He is aware, for example, of the fact that some nonhuman animals have some understanding, even some forms of language (*EG*, 175–76; *MRF*, 105).

A third issue in applied ethics treated by Gamwell is that of affirmative action, an issue that is almost as contentious as abortion, at least in the United States. He starts his treatment of affirmative action by highlighting the career of the Supreme Court justice William O. Douglas, who came down on the side of Blacks in every landmark civil rights case, but who was opposed to affirmative action because he saw it as a type of reverse discrimination. Affirmative action started in the 1960s as a means of soliciting minority candidates for socially desirable positions. It grew to include the favoring of minorities over those who had better test scores or who fared better according to other prevailing criteria. Opponents to affirmative action insist that the practice is inherently unjust; indeed, that it commits the same (or an analogous) sort of injustice that it is supposed to redress. The opponents hold that we should be blind to religion, race, gender, et cetera, such that *any* denial of this principle is an affront to human dignity (*PCV*, 143–44).

Gamwell's response is once again to emphasize the distinction between formative (in this case constitutional) principles and substantive principles of justice. The Fourteenth Amendment to the U S Constitution prescribes equal protection of the law to all. But there is debate regarding whether or not affirmative action is consistent with this amendment, with opponents alleging that affirmative action violates a basic moral principle essential to democratic politics (i.e., equal consideration of interests if not equal treatment) and defenders alleging that affirmative action is needed to ensure equal protection of the law, given a history of inequality before the law suffered by some citizens, most notably Blacks. Gamwell notes that *some* natural and historically created differences are pertinent to important decisions, as when relatively older people are exempted from military conscription or when those with disabilities are given preferential status when parking a car. But natural and historically created differences cannot *in themselves* justify different consideration and treatment. Regarding military conscription, for example, the exemption has very little to do with age and very much to do with the physical requirements of soldiering (*PCV*, 145–46).

Gamwell is skeptical as to whether the affirmative action debate can be settled by the constitutional right to equal protection of the law enshrined in the Fourteenth Amendment. In fact, both sides in the recent Supreme Court decision regarding affirmative action dealing with Harvard University and University of North Carolina cited the Fourteenth Amendment in their favor. Rather than a formative (in this instance, constitutional) purpose, affirmative action serves a substantive purpose: to help correct the consequences of generations of institutionalized racial discrimination.

Substantive principles, we have seen, admit of a wider range of disagreement than formative ones, even if the latter are also sometimes matters for debate (see Pettit 2016). Substantive justice, however, is illuminated by the formative principle to maximize access to emancipatory conditions. It is for this reason that Gamwell favors affirmative action, on the assumption that such maximization does not treat anyone else unfairly. Although I am not convinced that this assumption is defensible (see Dombrowski 2011, ch. 4), I am not a libertarian or someone who defends individual*ism* in contrast to a commitment to the common good. Gamwell seems to think that opposition to affirmative action comes only from libertarians in tandem with political conservatives. It should be noted, however, that at least some opponents to affirmative action are Rawlsian liberals like myself (*PCV*, 147–49).

There are many reasons to think that affirmative action is *not* conducive to general emancipation. At points Gamwell realizes this, but he thinks that affirmative action is nonetheless a practice in substantive justice that is more likely than its alternative to substantively support the formative principle to act in such a manner that is creative and that maximizes creativity in others. In any event, both sides to the affirmative action debate can benefit from Gamwell's argument that the formative standard that provides the criterion for debates at the substantive level is open to reasoned contestation at both formative and substantive levels (*PCV*, 150; *DP*, 219; *BTP*, ch. 7).

Whereas abortion and affirmative action tempt some people to look for (formative) constitutional solutions, despite the fact that reasonable people line up on either side of these issues, economic distribution is more clearly a substantive issue in that a policy regarding economic distribution is not generally viewed, not even by Rawls, as a constitutional essential. As a result, this issue in applied ethics most clearly illustrates the impact of Gamwell's distinctive approach to philosophy, from its most abstract to its most concrete levels of expression. Regarding this fourth issue in applied ethics, which was also treated above in a previous chapter, Gamwell develops a stance that is very much compatible with, indeed that is in some respects derived from, the Rawlsian stance on distributive justice. The relevant Gamwellian principle here is justice as general emancipation wherein we ought to maximize the conditions of creativity to which all have equal access. Economic provision is especially important to one's creative opportunities, for obvious reasons. Gamwell notices that income distribution in the United States tended toward equality from the end of World War II for several decades. But from the 1980s until the present the country has moved in the other direction. The point is not to defend complete equality of results in that the Rawlsian difference principle, with which Gamwell agrees, permits (even prescribes) some inequalities because as a result the empowerment of all is increased (*DP*, 290–311). Substantive issues in tax policy are crucial here, issues that should be informed by, if not determined in detail by, a metaphysics of general emancipation. Unreflective views from both the political right and left have contributed to the intransigence of poverty, which was drastically reduced in the postwar years. A key difficulty here is that at present mutuality is not affirmed for its own sake. This is because the quality of life is often defined in terms of the extent to which one enjoys benefits in a society devoted to production and distribution of goods and services used for private interests. The sort of liberalism defended by Gamwell, Rawls, and me, however, does not reduce politics to economic bargaining among competing interests. Of course, economic measures of "the good life" are parts of the story, but metaphysical speculation and argumentation indicate that there are wider and deeper aspects of a reflective person's life that should also be considered (*PCV*, 150–61; *BTP*, ch. 9).

Gamwell's overall approach to issues in applied ethics is to argue that, however particular the issue in question, one's response to the issue implies a conception of the comprehensive good. Creativity or novel unity-in-diversity is good whenever it is realized, but what we want is *maximal or optimal* creativity in the future as such. Justice as compound has as its goal general emancipation from those structures that serve to dampen creativity and to forestall flourishing. The word "emancipation" here has obvious resonances with Lincoln's thought. The cumulation of achievement in a human (or other) life increases its potential for significance for others. Debates in applied ethics often involve a tension between emancipation of any given individual and the widening character of general emancipation. Perhaps Gamwell's signal contribution to applied ethics is the idea that neither pole in this tension should be eliminated. Admittedly, a difficulty remains. Maximal or optimal creativity for all is an exceedingly abstract moral principle and vague with respect to counsels for practice. But this does *not* mean that the moral telos is altogether irrelevant to questions of justice (*DP*, 281–90).

Being a recipient of communicative respect as a result of a formative condition of emancipation is not an insignificant event, especially when such respect grounds democratic political association. In addition, such respect not only widens but also *localizes and applies* justice because participation in the democratic patterns of life requires that one be allowed to speak about *this* controversial issue and be given health care regarding *this* specific malady that one is at present experiencing. That is, justice as general emancipation includes Rawlsian and Gamwellian primary goods. It is the responsibility of individuals to make the most of the opportunities their families and communities present to them at the local level. Nonetheless, the legal order and substantive principles of justice are theoretically subservient to the comprehensive order of reflection, including the comprehensive good. This view is perfectly consistent with the realization that many individuals do a very poor job of taking advantage of the opportunities they are given. For example, equality of opportunity in education does not require that there be equal achievements. Rather, it means equal opportunity to be educated and equal opportunity to make the most of one's natural talents. Although justice may indeed require compensation for natural inequalities, this imperative is nonetheless constrained by the wider purpose of justice, which is to provide the widest possible context in which all reasonable individuals and associations can flourish (*DP*, 291–98).

The localizing *and widening* character of the comprehensive good means that, despite certain commendable features, an ethics of care might be too particularistic for a comprehensive theory of ethics. Analogously, libertarianism's failure to attend to the general conditions of emancipation counts against this view, as we saw in the first chapter of the present book. Again, like Rawls, Gamwell would require some inequalities, and permit others, but only if such inequalities increase the general conditions of emancipation. The inequalities that are permitted or required, however, deal with substantive principles rather than formative ones. There is no proper inequality regarding the latter. Further, formative principles have logical priority over substantive ones. Because the right to general emancipation requires a legal order, and because the requisite conditions for a legal order do not exist in a world community, citizens must participate in societies that are not universal, even if such societies are to be judged against certain universal standards. The very Rawlsian character to Gamwell's view of universal standards in applied ethics can be seen in the following priority rules loosely based on Gamwell:

1. The political association should be constituted as a full and free discourse, providing equal communicative respect for all.

2. The political order should: (a) maximize equality of public access, providing conditions of basic emancipation for all, and (b) maximize the general conditions of emancipation—both formal and material—to which there is equal access. (*DP*, 311, also 299–310)

To be specific, principle 1 takes priority over principle 2; and principle 2a takes priority over principle 2b. That is, one ought not leapfrog over principle 1 so as to address principle 2, nor do the same over 2a in order to address 2b.

These priority rules are not meant to deny the importance of economic provisions connected to principle 2b in the advance of one's creative opportunities. The fact that many American citizens live in poverty is an offense to the notion of a community of love. Neoclassical metaphysics entails an explicit or implicit call for a radical change in the way public discourse deals with the reality of grinding poverty. Such entailment is based on the commitment to mutuality in a metaphysics that is thoroughly processual *and* thoroughly relational. Also entailed in a thoroughly relational metaphysics are duties to future generations. In fact, Gamwell's teleological view of promoting mutuality *in the long run* provides a wide-angle vision that enables us to understand such duties to future generations better than in other attenuated views based loosely on Humean or positivist assumptions (*PCV*, 150–62; *DP*, 311–19). That is, there is much that a Gamwellian approach could contribute to an adequate response to the current climate crisis. In fact, perhaps the biggest problem involved in the development of such a response is the reluctance of people to view matters *comprehensively or metaphysically*. It is precisely this reluctance that is criticized throughout Gamwell's philosophy.

Gamwell's approach to applied ethics is a bit like the approach taken in virtue ethics in emphasizing the importance of understanding, especially self-understanding. The distinguishing feature of understanding, on Gamwell's account, is consciousness of universals and other abstractions. Reality, including moral reality, is discriminated *through* universals in a being with understanding. Further, as is widely known, discrimination through universals is integrally connected to the development of sophisticated language skills. We often think of such discrimination and such linguistic skills as distinctively human, but some nonhuman animals may have flashes of understanding and rudimentary language. Among the most important linguistic skills is the ability to talk about counterfactual alternatives, which, on the process account, were at one time future possibilities. The ability to entertain counterfactuals is what frees us up to consider alternative possibilities regarding acute problems in applied ethics. It is also helpful to consider the process philosophy commonplace that there is no such thing as a future actuality, only the possibility or probability of such (*DP*, 17–32).

Gamwell notes the widespread agreement among theologians that (predominantly human) subjectivity that is conditioned involves some sort of awareness of something Unconditioned. Indeed, the character of reality as such is unconditioned, as we have seen. Consciousness of the present implies difference from the past that conditions the present as well as from the future that one's present decisions will condition. That is, self-understanding is prospective in the sense that its object is a self that makes a difference. Freedom is analytic of *self*-understanding. We make the present self the best it can be by pursuit of the best, comprehensive telos. This comprehensive telos is the variable in light of which all lesser ends are evaluated in applied ethics. Some more or less *particular* purpose is chosen as a specification of *the* purpose by which human activity ought to be directed (*DP*, 33–46).

A moral agent *understands* what ought to be chosen. In different terms, action contrary to some specification of a moral duty is not culpable if done in ignorance of that specification. Admittedly, this understanding at times can be only implicit. In Whitehead's terms, "even at its brightest, there is a small focal region of clear illumination, and a large penumbral region of experience which tells of intense experience in dim apprehension" (Whitehead 1978, 267). But for a being with understanding, what we "understand" only implicitly can often, with effort, be brought to explicit attention (*MN*, 118–23).

One might suspect that a better approach to issues in applied ethics would come from the civic republicanism of Sandel due to his view of human persons as "encumbered selves" and his defense of a particular conception of a good society. But Gamwell makes it clear that the loss of the universal character of human rights would not be a small setback. That is, Gamwell faults Sandel for not formulating a universal telos to which universal rights contribute. Without a comprehensive good, political discourse can have no goods that are not historically specific. This opens up a Pandora's box of issues in applied ethics regarding women, gays, nonhuman animals, and future generations of human beings. (Gamwell offers the same criticism of the later Rawls on the questionable assumption that he had altogether abandoned the universal aspirations of *A Theory of Justice*, even though the original position is still assumed in *Political Liberalism*.) Although some scholars will continue to be skeptical of the value of Gamwellian abstractions for issues in practical philosophy, it seems to me to be a signal contribution of Gamwell to argue that some responses to moral and political problems must be better than others if moral deliberation itself is to have a point. And once we notice that some responses are *better* than others, we have presupposed the comprehensive purpose that lies behind (or lies ahead of) democratic theory. Indeed, the comprehensive telos of human life is the very reason for democracy itself (*DP*, 327–37).

Granted, when the comprehensive good is expressed in religious terms, there is the danger that the democratic process would be corrupted if such terms are advanced dogmatically or without a commitment to rational discourse. Indeed, the belief that human purpose and ultimate reality are not amenable to rational assessment is prevalent in many religious communities. Gamwell even wonders whether it is only this belief that many religious believers have in common. Religious believers are often at a loss to transcend mere assertion of their most strongly held positions. In this regard they are unfortunately much like many contemporary religious skeptics. Thus, the rationalization of society hoped for by Enlightenment thinkers, including Gamwell, waits on the rationalization of religion. One of Gamwell's favorite insights from Whitehead is that the affirmation of democracy divorced from discourse about the comprehensive purpose loses "its security of intellectual justification" (Whitehead 1967a, 36). Such intellectual justification is what Gamwell means by democracy *on purpose* (*DP*, 338–39).

Like Aristotle's virtue, Gamwellian emancipation is a matter of degree. Further, emancipation is cumulative in that it builds on the past in the effort to achieve maximal common humanity and solidarity with sentient life in general. A counterintuitive feature of Gamwellian emancipation is that it is both at once: self-widening—as more and more beings entitled to emancipation are included—as well as self-localizing—in that what is contributed among other things to the best possible future is present happiness. One of the key components of present happiness is communicative respect. Once again, it is hard when considering Gamwellian emancipation not to notice its resonance with Rawlsian theory as it relates to primary goods as well as to the imperative to maximize or optimize the general conditions to which there is equal access. That is, both Gamwell and Rawls see justice in terms of general emancipation (*DP*, 130, 283, 292–94).

It is the responsibility of individuals to make the most of the opportunities that are available to them. This puts Rawls and Gamwell somewhat at odds with some contemporary uses of "equity" that assume that *all* inequalities are the results of unjust structures rather than personal failings. Parents, for example, should take responsibility for their own offspring as constructive partners in the emancipatory process, but there are varying degrees to which parents fulfill their responsibilities in this regard (see Kearney 2023). But neither Rawls nor Gamwell wishes to push too far in this direction in that libertarian preference satisfaction is at odds with general emancipation. Only *some* inequalities enhance general emancipation. Gamwell is quite clear that there is a right to general emancipation in terms of the *opportunity* to participate as an equal in the emancipatory process once basic goods—both formal and material—are distributed regardless of merit (*DP*, 296, 299–301, 304–11). A further contrast with libertarian preference satisfaction is found in Gamwell's conception of general emancipation as the *maximization of mutuality*, which is, as he sees things, conducive to democracy at its best, which is, in turn, our best response to divine love (*DP*, 88, 92, 97, 108).

CHAPTER FOURTEEN

The Method of Reflective Equilibrium

In this final chapter I will be defending the views that: (1) reflective equilibrium should be seen as the overall method at work in philosophy, a method that is explicit in Rawls and, I will argue, implicit in Gamwell; and (2) reflective equilibrium should be seen as an ongoing process. The latter thesis is a novel one that helps both to clarify what reflective equilibrium is and to establish the cogency of the former thesis. It is precisely the processual character of reflective equilibrium that forges a crucial link between liberal political philosophers like Rawls and liberal process metaphysicians like Whitehead, Hartshorne, Gamwell, and me. In order to establish this link, however, it will be fruitful to first understand Nicholas Wolterstorff's interpretation of Rawls's theory, an understanding that will help us to better understand Gamwell, in particular. Like some of the previous chapters, the present chapter attempts to better understand Gamwell through close association with Rawls.

Wolterstorff's *Justice: Rights and Wrongs* was hailed on its dust jacket by one notable critic as the most important work on the subject since Rawls's *A Theory of Justice* in 1971. Quite a compliment! Wolterstorff's extremely interesting comments on Rawls raise important questions for how we should interpret Rawls's work, but also for how we should interpret Gamwell's. Specifically, Wolterstorff provides a most useful frame for considering Rawls's overall method of reflective equilibrium and for considering a "deep" dimension of Rawls's thought that brings Rawls close to Gamwell. Wolterstorff presses Rawls's defenders to account for their belief that human beings are free and equal, a belief that is an integral part of any effort to achieve reflective equilibrium in liberal democratic political theory. Wolterstorff's insistence in this regard (and his own traditional religious account of this belief) helps us develop a richer understanding of the method of reflective equilibrium. Granted, Wolterstorff is not criticizing the idea of reflective equilibrium per se. Rather, he asserts that there is an unacknowledged reliance on natural rights in Rawls. But as a result of his criticisms, we acquire a much better understanding of the method of reflective equilibrium that will be at work throughout the present chapter.

Wolterstorff makes the startling, but understandable, claim that Rawls's theory of justice is an inherent natural rights theory (hereafter I will drop "inherent" and refer simply to natural rights theory), but that Rawls "does nothing at all to develop an account of such rights. He simply assumes their existence" (Wolterstorff 2008, 15). This is why Wolterstorff largely ignores Rawls. Wolterstorff is concerned with developing an account of natural rights. As he puts it, "my interlocutors will be those [like Gamwell] who do not just appeal to such rights but have something to say about them" (Wolterstorff 2008, 15). Because Wolterstorff's claim will shock many readers, we should ask why he claims that Rawls's theory of justice is a natural rights theory. Wolterstorff's response to this question rests squarely on the work of two scholars, Michael Zuckert and Ronald Dworkin. But we should notice at the outset that because religious ethics has traditionally had two notable forms—divine command theory and natural law theory—the fact that Rawls's view is in a way a version of natural rights and natural law is notable. That is, it is perhaps the best kept secret in recent political philosophy that Rawls relies on natural rights; hence his view is deeper (in a positive sense) than Gamwell imagines and is closer to Gamwell's own view than he realizes (*DP*, 220, 258).

Zuckert's thesis is that, whereas John Locke understood rights, and therefore justice, to derive from "property" (he used the term to include life and liberty), Rawls understood rights, and therefore justice, to derive from fairness. There is no idiosyncratic use of "rights" here. The term is used in a familiar way to refer to legitimate claims. It seems that what Wolterstorff likes most about Zuckert's interpretation concerns Rawls's view of the inviolability of the human person. Whereas for Locke justice derives from the inviolability of the human person (i.e., from rights), which in turn is derived from property, Rawls takes almost the reverse stance: justice derives from fairness, and inviolability (i.e., rights) derives from justice. As Zuckert sees things, this stance jars our intuitive or commonsense notion of justice, in that we normally tend to think that justice follows from, and does not ground or serve as the source of, rights. In other words, the Rawlsian account of inviolability seems to be in a state of disequilibrium with our intuitive or commonsense notion of justice and with Gamwell's view.

Zuckert and Wolterstorff are in agreement with Rawls and Gamwell, and against utilitarian thinkers, in thinking that human beings are inviolable (*EG*, 115–26; *WTP*, 49, 52–53). For example, all four thinkers agree that the utilitarian critique of slavery is problematic because it condemns slavery only contingently. Under certain conditions, a utilitarian might have to permit, or even encourage, slavery, as is well known. By contrast, Zuckert and Wolterstorff agree with Rawls and Gamwell that we should condemn slavery as a matter of principle. The key criticism that Wolterstorff, with the aid of Zuckert, would like to make is that Rawls's defense of the inviolability of the person *should* be based on something like Locke's (and Wolterstorff's) concept of natural rights, a concept that relies on the biblical tradition of seeing a human person as an *imago Dei*, as being made in the image of God. Indeed, Zuckert suggests that Rawls's defense of inviolability is in fact parasitic on Locke's view. In this respect Zuckert and Wolterstorff are articulating the now familiar view (see Griffin 2007, ch. 7; also Habermas 2002) that various "post-religion" ethicists and political philosophers are living off the capital accumulated during the Judeo-Christian ages: they conveniently receive a great deal of insurance without having to pay any premiums. Here Gamwell is very much in agreement with these thinkers. Think of the reductionistic biologist who sees human beings as so much protoplasmic stuff, as strictly accidental byproducts of blind evolutionary history, but who also belongs to Amnesty International. The issue here is not the theory of evolution per se, which is perfectly compatible with many types of religious belief, but its reductionist materialist interpretation, which is very difficult to reconcile with any sort of belief in the inviolability of the human person. But Rawls muddies the water by speaking as if the inviolability of human persons is not prior to justice as fairness but is derived from it.

Zuckert is not alleging foul play or subterfuge on Rawls's part. Rather, he thinks that Rawls is led into genuine confusion as a result of his belief that there no more could be justice outside of (democratic) practices than there could be strikeouts outside of the practice of baseball. An athlete could swing a stick in the air three times, but outside of the practice of baseball this would not be a strikeout, as we have seen. Likewise, outside of certain political practices there could be no rights and hence no inviolability of the human person, on Zuckert's interpretation of Rawls, adopted by Wolterstorff. On this interpretation, a Rawlsian would presumably have to admit that "Hugo would be perfectly in the right to gratuitously kill Samuel if they met on a desert island." Rawls would be better served, Zuckert thinks, if he considered "more carefully the preconditions for his own edifice of fairness" (Zuckert 2002, 327). Once again, this is Gamwell's very point by defending transcendental arguments (*MN*, 8–12).

Now let us consider how Dworkin's thought, as filtered through Wolterstorff, can facilitate an appreciation of Rawls and Gamwell. Several features of Dworkin's liberal critique of Rawls do not figure in Wolterstorff's account. It is Dworkin's treatment of Rawlsian reflective equilibrium that positively influences Wolterstorff, who has complained about the "inarticulate" nature of Rawls's epistemology, such that interpreters of Rawls have to engage in an inordinate amount of exegetical industry in order to figure out what Rawls means by reasonableness, rationality, and reflective equilibrium (see Wolterstorff and Audi 1997, 69, 75, 77–79, 98–99, 109, 111–12, 148; *MRF*, 53–54). I assume, however, that reasonableness can be understood as the willingness to abide by fair terms of agreement and that rationality can be understood as the ability to follow arguments and the like. We have seen that whereas it takes a reasonable person to be willing to enter the Rawlsian original position and to abide by the decisions made there, it takes a rational person to do the deliberating.

Dworkin, however, correctly makes it clear that it is a mistake to assume that there is a direct, one-way argument from the original position to Rawls's famous two (actually three) principles of justice. This is a simplistic (because static) approach that is nonetheless the basis for the pedagogy through which many or most students come into contact with Rawls's thought. Dworkin rightly emphasizes that Rawls's more complex processual method consists in seeking reflective equilibrium "between our ordinary, unreflective moral beliefs and some theoretical structure that might unify and justify these ordinary beliefs" (Dworkin 1977, 155). The fact that Gamwell is a process philosopher is relevant here in the attempt to understand his own overall method, which includes, but is not exhausted by, very abstract argumentation. That is, his overall method is reflective equilibrium, as is implicit in his defense of the compound character of justice (*DP*, ch. 5).

On the one hand, the method involves the effort to provide a structure of principles that supports (i.e., that unifies *and* justifies) our ordinary, unreflective moral beliefs. On the other hand, we should also be prepared to alter or even abandon immediate convictions in the face of powerful theory. Here we should notice the importance of reflective equilibrium for Gamwell's philosophy, which stretches from the most abstract of metaphysical theories to work at the most concrete level in applied ethics. "We can expect to proceed back and forth between our immediate judgments and the structure of explanatory principles in this way, tinkering first with one side and then the other, until we arrive at what Rawls calls . . . reflective equilibrium in which we are satisfied, or as much satisfied as we can reasonably expect" (Dworkin 1977, 156). Dworkin notices, as few critics do, that for Rawls (and for Dworkin himself, if not for Wolterstorff) the conditions that are embodied in the description of the original position are not imposed from without, but are those that we either do in fact accept or could be led to accept as a result of the process of philosophical reflection (Dworkin 1977, 158–59; Rawls 1971, 21, 587).

Dworkin, along with many commentators, sees reflective equilibrium as part of a coherence theory of morality. But unlike most commentators, he sees two sorts of coherence. One of these is "natural," wherein human beings have a moral faculty that enables them to discover eternal and static moral reality, as in the intuition that slavery just *is* wrong. This faculty is analogous to the physical observations in science that are the clues to the existence and nature of physical laws. The second of these coherence models is processual and "constructive," in which the practitioner of the type of moral philosophy found in the model does not assume that principles of justice have a fixed, objective existence, as in the natural model. For example, the intuition that slavery is wrong is not a clue regarding the existence of an independent, eternal principle, but a stipulated feature of the general theory to be constructed. Gamwell, it will be remembered, thinks that *metaphysical* truth is part of a coherence theory, but other sorts of truth require more than coherence in order for them to be defensible (*MN*, 3–12).

Most commentators do not see the natural model as a type of coherence theory. Rawls would seem to agree with these commentators. Dworkin's classification of the natural model as a type of coherence theory seems to be the result of the analogy he draws with scientific observation. For example, if an astronomer has clear observational data that do not cohere with any existing theory, the astronomer understandably thinks that observational powers have temporarily outstripped explanatory powers and that the task is to try to have the latter catch up with the former so that coherence is eventually reached. By way of partial contrast, when "observations" are made by a moral faculty, the situation is a bit more complicated in that it is not automatically assumed that theory has to "catch up." This is because in the constructive model the "observations" regarding justice or injustice are more likely to be contested than in the natural model. There is something gained in the constructive model, however. Coherence is eventually reached owing to the responsibility and persistence of the moral agents who take initial intuitions regarding justice or injustice seriously along with the rational desire to be consistent. The point is not that scientific inquirers are not responsible or persistent. Rather, the idea is that, although these traits may facilitate coherence between observation and theory in science, they are not absolutely essential, as they are in the constructive model. That is, in the constructive model, moral philosophers themselves must take responsibility for the processual drive for coherence. I assume that this is close to Gamwell's view when dealing in different ways with issues both inside and outside of metaphysics (*EG*, 17–38).

As before, Rawls's constructivist notion of reflective equilibrium is a two-way process that goes back and forth between adjustments to conviction and adjustments to theory until the most adequate fit is achieved. (On the natural model this might look like "cooking" the evidence.) Once again, reflective equilibrium is a process notion rather than an algorithm that gives us the right answer once and for all. Although such an algorithm might not be found in the natural model either, it seems fair to claim that scientists at least hope to approximate such algorithmic thinking. If one's tentative theory of justice does not fit some particular intuition, this should serve as a warning that we should consider whether we really want to hold on to the intuition. Or perhaps it leads us to question the theory. The key point here is that the two-way process of reflective equilibrium is at odds with the natural model, which Dworkin thinks aims at the "timeless features of some independent moral reality" (Dworkin 1977, 166). It should be noted that, although Wolterstorff relies on Dworkin in his criticism of Rawls, Wolterstorff's own view of natural rights as ultimately resting on a theistic basis (on a traditional theistic basis at that, where God is seen as immutable) would seem to ally him with what Dworkin calls "the timeless features" of "the natural view." This gets Wolterstorff into trouble, from a Gamwellian point of view. Although there are certain similarities between Gamwell and Wolterstorff, we have seen that the former is a process, neoclassical theist who does not reify moral/political categories in the manner Wolterstorff prefers as a classical theist (*DG*, 165–78).

What is not in dispute among Dworkin, Wolterstorff, Gamwell, Rawls, and me is that a rights-oriented approach should be defended. For example, Wolterstorff and Rawls would agree with Dworkin that "there is a difference between the idea that you have a duty not to lie to me because I have a right not to be lied to, and the idea that I have a right that you not lie to me because you have a duty not to tell lies. . . . A theory that takes rights as fundamental is a theory of a different character from one that takes duties as fundamental" (Dworkin 1977, 171). The questions before us are how we should account for rights and how rights fit into the processual method of reflective equilibrium.

Although Dworkin does not give a great deal of evidence of agreeing with the conservative elements in Zuckert's and Wolterstorff's views of justice, he does think, along with them, that Rawls's view is ultimately a natural rights position: "It must be a theory that is based on the concept . . . of rights that are *natural,* in the sense that they are not the product of any legislation, or convention, or hypothetical contract. I have avoided that phrase because it has, for many people, disqualifying metaphysical associations. They think that natural rights are supposed to be spectral attributes worn by primitive men like amulets, which they carry into civilization to ward off tyranny" (Dworkin 1977, 176). Dworkin tries to reassure his readers that Rawls's natural rights are not, as perhaps they are in Wolterstorff, parts of a "metaphysically ambitious" project (177). Of course, in Gamwell's case there *is* a metaphysically ambitious project. But this project is part of a layered concern for issues with varying degrees of abstractness and concreteness, making his version of reflective equilibrium somewhat distinctive when compared to the projects defended by Rawls, Wolterstorff, and Dworkin.

Rights are connected to the practical political goal of protecting citizens. Nonetheless, Dworkin admits, to Wolterstorff's delight, that natural rights are *assumed* by Rawls without argument in that they are "not simply the product of deliberate legislation or explicit social custom, but are independent grounds for judging legislation and custom" (Dworkin 1977, 177). Simply put, Rawls's social contract assumes natural rights even if Rawls himself prefers to think of his view as "ideal-based" rather than "right-based," and even if at times he tries to distance himself from any association with natural law (see Rawls 1996, 406). Such a distance is due to the metaphysical associations with natural rights and natural law that are actually welcomed by Gamwell (*WTP,* 141).

Wolterstorff goes along with Zuckert and Dworkin in admitting that Rawls's presentation of his theory does not *appear* to be a natural rights theory. The argument that it is in fact a natural rights theory is strictly deductive, given other things that Rawls has to say. For example, it is basic to Rawls's theory that there be equal respect for all citizens, or at least for all reasonable/rational agents who *deliberate* in the original position. (More precisely, if the agents who deliberate in the original position are rational but not reasonable, this is because the information constraints they work under "stand for" reasonableness [Rawls 1999, 317].) Wolterstorff unfortunately refers to agents who *bargain* in the original position, which confuses the Rawlsian original position with the Hobbesian state of nature (Wolterstorff 2008, 16; Rawls 1971, 134–35). The equal respect that is owed to those deliberating in the original position is due to . . . due to what? The Rawlsian response to this question would seem to involve a natural right to equality of concern and respect, "a right they possess not by virtue of birth or characteristic or merit or excellence but simply as human beings with a capacity to make plans and give justice" (Dworkin 1977, 182; also see Wolterstorff 2008, 16). Once again, Gamwell is in agreement with this response as a result of his defense of general emancipation (*DP*, 300–301, 319).

Wolterstorff cites two passages from Rawls himself to support the claim that Rawls's theory of justice in *A Theory of Justice* is built on natural rights. The first is in the main body of the text, where Rawls refers to equality as it applies to the respect that is owed to persons irrespective of their social position. This sort of equality is "fundamental," according to Rawls. He says that this type of equality "is defined by the first principle of justice and by such natural duties as that of mutual respect; it is owed to human beings as moral persons. The natural basis of equality explains its deeper significance" (Rawls 1971, 511; see Wolterstorff 2008, 16). Rawls's language here regarding the *natural basis* of equality as *fundamental* indicates that he is not as opposed to Gamwell's metaphysical project as Gamwell thinks (*PCV*, ch. 2).

A second, more explicit, passage is found in a footnote. Its location outside the main body of the text Wolterstorff reads as a sign of Rawls's reluctance to parade the fact that his theory is built on natural rights, perhaps because of the aforementioned fear that he would be interpreted as advancing a Gamwellian metaphysically ambitious project. No doubt it is this fear that scares away many potential readers of explicitly process metaphysicians like Whitehead and Hartshorne and Gamwell, all of whom are political liberals who defend the concept of rights, it should be noted (see Morris 1991; Dombrowski 2019). This is unfortunate given their process contributions to political liberalism, most notably their defense of a version of theism wherein God is not an omnipotent king, the imitation of which gets in the way of democratic virtues, but is rather the ideal being-in-becoming who facilitates the liberal transition from force to persuasion (Whitehead 1967a, ch. 5; Hartshorne 1984c). This is no small accomplishment given that many or most people in the United States, in particular, and in the world, in general, are religious believers of some sort. Unfortunately, many of them have religious beliefs that contradict democratic virtues. Hence process theism is well positioned to try to persuade religious believers toward a better social world. Process or relational theism fits hand in glove with political liberalism even if it is but one among many reasonable comprehensive doctrines that are compatible with liberal citizenship, including many that are not religious. My hope in the present chapter is to add another process contribution to political theory by explicating the *dynamic* character of reflective equilibrium.

Now back to the second passage, where Rawls says that the fact that the capacity for moral personality is a sufficient condition for being entitled to equal justice "can be used to interpret the concept of natural rights":

> For one thing, it explains why it is appropriate to call by this name the rights that justice protects. These claims depend solely on certain natural attributes the presence of which can be ascertained by natural reason pursuing common sense methods of inquiry. The existence of these attributes and the claims based on them is established independently from social conventions and legal norms. The propriety of the term "natural" is that it suggests the contrast between the rights identified by the theory of justice and the rights defined by law and custom. But more than this, the concept of natural rights includes the idea that these rights are assigned in the first instance to persons, and that they are given a special weight. Claims easily overridden for other values are not natural rights. Now the rights protected by the first principle have both of these features in view of the priority rules. Thus justice as fairness has the characteristic marks of a natural rights theory. Not only does it ground fundamental rights on natural attributes and distinguish their bases from social norms, but it assigns rights to persons by principles of equal justice, these principles having a special force against which other values cannot normally prevail. Although specific rights are not absolute, the system of equal liberties is absolute practically speaking under favorable conditions. (Rawls 1971, 505–6)

It is to Wolterstorff's credit that he highlights this remarkable footnote, for philosophers should not be startled to hear about the natural rights dimension of Rawls's theory, a dimension that serves to highlight the similarities between Rawls and Gamwell. My purpose in what follows is to interpret this crucial statement in a way that differs somewhat from Dworkin's interpretation and a great deal from Zuckert's and Wolterstorff's static and religiously conservative interpretations.

Finding the best possible interpretation of this quotation is crucial if we are to confront head-on Wolterstorff's claim that the deepest issue in Rawlsian theory is one that is rarely discussed: the fact that the theory is based on natural rights and that these rights must somehow be located within the processual method of reflective equilibrium, a method that is congenial to Gamwell's wide-ranging interests. From Wolterstorff's point of view, a theory of justice that is based on natural rights *should* give us an account of these rights, and it *should* declare that a society is just to the extent that it honors these rights. In this regard, it is Wolterstorff's view, not Rawls's, that sees political philosophy in static terms amenable to deductive explication. Rawls, Wolterstorff alleges, does something different. He develops a theory of justice that appeals to only one natural right: the right of rational agents (Wolterstorff should say: reasonable/rational agents) to be treated with equal respect. On Wolterstorff's view, Rawls wistfully hopes that if this natural right is honored, then all of the others will be secured (Wolterstorff 2008, 17).

One of the classic debates in moral theory concerns the question of starting points. Should we start with particular moral judgments or with general (or universal) moral principles? We can call those who defend the former approach particularists and those who defend the latter generalists. The debate between the defenders of these two approaches is perhaps due to the fact that these thinkers are primarily interested in different questions. The particularist is primarily interested in responding to the question, Which actions are morally right (or wrong)? Whereas the generalist is primarily interested in the question, What are the criteria of right (or wrong) actions? Both of these views, it should be emphasized, are opposed to moral skepticism. But they combat moral skepticism in quite different ways. Despite the well-known and powerful Kantian and Gamwellian reservations regarding overreliance on particularism (*DP*, 40–47), some philosophers continue to insist that the best way to argue against moral skepticism is to start with particular moral judgments that are widely shared (e.g., that the mass killings at Auschwitz were unjust, that the treatment of Africans on the slave ships in the middle passage was immoral) and then try to work out the theoretical criteria for moral (or immoral) action later. Most of the major figures in the history of moral theory have made some contribution to this debate.

I understand Rawls's contribution to lie in his processual method of reflective equilibrium, which in effect asks the question, *why* does one have to choose between particular moral beliefs and general (or universal) moral principles when searching either for starting points in political philosophy (which is only one part of moral philosophy) or for the source of justificatory warrant? Rawls thinks it makes better sense to make use of *both* sorts of belief in the articulation and defense of moral theory. I think that Gamwell might agree with this assessment, given his brilliant work in *both* metaphysics and practical/political philosophy (e.g., *MN*, chs. 1 and 5). We sometimes begin a conversation in moral philosophy with the statement of a particular judgment; in other conversations we start with an affirmation of a moral principle, as in a statement of the golden rule. There is no good reason to restrict ourselves to only one of these starting points or sources of moral judgment. Or better, given that both particular moral judgments and general (or universal) moral principles are necessary conditions for, and perhaps jointly sufficient conditions for, moral discourse, the burden of proof should be on the person who wishes to crowd out one or the other of these features.

A partial response to Wolterstorff is available at this point. One of the reasons, but not the only one, why Rawls does not talk more about natural rights is that they collectively function only as a *part* of a theory of justice, rather than as its cornerstone, as in Wolterstorff. That is, Wolterstorff needs to manage his expectations regarding the place of natural rights within the processual method of reflective equilibrium. He should not expect natural rights to play as large a role in Rawls's and Gamwell's thought as they play in Locke's thought. There are many ways to incorporate the strengths of both particularism and generalism, of course, and reflective equilibrium is only one of them. But by pointing out the hybrid character of the method we can trim Wolterstorff's expectation that if natural rights are in play they must take center stage. As in process thought in general, reflective equilibrium is thoroughly *relational* in character. This partial response is also instructive in the effort to understand Gamwell in that he believes in a *metaphysical* basis or cornerstone for political philosophy (*EG*, chs. 5–6). My claim is that some sort of rapprochement between processual reflective equilibrium and Gamwellian metaphysics should be reached. Indeed, it is a commonplace in Gamwell's philosophy to *invite* dialogue, even in metaphysics and in the relationship between religion and politics.

The mereological character of natural rights in Rawls's thought (i.e., the fact that it is only one part of the whole theory) is signaled by the fact that he prefers to label his view "conception-based" or "ideal-based," rather than "rights-based," despite the obvious part that rights play. But his view is nonetheless "right-based," in the singular, so as to signify the Rawlsian commonplace that the right is prior to the good (Rawls 1999, 400–401; Freeman 2007a, 18–19, 24). As Samuel Freeman sees the issue, in Rawls's revival of "the natural rights theory of the social contract" there is a transition to a reflective equilibrium that involves "separate strands of argument," much like Peircean strands of cable that mutually reinforce one another and unlike the metaphor that a chain of argument is only as strong as its weakest link. That is, the cable metaphor comes closer to what reflective equilibrium is all about than the chain metaphor does—indeed, the chain metaphor has become so familiar that it is usually not even perceived as a metaphor (Freeman 2007b, x, 42). Likewise, as should now be clear, there are many layers of Gamwellian argumentation, many strands of argument that mutually reinforce each other in reflective equilibrium, as the present book attempts to show.

By considering the many situations in which moral questions arise (i.e., by trying to incorporate the legitimate insights of moral particularists), we are inevitably led, whether explicitly or implicitly, to moral principle and to a region much wider than, but admittedly not at odds with, natural rights. Most people have both general and particular initial beliefs, including both general and particular beliefs about natural rights. But the key question is, How are we to bring these disparate beliefs into some sort of consistent Gamwellian whole? Particular beliefs, including particular beliefs about natural rights, can lead to disaster if they are not examined from some sort of reticulative perspective like that taken by the person who aspires to reflective equilibrium or the person who thinks systematically along the lines of Whitehead or Hartshorne or Gamwell. Robert Nozick's version of libertarianism, to cite one example, involves some extremely questionable judgments based on a runaway version of natural rights. Do we really want to privatize both the national park system and the public school system, as seems to be required by libertarian theory? (*BP*, ch. 2).

Although there are clear differences between natural rights and natural duties, an important similarity between the two should not escape our notice. Natural duties are those that all reasonable beings already agree to and thus need not be adjudicated by a fair decision-making procedure. We do not need a social contract to determine that cruelty is wrong. The natural duty not to be cruel holds between persons regardless of their institutional relationships, hence "the propriety of the adjective 'natural' " (Rawls 1971, 115). No matter what comprehensive doctrine one believes in, if the doctrine is reasonable it includes the belief that we have a duty not to be cruel and a duty not to murder. This latter duty would thus apply even on a desert island, contra Zuckert (Freeman 2007b, 418, 422). Once again, Gamwell's metaphysical support for the concepts of natural rights and duties (i.e., those that are the deliverances of the way of reason antecedent to any social contract) is conducive to both Rawlsian and Gamwellian liberal political philosophy.

Likewise, there is something antecedent about natural rights. These are the rights that are presupposed by the process of reflective equilibrium, as Wolterstorff rightly notes and as would, I assume, be held by Gamwell. But this need not be a problem, as Wolterstorff assumes. Resolution of moral conflicts is not to be determined by which of those beliefs is general and which is particular, but by which belief seems most likely to be true after thoroughly considering the issue. Once again, appeal to particular natural rights is only a part of the process of developing a defensible theory of justice. That the original position, or some other abstract device used to develop a fair decision-making procedure, is needed indicates that the critic who alleges that reflective equilibrium leans more in the direction of Gamwellian generalism than particularism is on to something. But the method is hardly an attempt to run roughshod over particular moral beliefs. It is quite possible for theory as well as intuition to be overridden. The process of reflective equilibrium here looks similar to Whitehead's famous metaphor in *Process and Reality* defended by Gamwell. Theory is like an airplane that takes off from the ground (of particular intuitions) so as to develop an abstract account of the phenomena in question, making sure eventually to touch ground again (Whitehead 1978, 5; *EG*, 31, 35, 57).

The place of natural rights in Rawlsian political theory is further contextualized when a distinction is made between narrow reflective equilibrium, as I have described it thus far in political liberalism, and the effort to find wide equilibrium between political principles and nonpolitical principles in philosophy of mind, science, and so on (see Daniels 1979). In both endeavors there is an understandable reluctance to give up on a seemingly well-established belief (e.g., that cruelty is wrong) when challenged by an untested one. And in both there is the requirement of intellectual honesty, such that an inconsistent or poorly supported belief is relinquished in the face of a more powerful one that is internally consistent. Further, reflective equilibrium in its widest sense also involves the effort to reach coherence between one's view of justice and one's comprehensive doctrine, indeed between justice and Gamwellian metaphysics.

The starting points in the process of reflective equilibrium can be seen as shared notions latent in common sense (Rawls 1999, 327), but this does not mean that they are self-evident. Both Rawls and Wolterstorff are understandably opposed to the idea of self-evident starting points (see Rawls 1971, 20–21, 48–50). Or at least self-evident starting points, if such things exist, would have to be analyzed critically along with other proposed starting points (Rawls 1999, 288–91). Wolterstorff even goes so far as to claim that the appeal to self-evident rights in the US Declaration of Independence is "a piece of epistemological bluster" (Wolterstorff 2008, 319). To say that our starting points have some basis in our common democratic heritage is not necessarily to say that they are static moral truths. In fact, they are open to revision. As Whitehead put a related point, the deadly foe of morality is not change, but stagnation (Whitehead 1967a, 269). Nonetheless, some starting points—for example, that cruelty is wrong—when revised put *all* of our other moral beliefs into a dangerous disequilibrium. This danger plays into Gamwell's hands as a metaphysician who encourages that attention be paid to the *comprehensive* question.

It is often noticed that behind the initial beliefs that get the process of reflective equilibrium started lies a Rawlsian view of the human person. At times Rawls distinguishes between *conceptions* of the human person and *ideals* of the human person (Rawls 1999, 321–22, 352). (This is different from the aforementioned distinction from Hart between "concept" and "conception.") The former are connected to issues in philosophy of mind regarding, say, personal identity over time, whereas the latter are connected to issues in moral philosophy regarding how a human person ought to act and what a human person ought to be. It should be emphasized that, although there may well be useful connections between conceptions of and ideals of the human person, conceptions of the human person underdetermine moral theory. Even if Rawls himself seems to believe in a Kantian conception of the human person (as free, equal, reasonable, and rational), which pushes strongly in the direction of human rights, he is well aware that competing conceptions of the human person must be considered in a politically liberal society. Gamwell's view of the human person is not much different from that in Rawls (and Kant), with the signal difference that such a view is explicitly religious and rooted in a metaphysical stance in Gamwell, in contrast to the Rawlsian and Kantian views, which are religious and metaphysical only implicitly.

Granted, there are only a finite number of conceptions of the human person that see human persons, as Gamwell does, as reasonable. And granted, each conception of the human person makes some moral theories more probable than others. But even if one grants these points, one is still able to defend the thesis that conceptions of the human person underdetermine moral theory. For example, to grant that a human person is made in the image of God still leaves unresolved many of the most important issues in political philosophy, as Gamwell realizes. Among Catholics, say, who believe in the *imago Dei* hypothesis, we find liberation thinkers who are heavily influenced by Marxist thought, Opus Dei members who consort with fascism, and political liberals, broadly construed. It is to be hoped that this last group will continue to flourish in the future.

The treatment thus far of the problem that the process of reflective equilibrium is meant to solve makes it possible both to better situate the place of natural rights in Rawls's view and to better understand the place of starting points within the process of reflective equilibrium. But one of the difficulties that any interpreter of Rawls must confront is how to navigate among three different methods or types of justification in his thought: (1) the processual method of reflective equilibrium; (2) the original position, which can be understood as that part of reflective equilibrium wherein particular beliefs or intuitions regarding justice are put to the test of objective rationality; and (3) public reason, which is more restrictive than reflective equilibrium in general because it concerns only those values that can be affirmed by all reasonable beings regardless of the comprehensive doctrines that they affirm. Regarding 3 it can be said that not all considered judgments, not even for Gamwell, meet the publicity criterion (e.g., those that concern many particular religious beliefs that are not amenable to abstract reasoning, as in which day will be considered the sabbath). Like the original position, public reason can profitably be seen as part of the process of reflective equilibrium, the part that deals with concepts that constitute an overlapping consensus with other reasonable citizens on the subject of justice. The original position is admittedly, in a way, deductive and nonprocessual, as are the most abstract metaphysical arguments in Gamwell, like the ontological argument, but reflective equilibrium as a whole is a process.

However these three methods or types of justification are related, it is requisite that we understand Gamwellian or Rawlsian reflective equilibrium itself as including three moments: identifying initial beliefs or intuitions about justice, trying to account for these from some objective point of view, and trying to reach equilibrium when the previous two moments diverge. Equilibrium, it should be noted, is a goal or an ideal rather than an accomplished fact. Thus, we should be wary of having our starting points do too much work for us. We should also distinguish between descriptive and deliberative understandings of reflective equilibrium. Whereas the former enables us to better understand the implications of what we already believe, the latter enables us to better understand what we ought to believe. The former provides some reason for a conservative understanding of reflective equilibrium, and the latter does the same for a radical understanding of it, as when Norman Daniels has us notice that a society that conformed to Rawls's three principles of justice (the first principle—the equal liberty principle—plus the two parts of the second principle, the equality of opportunity principle and the difference principle), principles that are also defended by Gamwell, would be more egalitarian than any existing society, including the social welfare states (Daniels 2003, 243). Although there is no compulsion to steer the method of reflective equilibrium into the descriptive mode, it must be admitted that the method does require that we account for those judgments concerning which we are most confident, including judgments regarding natural rights (Scanlon 2003, 142–44).

The Rawlsian *original position* (a decision-making procedure that helps us to achieve a certain degree of objectivity regarding the concept of justice) requires that we deliberate about justice behind a *veil of ignorance* regarding the particularities of our existence such that we should decide what a just society would look like if we did not know, for example, what our race would be in such a society. In this decision-making procedure, reasonable/rational agents would universally agree that basic goods (whether material or formal) would be distributed equally to everyone in society, and all of the goods beyond what it would take to fund the basic goods could be distributed unequally, but only if such unequal distribution was in principle open to all and to everyone's advantage, especially the least advantaged. This is the radical understanding of reflective equilibrium toward which Rawls's theory of justice, and Gamwell's appropriation of this theory, points (*DP*, ch. 6).

One of the most common mistakes that interpreters of Rawls make is to assume that Rawlsian justification occurs only within the deliberation in the original position. But Rawls is quite clear, as is Gamwell in his view of justice as compound, that "justification is a matter of mutual support of many considerations" (Rawls 1971, 507; *DP*, ch. 5). That is, reflective equilibrium is both thoroughly processual *and* thoroughly process-relational in that all of the elements can be revised in light of the others. If there are no good grounds for doubting our beliefs, it is reasonable to grant them initial credibility and fallible authority. It is not merely *that* we believe them that counts, but that they are credible, as Wolterstorff would otherwise admit as a reformed epistemologist. The stance of reformed epistemology involves an innocent-until-proven-guilty quality: we should be free to believe whatever we wish until the belief is shown to be inconsistent, contradicted by the facts, and so on. Rawls is rightly most famous, however, for the deliberations that occur in the original position, so it makes sense for Thomas Scanlon to say that if we had to choose between the descriptive and the deliberative understandings of the processual method of reflective equilibrium, the latter deserves the nod. At least in principle, our initial judgments can change significantly over the course of time in that reflective equilibrium is not only a process, but a "Socratic" process. It is because this method is self-correcting that Scanlon says that it is "the best way of making up one's mind about moral matters and about many other subjects. Indeed, it is the only defensible method" (Scanlon 2003, 149). This includes Gamwell's use of the method, which in turn includes use of transcendental arguments at the most abstract metaphysical level, but which in turn are open to the dialectical criticism that is the hallmark of reflective equilibrium, especially at more concrete levels.

Scanlon's claim is remarkable. But I do not think that he hyperbolizes, for the process of reflective equilibrium is exactly what is required if we are to avoid the twin evils of reifying either particular moral judgments or general (or universal) moral principles. Gamwell is especially interested in avoiding such reification. The results of other proposed philosophical methods, in Gamwell's case especially the transcendental method, are subject to dialectical criticism.

It must be admitted that at times Rawls gives the impression that principles of justice are *given* to us by practical reason, but because it is *our* practical reason that does the giving, I assume that there is no big problem with this impression, in that human actions are shaped by self-examination and criticism. And it is this criticism that prevents contractarianism from degenerating into conventionalism, an eventuality that would be understandably resisted energetically by Gamwell. Reflective equilibrium is an ideal, it will be remembered, rather than an already accomplished fact; the process of modifying ideas and rejecting recalcitrant ones is ongoing. This asymptotic effort is complicated considerably in the later Rawls by the fact that one must also bring into equilibrium the principles of justice operative in politics with one's own comprehensive doctrine, an effort that is encouraged by Gamwell. The complications are especially noteworthy if the comprehensive doctrine in question does not have an obvious place for human autonomy (Freeman 2007a, 6, 27, 38, 40, 240; Rawls 1996, 385; *DG*, 3–8).

To say that the method of reflective equilibrium is processual is to say that one always begins one's thinking about justice in the middle of things. One "starts" with intuitive considerations, but one does not exactly ground them in terms of a *reified* foundationalism, as Wolterstorff hopes to do in spite of his reformed epistemology. One "then" moves to the original position, but the rational deliberations found there are framed by the reasonable, which includes the *desire* to abide by fair terms of agreement, a desire that is implied in the willingness to deliberate under the constraints imposed by the veil of ignorance. As Burton Dreben emphasizes regarding the process of reflective equilibrium (Dreben is almost alone among scholars in explicitly referring to reflective equilibrium as a *process*), the key phrases in Rawls, which have hardly been noticed, are "working through" or "working out." One tries to explicate both the benefits of living in a liberal democracy and the conceptual details of what such a society would look like. This involves the Gamwellian search for a liberal constitutional democracy that is stable, but stable for the right reasons. This search, in turn, involves dialectic, as Rawls himself admits when he compares reflective equilibrium to Aristotle's dialectical procedure in the *Nicomachean Ethics*. In Aristotle there are starting points (*archai*), received opinions (*endoxa*), commonplaces (*topoi*), and, of course, habits ("ethics" is derived from the Greek word for habit, *ethos*) that enable us eventually to move dialectically *to* principle and *to* Gamwellian transcendental argument. But it is also possible to move *from* principle and transcendental argument deductively. Both dialectic and deduction are required (see Hardie 1968, ch. 3; Rawls 1971, 45; *MRF*, 192–205).

Dreben confuses matters a bit when he compares the back-and-forth dialectical character of the process of reflective equilibrium with circular reasoning, which does not bother him. But because circular reasoning *does* bother most philosophers, including Gamwell, it is better to stick with the claim that reflective equilibrium involves the give-and-take movement of dialectic at its best, wherein conceptual snags are untangled and inconsistencies exposed (Dreben 2003, 338). I would like to emphasize that Wolterstorff is to be commended for defending theistic philosophy with a capital "P." But I am not convinced that (1) theism has to be defended in the traditional, static terms Wolterstorff uses (Gamwellian neoclassical theism seems much more defensible) or that (2) philosophy with a capital "P" is appropriate regarding some of the more concrete issues in political thought, where the goal is to articulate fair terms of agreement among reasonable people with different, sometimes uncompromisingly different, comprehensive doctrines, including both religious and nonreligious ones. That is, Rawlsian political philosophy is no less important or difficult because it is largely done with a lower-case "p," although conceptual space is needed in order to engage in Gamwellian transcendental argument with an uppercase "P," which might support political philosophy, but is not exactly political philosophy itself. As Hartshorne puts a related point, liberals are those who know that they are not God (Hartshorne 1984a, 9), as mentioned earlier.

To those who fear that the process of reflective equilibrium is relativistic, I would respond that although coherence is a necessary condition for justification in political philosophy, it is not sufficient, as it might be in Gamwellian metaphysics. Common presuppositions in liberal democracies (e.g., that slavery and cruelty are wrong) and considered moral judgments in liberal democracies (e.g., that deviations from equality require justification) provide stable points that enable us to stave off the horrors of relativism. We might even say that reflective equilibrium can profitably be seen as an opposition not so much to foundationalism per se as to strong foundationalism. That is, the method of reflective equilibrium is perfectly compatible with Gamwellian weak or modest foundations. We should both allow the defender of slavery to state the case for slavery *and* insist that the extremely heavy burden of proof is on him, not his opponent. As Lincoln observed, if slavery is not wrong, nothing is wrong, a sentiment that is shared by both Rawls and Gamwell (Rawls 2001, 29; *WTP*, ch. 3).

Further, the method under consideration here is not equilibrium at any cost, which would indeed be relativistic. Rather, it is a method that involves a reflective, dialectically responsible process. Theories of justice should be viewed historically (i.e., processually) as involving conceptions that are gradually purified in the Gamwellian fire of reasonable/rational criticism, with the best available conceptions (considered judgments) providing preliminary standards for further dialectical criticism. The provisional fixed points mentioned above (e.g., Lincoln's claim that if slavery is not wrong, nothing is wrong) are sufficient to hold the wolf of relativism at bay. This is consistent with the claim that the content of public reason is not fixed, particularly if it is an expression of an especially dynamic society. Think, say, of how attitudes toward class, race, and gender have changed in liberal democracies over the past several decades. But even in the swift stream of contemporary history, the goal should remain to reach equilibrium between our real beliefs and what would be chosen in the original position behind a veil of ignorance and in terms of Gamwellian transcendental arguments in metaphysics. Overlapping consensus among reasonable beings is at least partially in place already, so this goal is not utopian in the pejorative sense of the term. Society's political conception should be publicly, though never finally, justified, as Rawls himself urges (Rawls 1996, 388–89) and as Gamwell defends in terms of "public liberties" (*DP*, ch. 4).

Or, more precisely, the realistic goal is that reasonable people would come to agree on a family of politically liberal views, of which Rawlsian justice as fairness or Gamwellian reformed liberalism are but two representatives, albeit the most egalitarian members of the family. The Rawlsian hope for justice as fairness, in particular, is that other politically liberal views would cluster around it for comparison and contrast. It can be seen as a carefully defended center of the focal class in the process of political justification.

It is to be hoped that the processual character of the method of reflective equilibrium will become better known to both political philosophers, in general, and to process thinkers who are political liberals, in particular, such that these two groups could help to further "work out" both the concept of justice, which is, as Rawls emphasizes (Rawls 1971, 3), the first virtue of social institutions, just as truth is the first virtue of systems of thought, as well as the Gamwellian connection between the transcendental character of arguments in metaphysics and their political ramifications (*MN*, ch. 5).

It *is* well known that from the time of his doctoral dissertation and his first publication, Rawls was very much interested in a procedure that would correct our considered moral beliefs against a set of moral principles, a procedure that came to be known as reflective equilibrium. I have argued in this chapter, however, for a feature of reflective equilibrium that is not well known: that such equilibrium is not really a permanent state but a process (see Rawls 1999, ch. 1). This realization changes things significantly, I think. For example, the familiar charge that Rawls's method is ahistorical and hence irrelevant to the flux of historical events begins to look inaccurate in the extreme. A similar charged leveled against Gamwellian transcendental metaphysics as too abstract would also be very unfair.

In this regard it is worthwhile to consider the way that Rawls's views in *A Theory of Justice* were later clarified in *Political Liberalism*. As a result of the aftermath of the wars of religion, some defended a liberal, Enlightenment, comprehensive doctrine in an effort to replace religious comprehensive doctrines. In turn, this *comprehensive* liberalism is replaced by Rawlsian *political* liberalism, which is meant to be congenial to both religious comprehensive doctrines and skeptical comprehensive doctrines. For this reason, Rawls's explicit flirtation with natural rights (and with their implicit religiosity) in *A Theory of Justice* ends at the level of public, political discourse in *Political Liberalism*, even if the affair can nonetheless continue in the nonpublic realm of associational freedom. This concession should, I think, be seen as very good news from the perspective of process metaphysicians like Gamwell who wish to give metaphysical support to the view that human beings are to be characterized by their responses to the comprehensive question.

Gamwell is as much a defender of transcendental argumentation in metaphysics *and* political thought as any other contemporary philosopher. But in addition to transcendental argument there is the need for some other type of rational pursuit. This additional requirement is highlighted in the distinction between formative and substantive principles. It is also highlighted by Hart's distinction between concepts and conceptions. And both of these distinctions are amplified by the Rawlsian four-stage sequence, which is a friendly amendment to Gamwell's views. However, the limits of transcendental argument in Gamwell, which admittedly are less extensive than such limits in other philosophers who have little or no confidence in transcendental arguments, are best understood in terms of the *inclusion* of transcendental arguments within the larger whole of reflective equilibrium. Whether we are considering comprehensive variables or the general contours of a just society or quotidian problems of a practical sort, the Gamwellian direction is to stay entangled in rational argument of a dialectical sort with other rational inquirers.

Coda

The following can be said by way of summation. Regarding the conditions of reality as such, it is necessarily true that "something exists" (in that denial of this claim is a semantic and pragmatic contradiction) and that "God exists" (for the same reason in that denial of theism is contradictory, given the logic of a modal version of the ontological argument). But the something that exists is in process and the God whose necessary existence is the conclusion of the ontological argument is inadequately described by classical theists, who have unfortunately dominated the concept of God in the Abrahamic religions for several centuries. The neoclassical concept of God is a noticeable advance over the classical concept, yet it preserves the best insights in classical theism. Regarding the conditions of human subjectivity as such, it is necessary for reasonable human subjects to tolerate differences of opinion (within limits of the reasonable, of course) in a democratic setting and to engage in communicative respect with one's interlocutors in a society that is at least somewhat just. It is precisely such reciprocal communicative respect that makes participation in the public square appropriate for all rational subjects, regardless of whether or not their responses to the comprehensive question are theistic. In addition to the above formative claims, a substantively just society would be one where basic goods (both material and formal) would be provided for everyone in society; any deviations from equality should be open to all and for the benefit of all, especially the least advantaged. All of the above claims are fallible and open to contestation, including those that deal with necessary truth. Finally, the twin dangers to democracy are authoritarianism and a refusal to discourse rationally about contested claims, especially those involving the comprehensive order of reflection. The first danger understandably receives a great deal of attention; the latter danger is unfortunately largely ignored. Gamwell is almost alone in emphasizing the connection between these two dangers: when reason is seen as anemic, those who hunger for power are well fed.

Works Cited

Gamwell Sources

Gamwell, Franklin. *Beyond Preference: Liberal Theories of Independent Associations.* University of Chicago Press, 1984.

———. *By the People, For the People: A Political Voice for Progressive Christians.* Wipf and Stock, 2010.

———. *Democracy on Purpose: Justice and the Reality of God.* Georgetown University Press, 2002.

———. *The Divine Good: Modern Moral Theory and the Necessity of God.* Harper, 1990.

———. *Existence and the Good: Metaphysical Necessity in Morals and Politics.* State University of New York Press, 2011.

———. *The Meaning of Religious Freedom: Modern Politics and the Democratic Resolution.* State University of New York Press, 1995.

———. *On Metaphysical Necessity: Essays on God, the World, Morality, and Democracy.* State University of New York Press, 2020.

———. *Politics as a Christian Vocation: Faith and Democracy Today.* Cambridge University Press, 2005.

———. *Religion among We the People: Conversations on Democracy and the Divine Good.* State University of New York Press, 2015.

Other Sources

American State Papers and The Federalist. 1952. University of Chicago Press.

Anselm, St. 1982. *Basic Writings.* Translated by S. N. Deane. Open Court.

Apel, Karl-Otto. 1980. *Toward a Transformation of Philosophy.* Routledge and Kegan Paul.

———. 1984. *Understanding and Explanation: A Transcendental-Pragmatic Perspective.* MIT Press.

Aquinas. See Thomas Aquinas, St.

Arendt, Hannah. 1966. *The Origins of Totalitarianism.* Harcourt, Brace, and World.

Aristotle. 1934. *Nicomachean Ethics.* Translated by Harris Rackham. Loeb Classical Library. Harvard University Press.

Augustine, St. 1993. *On Free Choice of the Will.* Translated by Thomas Williams. Hackett.

Barry, Brian. 1995. *Justice as Impartiality.* Clarendon Press.

Bellah, Robert. 1974. "Civil Religion in America." In *American Civil Religion*, edited by Russell Richey and Donald Jones. Harper and Row.

Berger, Peter. 1967. *The Sacred Canopy: Elements of a Sociological Theory of Religion.* Doubleday.

Burns, Elizabeth. 2013. "Ontological Arguments from Experience: Daniel A. Dombrowski, Iris Murdoch, and the Nature of Divine Reality." *Religious Studies* 49 (4): 459–80.

Burt, John. 2013. *Lincoln's Tragic Pragmatism.* Harvard University Press.

Cross, Richard. 2005. *Duns Scotus on God.* Ashgate.

Daniels, Norman. 1979. "Wide Reflective Equilibrium and Theory Acceptance in Ethics." *Journal of Philosophy* 76 (5): 256–82.

———. 2003. "Democratic Equality: Rawls's Complex Egalitarianism." In *The Cambridge Companion to Rawls*, edited by Samuel Freeman. Cambridge University Press.

Devenish, Philip. 1993. "Review of David Ray Griffin, *Evil Revisited.*" *Journal of Religion* 73: 280–81.

Dewey, John. 1934. *Our Common Faith.* Yale University Press.

———. 1957. *Reconstruction in Philosophy.* Beacon.

Dombrowski, Daniel. 1988. *Hartshorne and the Metaphysics of Animal Rights.* State University of New York Press.

———. 1996. *Analytic Theism, Hartshorne, and the Concept of God.* State University of New York Press.

———. 1997. *Babies and Beasts: The Argument from Marginal Cases.* University of Illinois Press.

———. 2001. *Rawls and Religion: The Case for Political Liberalism.* State University of New York Press.

———. 2004. *Divine Beauty: The Aesthetics of Charles Hartshorne.* Vanderbilt University Press.

———. 2005. *A Platonic Philosophy of Religion: A Process Perspective.* State University of New York Press.

———. 2006. *Rethinking the Ontological Argument: A Neoclassical Theistic Response.* Cambridge University Press.

———. 2009. *Contemporary Athletics and Ancient Greek Ideals.* University of Chicago Press.

———. 2011. *Rawlsian Explorations in Religion and Applied Philosophy.* Pennsylvania State University Press.

————. 2016. *A History of the Concept of God: A Process Approach*. State University of New York Press.

————. 2017. *Whitehead's Religious Thought: From Mechanism to Organism, From Force to Persuasion*. State University of New York Press.

————. 2019. *Process Philosophy and Political Liberalism*. Edinburgh University Press.

————. 2020. "Plato and Panpsychism." In *The Routledge Handbook of Panpsychism*, edited by William Seager. Routledge.

————. 2022. *Pre-liberal Political Philosophy: Rawls and Plato, Aristotle, Augustine, Aquinas*. Brill.

————. 2023. *Process Mysticism*. State University of New York Press.

————. 2024. "John Burt's Lincoln and Process Thought." *Religions* 15 (8): 1–14.

Dombrowski, Daniel, and Robert Deltete. 2000. *A Brief, Liberal, Catholic Defense of Abortion*. University of Illinois Press.

Dreben, Burton. 2003. "On Rawls and Political Liberalism." In *The Cambridge Companion to Rawls*, edited by Samuel Freeman. Cambridge University Press.

Dworkin, Ronald. 1977. *Taking Rights Seriously*. Harvard University Press.

————. 2006. *Is Democracy Possible? Principles for a New Political Debate*. Princeton University Press.

————. 2011. *Justice for Hedgehogs*. Harvard University Press.

————. 2013. *Religion without God*. Harvard University Press.

Eberle, Christopher. 2002. *Religious Conviction in Liberal Politics*. Cambridge University Press.

Emerson, Ralph Waldo. 1885. "Self-Reliance." In *Essays*. Hurst.

Finnis, John. 1980. *Natural Law and Natural Rights*. Clarendon Press.

Foot, Philippa. 1995. "Does Moral Subjectivism Rest on a Mistake?" *Oxford Journal of Legal Studies* 15:1–14.

Freeman, Samuel. 2007a. *Justice and the Social Contract: Essays on Rawlsian Political Philosophy*. Oxford University Press.

————. 2007b. *Rawls*. Routledge.

Friedman, Milton. 1962. *Capitalism and Freedom*. University of Chicago Press.

Friedman, Milton, and Rose Friedman. 1981. *Free to Choose*. Harcourt, Brace, and Jovanovich.

Frost, Robert. 1969. *The Poetry of Robert Frost*. Holt, Rinehart, and Winston.

Gewirth, Alan. 1978. *Reason and Morality*. University of Chicago Press.

Goldmann, Lucien. 1971. *Immanuel Kant*. Translated by Robert Black. NLB Press.

Greenawalt, Kent. 1988. *Religious Convictions and Political Choice*. Oxford University Press.

Griffin, David Ray. 2001. *Reenchantment without Supernaturalism: A Process Philosophy of Religion*. Cornell University Press.

————. 2007. *Whitehead's Radically Different Postmodern Philosophy*. State University of New York Press.

Habermas, Jurgen. 1984. *The Theory of Communicative Action*. Vol. 1, *Reason and Rationalization of Society*. Beacon.

———. 1987. *The Theory of Communicative Action*. Vol. 2, *Lifeworld and System: A Critique of Functionalist Reason*. Beacon.

———. 2002. *Religion and Rationality: Essays on Reason, God, and Modernity*. MIT Press.

Hadot, Pierre. 1995. *Philosophy as a Way of Life*. Translated by Michael Chase. Blackwell.

Hardie, W. F. R. 1968. *Aristotle's Ethical Theory*. Clarendon Press.

Hart, H. L. A. 1961. *The Concept of Law*. Clarendon Press.

Hartshorne, Charles. 1934a. "Ethics and the New Theology." *International Journal of Ethics* 45 (1): 90–101.

———. 1934b. *The Philosophy and Psychology of Sensation*. University of Chicago Press.

———. 1937. *Beyond Humanism*. Willet, Clark.

———. 1941. *Man's Vision of God*. Harper.

———. 1948. *The Divine Relativity*. Yale University Press.

———. 1953a. *Philosophers Speak of God*. University of Chicago Press.

———. 1953b. *Reality as Social Process*. Beacon Press.

———. 1962. *The Logic of Perfection*. Open Court.

———. 1965. *Anselm's Discovery*. Open Court.

———. 1967. *A Natural Theology for Our Time*. Open Court.

———. 1970. *Creative Synthesis and Philosophic Method*. Open Court.

———. 1973. *Born to Sing*. Indiana University Press.

———. 1981. *Whitehead's Philosophy*. University of Nebraska Press.

———. 1983. *Insights and Oversights of Great Thinkers*. State University of New York Press.

———. 1984a. *Creativity in American Philosophy*. State University of New York Press.

———. 1984b. *Existence and Actuality*. Edited by John Cobb and Franklin Gamwell. University of Chicago Press.

———. 1984c. *Omnipotence and Other Theological Mistakes*. State University of New York Press.

———. 1987a. "A Metaphysics of Universal Freedom." In *Faith and Creativity*, edited by George Shields and George Nordgulen. CBP Press.

———. 1987b. *Wisdom as Moderation*. State University of New York Press.

———. 1990. *The Darkness and the Light*. State University of New York Press.

———. 1991. *The Philosophy of Charles Hartshorne*. Edited by Lewis Hahn. Open Court.

———. 2011. *Creative Experiencing*. Edited by Donald Viney and Jincheol O. State University of New York Press.

Hauerwas, Stanley. 1993. *Unleashing the Scripture*. Abingdon Press.

Heidegger, Martin. 1962. *Being and Time*. Translated by John Macquarrie and Edward Robinson. Harper.

Hollenbach, David. 1994. "A Communitarian Reconstruction of Human Rights." In *Catholicism and Liberalism*, edited by R. Bruce Douglass and David Hollenbach. Cambridge University Press.

———. 1998. "Is Tolerance Enough?" *Conversations on Jesuit Higher Education* 13:5–15.

Homer. 1937. *Odyssey*. Translated by W. H. D. Rouse. New American Library.

Hume, David. 1980. *Dialogues concerning Natural Religion*. Hackett.

Jaspers, Karl. 2011. *The Origin and Goal of History*. Translated by Michael Bullock. Routledge.

Jefferson, Thomas. 1999. *Political Writings*. Edited by Joyce Appleby and Terence Ball. Cambridge University Press.

Kant, Immanuel. 1965. *Critique of Pure Reason*. Translated by Norman Kemp Smith. St. Martin's.

———. 1993. *Grounding for the Metaphysics of Morals*. Translated by James Ellington. Hackett.

———. 1997. *Critique of Practical Reason*. Translated by Mary Gregor. Cambridge University Press.

Kearney, Melissa. 2023. *The Two-Parent Privilege*. University of Chicago Press.

Kuhn, Thomas. 1970. *The Structure of Scientific Revolutions*. 2nd ed. University of Chicago Press.

Lee, Tori. 2023. "Franklin I. 'Chris' Gamwell, Religious Ethics Scholar Devoted to Justice, 1937–2023." *UChicago News*, September 18. https://news.uchicago.edu/story/franklin-i-chris-gamwell-religious-ethics-scholar-devoted-justice-1937-2023.

Livingston, Richard. 2023. "Refiguring the Relation between Being and God." 50th Anniversary of the Center for Process Studies Conference, Claremont, CA, April 21.

Locke, John. 1983. *A Letter concerning Toleration*. Hackett.

MacIntyre, Alasdair. 1981. *After Virtue*. University of Notre Dame Press.

———. 1988. *Whose Justice? Which Rationality?* University of Notre Dame Press.

Macpherson, C. B. 1962. *The Political Theory of Possessive Individualism: Hobbes to Locke*. Clarendon Press.

Malone-France, Derek. 2012. *Faith, Fallibility, and the Virtue of Anxiety*. Palgrave Macmillan.

Maritain, Jacques. 1998. *Man and the State*. Catholic University of America Press.

Marty, Martin. 1988. "The Virginia Statute Two Hundred Years Later." In *The Virginia Statute for Religious Freedom*, edited by Merrill Peterson and Robert Vaughan. Cambridge University Press.

Marx, Karl. 1970. *Critique of Hegel's Philosophy of Right*. Translated by Joseph O'Malley and Annette Jolin. Cambridge University Press.

Mead, Sidney. 1963. *The Lively Experiment: The Shaping of Christianity in America*. Harper and Row.

Milbank, John, ed. 1999. *Radical Orthodoxy*. Routledge.

Mill, John Stuart. 1874. *Three Essays on Religion*. Holt.

Morowitz, Harold, and James Trefil. 1992. *The Facts of Life: Science and the Abortion Controversy*. Oxford University Press.

Morris, Randall. 1991. *Process Philosophy and Political Ideology*. State University of New York Press.

Murdoch, Iris. 1970. *The Sovereignty of Good*. Routledge.

———. 1993. *Metaphysics as a Guide to Morals*. Penguin.

Murray, John Courtney. 1960. *We Hold These Truths: Catholic Reflections on the American Proposition*. Sheed and Ward.

Neville, Robert. 2019. *Metaphysics of Goodness*. State University of New York Press.

Niebuhr, Reinhold. 1941–1943. *The Nature and Destiny of Man*. 2 vols. Scribner's.

Nozick, Robert. 1974. *Anarchy, State, and Utopia*. Basic Books.

Nussbaum, Martha Craven. 2006. *Frontiers of Justice*. Harvard University Press.

Odin, Steve. 2016. *Tragic Beauty in Whitehead and Japanese Aesthetics*. Lexington.

Ogden, Schubert. 1966. *The Reality of God and Other Essays*. Harper and Row.

Ong, Walter. 1998. "Response to Hollenbach." *Conversations on Jesuit Higher Education* 14:43–44.

Peirce, Charles Sanders. 1935. "How to Make Our Ideas Clear." In *The Collected Papers of Charles Sanders Peirce*, vol. 5, edited by Charles Hartshorne and Paul Weiss. Harvard University Press.

Petek, Joseph. 2022. *Unearthing the Unknown Whitehead*. Lexington Books.

Pettit, Joe. 2016. "Racial Justice: Easy to Understand, Very Difficult to Achieve." *Political Theology Today*, July 12.

Plaskow, Judith. 1980. *Sex, Sin, and Grace: Women's Experience and the Theologies of Reinhold Niebuhr and Paul Tillich*. University Press of America.

Plato. 1977. *Platonis opera*. 5 vols. Edited by John Burnet. Clarendon Press.

———. 1999. *The Collected Dialogues of Plato*. Edited by Edith Hamilton and Huntington Cairns. Princeton University Press.

Pogge, Thomas. 2007. *John Rawls: His Life and Theory of Justice*. Oxford University Press.

Popper, Karl. 1963. *The Open Society and Its Enemies*. 2 vols. Routledge and Kegan Paul.

———. 1972. *Objective Knowledge*. Clarendon Press.

Rawls, John. 1971. *A Theory of Justice*. Harvard University Press.

———. 1996. *Political Liberalism*. Columbia University Press.

———. 1999. *Collected Papers*. Edited by Samuel Freeman. Harvard University Press.

———. 2001. *Justice as Fairness*. Edited by Erin Kelly. Harvard University Press.

———. 2007. *Lectures on the History of Political Philosophy*. Edited by Samuel Freeman. Harvard University Press.

Rorty, Richard. 1979. *Philosophy and the Mirror of Nature*. Princeton University Press.

———. 1982. *Consequences of Pragmatism*. University of Minnesota Press.

Sandel, Michael. 1996. *Democracy's Discontent: America in Search of a Public Philosophy*. Harvard University Press.

————. 1998. *Liberalism and the Limits of Justice.* 2nd ed. Cambridge University Press.

Sartre, Jean-Paul. 2007. *Existentialism Is a Humanism.* Translated by Carol Macomber. Yale University Press.

Scanlon, Thomas. 2003. "Rawls on Justification." In *The Cambridge Companion to Rawls,* edited by Samuel Freeman. Cambridge University Press.

Schilbrack, Kevin. 2013. *Philosophy and the Study of Religions: A Manifesto.* Wiley-Blackwell.

Schleiermacher, Friedrich. 1989. *The Christian Faith.* Translated by H. R. Mackintosh. T. and T. Clark.

Shields, George, and Donald Viney. 2003. "The Logic of Future Contingents." In *Process and Analysis,* edited by George Shields. State University of New York Press.

Smith, John. 1963. *The Spirit of American Philosophy.* Oxford University Press.

Spinoza, Baruch. 1992. *Ethics.* Translated by Samuel Shirley. Hackett.

Stout, Jeffrey. 2004. *Democracy and Tradition.* Princeton University Press.

Strauss, David. 2010. *The Living Constitution.* Oxford University Press.

Strauss, Leo. 1964. *The City and Man.* University of Chicago Press.

Taylor, Charles. 1989. *Sources of the Self.* Harvard University Press.

Thomas Aquinas, St. 1972. *Summa theologiae.* Blackfriars edition. McGraw-Hill.

Tocqueville, Alexis de. 1945. *Democracy in America.* 2 vols. Knopf.

Vishio, Alex. 2005. Review of *Real Ethics: Rethinking the Foundations of Morality,* by John Rist. *Journal of Religion* 85 (2): 336–38.

Walzer, Michael. 1977. *Just and Unjust Wars.* Basic Books.

Weber, Max. 2019. *Economy and Society.* Translated by Keith Tribe. Harvard University Press.

Weithman, Paul. 2002. *Religion and the Obligations of Citizenship.* Cambridge University Press.

————. 2011. *Why Political Liberalism?* Oxford University Press.

Whitehead, Alfred North. 1927. *Symbolism.* Macmillan.

————. 1941. *The Philosophy of Alfred North Whitehead.* Edited by Paul Schilpp. Northwestern University Press.

————. 1958. *Function of Reason.* Beacon Press.

————. 1967a. *Adventures of Ideas.* Free Press.

————. 1967b. *The Aims of Education.* Free Press.

————. 1967c. *Science and the Modern World.* Free Press.

————. 1968. *Modes of Thought.* Free Press.

————. 1978. *Process and Reality.* Edited by David Ray Griffin and Donald Sherburne. Free Press.

————. 1996. *Religion in the Making.* Fordham University Press.

Wilmot, Brett. 2021. "God and the Problem of Evil." *Religions* 12: 1–18.

Wolterstorff, Nicholas. 1983. "Can Belief in God Be Rational If It Has No Foundations?" In *Faith and Rationality,* edited by Alvin Plantinga and Nicholas Wolterstorff. University of Notre Dame Press.

———. 2008. *Justice: Rights and Wrongs*. Princeton University Press.
Wolterstorff, Nicholas, and Robert Audi. 1997. *Religion in the Public Square*. Rowman and Littlefield.
Zuckert, Michael. 2002. *Launching Liberalism: On Lockean Political Philosophy*. University Press of Kansas.

Name Index

Abraham, 53, 132, 239

Adam, 111

Anselm, St., 49–51, 64

Apel, Karl-Otto, 5, 35, 80, 92–96, 98,
   100, 105, 118, 121, 124, 133

Arendt, Hannah, 79

Aristotle, 4–5, 9, 13, 18, 20, 36–38,
   53, 66, 69, 73–87, 89–90, 96, 98,
   115–117, 125, 158, 162, 181–182,
   188, 190–191, 196, 206–207, 214,
   234

Audi, Robert, 220

Augustine, St., 6, 104, 110–111,
   120

Barry, Brian, 28

Bellah, Robert, 177

Berger, Peter, 79

Bernardin, Joseph, 159

Buddha, 71, 132

Burns, Elizabeth, 86

Burt, John, 8, 167, 172

Calhoun, John C., 126

Calvin, John, 173

Confucius, 132

Daniels, Norman, 229, 232

Descartes, Rene, 108, 152

Dewey, John, 22–24, 29, 31, 157

Douglas, William O., 208

Dreben, Burton, 234

Duns Scotus, 52

Dworkin, Ronald, 141–143, 218,
   220–224, 226

Eberle, Christopher, 145

Eleatic Stranger, 38

Emerson, Ralph Waldo, 183

Euclid, 68

Euthyphro, 33, 142

Finnis, John, 190

Foot, Philippa, 192

Franklin, Benjamin, 168, 174

Freeman, Samuel, 145, 228–229, 233

Friedman, Milton, 2, 17–20, 22–23

Frost, Robert, 24, 122

Gewirth, Alan, 2, 20–21, 23, 120

Goldmann, Lucien, 74

Greenawalt, Kent, 133, 140–141, 168

Griffin, David Ray, 151, 219

Habermas, Jurgen, 6, 79, 99–101,
   105, 118, 120, 124, 148, 156, 219

Hadot, Pierre, 107

Hardie, W. F. R., 234

Hart, H. L. A., 9, 172, 196, 203, 230, 237

Hartshorne, Charles, 2–4, 10, 25–26, 29–45, 47, 53–54, 56, 64, 66, 68, 78, 82, 110, 113, 146, 152, 154, 156, 165, 205–206, 224, 228, 235

Hauerwas, Stanley, 179

Heidegger, Martin, 85

Hobbes, Thomas, 9, 118, 120, 150, 181–182, 185, 224

Hollenbach, David, 188–190, 194, 196

Homer, 113

Hume, David, 35, 37, 44–45, 83, 116, 120, 142, 199, 212

Jaspers, Karl, 132

Jefferson, Thomas, 8, 167–172, 174

Kant, Immanuel, 1, 4–5, 13–14, 19, 25–26, 35, 37, 42, 45, 47, 49–50, 56–58, 73–87, 89, 91–96, 99, 112, 116–117, 119–120, 127, 134, 142, 149, 154–155, 157, 177–178, 189, 195, 226, 230

Kearney, Melissa, 214

King, Jr., Martin Luther, 6, 106, 158, 173

Kuhn, Thomas, 182

Lee, Tori, 11

Leibniz, Gottfried, 152

Lincoln, Abraham, 8–9, 51, 122, 126, 167, 172–174, 176, 210, 235

Locke, John, 23, 218–219, 227

Luther, Martin, 191

MacIntyre, Alasdair, 5, 35, 80, 89–92, 96, 98–99, 179, 184

Macpherson, C. B., 181

Madison, James, 167, 174

Maritain, Jacques, 190

Marty, Martin, 167

Marx, Karl, 74, 156, 165, 182, 231

Matthew, St., 117, 165

Mead, Sidney, 174

Milbank, John, 179

Mill, John Stuart, 134, 157

Moliere, Jean Baptiste, 59

Morowitz, Harold, 205

Morris, Randall, 29, 156, 224

Murdoch, Iris, 35, 86

Murray, John Courtney, 7, 133, 138–140, 168

Neville, Robert, 86

Niebuhr, Reinhold, 6, 35, 111–114

Nietzsche, Friedrich, 89

Nozick, Robert, 77, 228

Nussbaum, Martha, 162

Obama, Barack, 6

Odin, Steve, 72

Ogden, Schubert, 110

Ong, Walter, 196

Pandora, 213

Parmenides, 48

Paul, St., 104, 197

Peirce, Charles Sanders, 94, 124, 228

Petek, Joseph, 41

Pettit, Joe, 209

Plaskow, Judith, 112

Plato, 3, 36–38, 48, 60, 85–86, 91, 106, 111, 164, 191

Pogge, Thomas, 145

Popper, Karl, 44, 47, 81, 176

Rawls, John, 7–13, 21, 56–57, 77, 97–98, 100–101, 103, 105, 117, 127, 133–139, 141, 145–166, 168, 173, 177, 179, 181–201, 203–205, 207, 209–211, 213–214, 217–237

Rorty, Richard, 5, 80, 91–92, 98–99,
 152, 161, 190

Sandel, Michael, 181, 183–184, 213
Sartre, Jean-Paul, 39
Scanlon, Thomas, 164, 232–233
Schilbrack, Kevin, 162
Schleiermacher, Friedrich, 41–42
Shields, George, 70
Smith, John, 23
Socrates, 92, 176, 233
Sophocles, 86
Spinoza, Baruch, 53
Stout, Jeffrey, 9, 179–180
Strauss, David, 8, 167–170, 172
Strauss, Leo, 156, 165, 167

Taylor, Charles, 184
Tertullian, 106
Thomas Aquinas, St., 41, 55, 84–85,
 104, 139, 158, 190–192

Tocqueville, Alexis de, 23
Tracy, David, 10–11
Trefil, James, 205
Trump, Donald, 51

Viney, Donald, 70

Walzer, Michael, 178
Weber, Max, 93, 133
Weithman, Paul, 145
Whitehead, Alfred North, 2–3, 10,
 19, 25–26, 29–42, 56–57, 79, 82,
 84, 87, 96, 110, 113, 124–125,
 148, 156, 166, 173–174, 206–207,
 213–214, 217, 224, 228–230
Wittgenstein, Ludwig, 46, 52, 162
Wolterstorff, Nicholas, 10, 34, 145,
 161, 217–234

Zuckert, Michael, 218–220, 223, 226,
 229